State-Business Relations and Economic Transformation in South Africa and Zimbabwe

State-Business Relations and Economic Transformation in South Africa and Zimbabwe

Unfinished Transformation

Sinan Baran

LEXINGTON BOOKS
Lanham • Boulder • New York • London

Published by Lexington Books
An imprint of The Rowman & Littlefield Publishing Group, Inc.
4501 Forbes Boulevard, Suite 200, Lanham, Maryland 20706
www.rowman.com

86-90 Paul Street, London EC2A 4NE

British Library Cataloguing in Publication Information Available

Library of Congress Cataloging-in-Publication Data

Names: Baran, Sinan, author.
Title: State-business relations and economic transformation in South Africa and Zimbabwe : unfinished transformation / Sinan Baran.
Description: Lanham : Lexington Books, 2023. | Includes bibliographical references and index.
Identifiers: LCCN 2023009219 (print) | LCCN 2023009220 (ebook) | ISBN 9781666920024 (cloth) | ISBN 9781666920031 (ebook)
Subjects: LCSH: Industrial policy--South Africa. | Industrial policy--Zimbabwe. | Mineral industries--South Africa. | Mineral industries--Zimbabwe. | South Africa--Economic policy. | Zimbabwe--Economic policy. | South Africa--Foreign economic relations--China. | Zimbabwe--Foreign economic relations--China. | China--Foreign economic relations--South Africa. | China--Foreign economic relations--Zimbabwe.
Classification: LCC HD3616.A356 B373 2023 (print) | LCC HD3616.A356 (ebook) | DDC 338.968--dc23/eng/20230227
LC record available at https://lccn.loc.gov/2023009219
LC ebook record available at https://lccn.loc.gov/2023009220

Contents

Acknowledgments

These pages owe their existence to numerous people and institutions. First and foremost, I would like to give a special thanks to the constant advice, support, and guidance of Dr Stefan Andreasson. In particular, I would like to thank his great patience for answering my endless questions and giving invaluable recommendations on this current study. His support and encouragement have contributed to my development as an academic researcher in this field. I wish to extend my thanks to Dr Andrew Thomson, who has also contributed to this book with his valuable reviews. In addition to them, Prof John Barry and Prof Padraig Carmody provided comprehensive and valuable feedback on drafts of the chapters leading to this ultimate version of the manuscript. I would like to express my deepest gratitude to the distinguished staff of Lexington Books, especially its associate acquisitions editor of African and Africana Studies and Geography Sydney Wedbush, and anonymous reviewer, for their great contributions to the finalization of this book.

Besides, I would not have been able to afford to undertake this endeavour without the huge financial assistance of the Turkish Ministry of National Education. Also, I am grateful for the financial support of the School of History, Anthropology, Philosophy, and Politics at Queen's University of Belfast during my vacation to South Africa to complete my fieldwork. I am also indebted to many people from South Africa and Zimbabwe whom I interviewed, and the great help of Prof Patrick Bond for finding accommodation in Melville and exploring Johannesburg during my fieldwork.

I want to express my special appreciation to the love of my life Berrak for her endless patience, support, and love and our beloved son Teoman. My acknowledgements would not be complete without thanking my mum, Munire; dad, Mustafa; and brother, Emre for their invaluable existence in my life.

List of Abbreviations

ANC	African National Congress
ASEAN	Association of Southeast Asian Nations
B-BBEE	Broad-Based Black Economic Empowerment
BEE	Black Economic Empowerment
BRIC	Brazil, Russia, India, China
BRICS	Brazil, Russia, India, China, South Africa
CEO	Chief Executive Officer
CIC	Chinese Investment Corporation
COSATU	Congress of South African Trade Unions
CZI	Confederation of Zimbabwe Industries
DMR	Department of Mineral Resources (South Africa)
DRC	Democratic Republic of Congo
ECLA	Economic Commission for Latin America
EFF	Economic Freedom Fighters
ESAP	Economic Structural Adjustment Programme
EU	European Union
FDI	Foreign Direct Investment
FOCAC	Forum on China-Africa Cooperation
GATT	General Agreements of Tariff and Trade
GDP	Gross Domestic Product
GEAR	Growth, Employment, and Redistribution
GNI	Gross National Income
HDI	Human Development Index
HDSAs	Historically Disadvantaged South Africans
HRD	Human Resources Development
IBSA	India-Brazil-South Africa Dialogue Forum
IDC	Industrial Development Corporation
IEE	Indigenisation and Economic Empowerment
IFIs	International Financial Institutions

IMF	International Money Fund
JCI	Johannesburg Consolidated Investment
JSE	Johannesburg Stock Exchange
LSE	London Stock Exchange
MDC	Movement for Democratic Change
MOFCOM	Ministry of Commerce (China)
MPRDA	Mineral and Petroleum Resources Development Act
MWS	Modern World-System
NAIL	New Africa Investment Limited
NAM	Non-Aligned Movement
NICs	Newly Industrialised Countries
NP	National Party
NPAT	Net Profit after Tax
NUM	National Union of Mineworkers
OECD	Organisation for Economic Co-operation and Development
RDP	Reconstruction and Development Programme
SACP	South African Communist Party
SADC	Southern African Development Community
SANNC	South African Native National Congress
SAP	Structural Adjustment Programme
SBN	State-Business Nexus
SBRs	State-Business Relations
TCC	Transnational Capitalist Class
UDI	Unilateral Declaration of Independence
UK	United Kingdom
UNCTAD	United Nations Conference on Trade and Development
UNDP	United Nations Development Programme
UNSC	United Nations Security Council
US	United States
ZANU-PF	Zimbabwean African National Union-Patriotic Front
ZAPU	Zimbabwe African People's Union

Introduction

This book is an examination of the state-business nexus (SBN) in South Africa and Zimbabwe, which share a common history of white settler colonialism before each country's transition to majority rule.[1] By means of a comparative case study of the mining industries in each country, the book offers an explanation of why state-business relations (SBRs) are likely to either consolidate or fracture over time. The overall aim of the study is to understand why states in developing regions become more or less fragile in the context of transition. This study examines the posttransition trajectories of South Africa and Zimbabwe following the end of minority rule and the transitions to majority-rule democracy (in 1980 in Zimbabwe and in 1994 in South Africa). The two majority governments in Harare and Pretoria have needed to deal with deep divisions in each country relating to race, inequality, and underdevelopment. Specifically, as a consequence of these unresolved post-transition divisions, underdevelopment has persisted in these two countries. Although the countries share several historical similarities, both South Africa and Zimbabwe had sharply divergent trajectories after their respective transitions in terms of their SBRs. This study explores the policy choices related to the historically significant mining industries in the two countries to examine the nature of and reasons for those different trajectories.

Although the literature on the SBRs in developing countries has focused on collaboration between the government and business for enhancing economic growth (Cali & Sen, 2011; Maxfield & Schneider, 1997; Evans, 1995; Amsden, 1992 [1989]), prodevelopmental outcomes of it (Taylor, 2012; Maxfield & Schneider, 1997) and the importance of cooperation between the public and private sector (Te Velde, 2006) the current study focuses on the variations of SBRs. The consolidation and fracturing of SBRs in South Africa and Zimbabwe therefore are one of the most significant outcomes of these posttransition periods. During the last decade, a considerable literature has grown up around the theme of the relationship between the majority governments and the business in South Africa and Zimbabwe (*see* Southall,

2012; Seekings & Nattrass, 2011; Nattrass & Seekings, 2010; Van Wyk, 2009; Handley, 2008; Andreasson, 2007; Taylor, 2007). However, a comparison of SBRs regarding the mining industry from the MWS perspective in South Africa and Zimbabwe has not yet been attempted. Although China's effects on the mining industries of southern Africa have been analysed during the last decade (Burgess & Beilstein, 2013; Shelton & Kabemba, 2012; Gonzalez-Vicente, 2011) the effects on the business environment in the mining industry of South Africa and Zimbabwe remain debatable.

In the last two decades, there has been a surge of interest in the effects of implementation of liberalisation and indigenisation policies by the majority governments of South Africa and Zimbabwe to complete economic transformation, as well as to address the social pressures in their posttransition communities (Nyabereka, 2017; Magure, 2013; 2012; Fine *et al.*, 2011; Andreasson, 2010a; 2006; 2003; Tangri & Southall, 2008; Brett, 2005; Raftopoulos & Phimister, 2004; Bond & Manyanya, 2003; Bond, 2000; Dashwood, 2000; Williams & Taylor, 2000; Carmody, 1998). Indeed, a wide range of domestic and foreign pressures have triggered these policy choices in South Africa and Zimbabwe. Pressures from international financial institutions such as the International Monetary Fund (IMF) and the World Bank affected the Zimbabwean neoliberal transformation to some extent during the early 1990s (Andreasson, 2007). On the other hand, the African National Congress (ANC) and then President Nelson Mandela were under pressure from domestic conglomerates during the early years of majority rule in South Africa to transform the South African economy into a neoliberal model (Bond, 2000).[2]

In the general sense, the aim of the book is to explain changes in the SBRs in noncore areas of the Modern World-System (MWS) during the economic transformation period. It argues that in countries with significant extractive industries such as South Africa and Zimbabwe, the shifts in policy choices of the governments (in this study in regard to the mining industries) affect the SBN differently depending on their location on the periphery or the semiperiphery of the MWS as outlined by Wallerstein and the subsequent MWS analysis of the links between the location in the MWS and developmental outcomes (*see* Babones & Chase-Dunn, 2012; Wallerstein, 2011a; 2006; 1989; 1980; 1979a; 1975; 1974a; 1974b; Gowan, 2004; Goldfrank, 2000; Chase-Dunn & Hall, 1997; Chase-Dunn & Grimes, 1995; Arrighi & Drangel, 1986; Hopkins & Wallerstein, 1982; 1980; Petras, 1981; Chase-Dunn & Rubinson, 1977). This study claims that semiperipheral countries are more unsusceptible than countries located in the periphery in terms of being vulnerable to shifts in policy choices during periods of transition. The reason behind that difference is based on not only weaker state structures in the periphery than their counterparts in the semiperiphery, but also the differences in the division of labour within these noncore areas (Wallerstein, 2011, p. 355; Chase-Dunn & Rubinson, 1977, p. 456).

In addition, China's increasing economic and political presence across Africa is a vital emerging phenomenon in African studies which is taken into consideration in this comparative case study (*see* Garcia, 2017a; 2017b; Besada & O'Bright, 2016; Mason, 2016; Taylor, 2014; 2006; Alden, 2013; Breslin, 2013; Carmody, 2013; 2011; Cheru & Obi, 2010; Brautigam, 2009; Alden *et al.*, 2008; Le Pere & Shelton, 2007; Marks & Manji, 2007). In fact, China has transformed nearly all of the continent's economies during the first decades of the twenty-first century with aid, trade, and infrastructural investments (Brautigam, 2009). As an emerging semiperipheral power, China has become the most significant actor of the rising global south within the MWS during the twenty-first century (Hung, 2017; Moyo & Yeros, 2015). Chinese state-owned and private investments have changed the characteristics of investors in sub-Saharan Africa, which was dominantly Western before the early 2000s. Indeed, overtaking Western private investors with an expansionist investment policy has also changed the business environment in the continent (Mason, 2017; Burgess & Beilstein, 2013; Carmody & Taylor, 2010; Schoeman, 2007). The image of Africa has changed considerably during the early 2000s, from civil wars to economic development, with the help of the commodity boom and investments from China (Le Pere & Shelton, 2007; Taylor, 2006). Similarly, both South Africa and Zimbabwe have also developed important trade and political relations with China and have benefitted from the Chinese presence in the continent (Alao, 2014; Chun, 2014; Grim *et al.*, 2014; Shelton & Kabemba, 2012; Le Pere & Shelton, 2007). I shall answer the query "Why do SBRs have the tendency to consolidate or fracture over time in posttransition communities, such as South Africa and Zimbabwe?" which is the key research question of the current study.

The explanation of changes in SBRs, which is about whether or not governments and business sectors can end up producing mutually trustworthy and otherwise effective relations, will also take into account the impact of China's economic and political presence in both South Africa and Zimbabwe. Effective SBRs are crucial for economic productivity to enhance and accelerate development (Qureshi & Te Velde, 2013; Cali & Sen, 2011; Cali *et al.*, 2011; Sen & Te Velde, 2009). However, the deep divisions from minority rule related to the structures of the mining industries, which have been predominantly white, are obstacles to stabilising the relations between the governments and businesses. This book proposes the argument that a country's location in the MWS, major policy shifts related to the mining industries, and the increasing economic and political presence of China have a distinct and significant effect on SBRs in these posttransition communities (for SBRs in developing countries, particularly in South Africa and Zimbabwe, *see*

Qureshi & Te Velde, 2013; Taylor, 2012; 2007; Seekings & Nattrass, 2011; Nattrass & Seekings, 2010; Te Velde & Leftwich, 2010; Sen & Te Velde, 2009 Van Wyk, 2009; Handley, 2008; Ponte *et al.*, 2007; Te Velde, 2006; Evans, 1997; Haggard & Kaufman, 1997; Haggard *et al.*, 1997; Maxfield & Schneider, 1997; Schneider & Maxfield, 1997).

KEY ASSUMPTIONS OF THE STUDY

It is the argument in this book that the mining industries are perfect places to understand how these competing policy preferences play out and why they are vital, as they had substantial roles in each country's national economy during both the previous settler rule and the posttransition periods. The mining industry is one of the most visible examples in South Africa and Zimbabwe of not only the inequality between the races but also the unfair wealth and income redistribution. Moreover, the fracturing or consolidation of SBRs is also visible in the mining industry. It is the key empirical focus of this research project.

China's insignificant or significant economic and political presence in southern Africa has different outcomes for the variation of the SBRs of both countries. The discarding of liberalisation policies has created opportunities for China from the early 2000s, but implementing indigenisation policies in South Africa and Zimbabwe has sometimes restricted these opportunities for China, as well as for other foreign investors. Indigenisation policies are therefore not attracting foreign investors because of their high demands, and this causes a breakdown of SBRs. Chinese private and state-owned mining companies have invested in South Africa and Zimbabwe, and the trade volumes of each country with China soared after the millennium. Also, beyond South Africa and Zimbabwe, whether the Chinese presence has been either beneficial or not for African countries in terms of aid, infrastructure, and trade relations is an ongoing discussion. Furthermore, the effects of the Chinese presence in South Africa remains debatable within the literature. This study is therefore designed to assess the effects of China on South Africa and Zimbabwe in terms of SBRs.

The first assumption of this book is if a peripheral country has strong ties with the core and applies a policy of liberalisation in its mining sector, it would be expected that SBRs would be consolidating. This consolidation might be compatible with the historical experience of peripheral countries since core countries shape the nature of the MWS and there would be no major disagreements between periphery and core regarding SBRs. The core economically controls the periphery through unequal exchange and private transnational economic actors (Chase-Dunn & Rubinson 1977, p. 462; the unequal exchange between the core and periphery has been analysed in the MWS and political economy literature during the last decade *see* Garcia & Bond, 2015; Bieler & Morton, 2014; Xiong, 2014; Austin *et al.*, 2012; Kollmeyer, 2009).[3] In contrast to this indirect control, core countries have directly controlled peripheral areas for political reasons. Moreover, peripheral economic elites have been tied to the needs of core capital (Chase-Dunn & Rubinson 1977, pp. 467–68). Corporations from core countries have thus suppressed or limited the development of national business classes in peripheral countries. In this case, foreign companies which establish economic ties to the periphery prefer policies of liberalisation as such policies allow them to maintain their businesses in these areas without restrictions. The motivation behind the application of the Washington Consensus, which was essential for implementing SAPs in developing countries, was to separate business from the state apparatus (Schneider & Maxfield, 1997, p. 4). This compatible bilateral relation keeps governments of the periphery to core institutions and states, which provides the reproduction of the MWS through capital accumulation and the unequal exchange between them (Hopkins *et al.*, 1982).

The second assumption of this book is a little more complicated than the first one. Therefore, if a country is located in the periphery of the MWS and pursues a policy of indigenisation in governing its mining industries, it is expected that the SBRs are fracturing. If this country is to experience a shift away from its previous ties to the core and towards the emerging semiperiphery (China), SBRs would be consolidating along with a new set of relevant actors (China), such as domestic and foreign mining companies. Since core-like activities are present in the semiperiphery, such as China and South Africa (*see* Wallerstein, 2006; 1982; 1974a; Goldfrank, 2000; Arrighi & Drangel, 1986; Chase-Dunn & Rubinson, 1977), new powerful corporate actors might bring the required technology and capital to replace the established ones over the long term in the periphery. Goldfrank (2000, p. 169) stated that "semi-peripheral states are said to stabilize the world-system through subimperial practices deflecting and absorbing some of the peripheral opposition to the core." Thus, agricultural or mineral-extracting activities in peripheral countries, which are enabled by the technology and finance of the core, can be replaced by that of semiperipheral countries. Semiperipheral states are properly "recognized as *intermediate* between core and periphery in terms of the capital intensity, and skill and wage levels of their production processes" (Goldfrank, 2000, p. 169). The investments from the semiperiphery might, therefore, lead to the consolidation of SBRs over time.

The third assumption of this book is if a country is located in the semiperiphery of the MWS and pursues a policy of liberalisation in governing its mining industries, it is expected that this country retains strong ties with the core. As a result, SBRs will be consolidated in this semiperipheral country.

Business in semiperipheral countries welcomes economic liberalisation, particularly privatisation policies similar to those in the periphery. According to the neoclassical perspective on the function of the state, its role ought to be restricted to making laws to provide macroeconomic stability and nonintervention in the private sector (Cali & Sen, 2011, p. 1542). Policies of this kind should, therefore, provide a consensus between the state and business in semiperipheral countries. Similarly, periphery liberalisation is always the safe bet if actors want SBRs to remain consolidated, and the potential for different outcomes only comes into play when countries implement indigenisation policies.

The last assumption of this book is also a little more complicated than the previous one. If a country is located in the semiperiphery of the MWS and pursues a policy of indigenisation in its mining industries, it is expected that the SBRs are consolidating. If this country is to experience a shift away from its previous ties to the core towards the emerging semiperiphery (China), SBRs would be fracturing because new actors (China) might not provide consolidation as it brings competition with the domestic actors and might take the place of them over time. Chase-Dunn and Rubinson (1977, p. 472) argued that "upwardly mobile semiperipheral countries tend to employ more state-directed and state-mobilized development policies than do core countries." It is expected that state-led development policies of this type (for example, indigenisation policies) might create a consensus between the state and business, as happened in East Asia (Cali & Sen, 2011; Maxwell & Schneider, 1997). However, such state-led development policies cause a flight of core capital and open up space for upwardly mobile semiperipheral countries, such as China. As a result of the competition between domestic actors and foreign semiperipheral investors, indigenisation policies might cause fracturing of SBRs over time.

Both the choices made about policy in the mining industries (liberalisation or indigenisation) and the degree of Chinese influence over time (relatively absent or increasing) are decisive factors shaping SBRs in the periphery and semiperiphery of the MWS. Indeed, this book argues that semiperipheral countries are less fragile than countries located in the periphery in terms of being susceptible to pressures from external powers and to shifts in policy choices during periods of transition. Liberalisation policies might be only short- and medium-term repairs for the consolidation of SBRs in postminority regimes. Hence, both postcolonial semiperipheral and peripheral countries inevitably embrace indigenisation policies over time, as they could not transform their institutions on behalf of the wider populations in posttransition societies (Kragelund, 2012; Verhoef, 2004; Tevera, 1996).

These assumptions generate several important questions about the nature and durability of SBRs in semiperipheral and peripheral regions of the MWS (and the global economy more generally). Why do semiperipheral states seem less fragile or vulnerable than those in the periphery when it comes to adapting to, accommodating, or resisting pressures from external actors? What are the advantages of semiperipheral countries compared with peripheral ones in this regard? To what extent do government policy choices about pursuing indigenisation or liberalisation in their mining industries affect the SBRs in peripheral and semiperipheral countries such as Zimbabwe and South Africa respectively? To what extent does Chinese influence over mineral extraction industries directly affect SBRs in countries located in semiperipheral and peripheral regions?

HISTORICAL BACKGROUND

The black majorities in South Africa and Zimbabwe desired to transform racially segregated economies when they took over governments respectively. The first phase of the transformation was the liberalisation of the inherited economies as they were isolated from the global market during the last years of minority rules. The liberalisation of the economy is not enough to complete transformation in postcolonial societies, such as South Africa and Zimbabwe, because the inherited economic structure caused disadvantages to the indigenous population. Therefore, the black majority governments of South Africa and Zimbabwe applied respective indigenisation policies in order to complete the economic transformation and redress the inherited disadvantages of previous regimes in postcolonial communities. The basic requirements of economic transformation, namely Black Economic Empowerment (BEE) in South Africa were equality for all citizens, sustainability, accessibility to skills and self-employment, which were restricted under the apartheid regime, and reversing the underdevelopment of black communities (Davies, 2012; DTI, 2003).

On the other hand, the Indigenisation and Economic Empowerment (IEE) Act of 2007 focused primarily on the equitable ownership among the indigenous Zimbabweans for the economic activities of the country (Zvoushe *et al.*, 2017, p. 123; MacLean *et al.*, 1997, p. 159). Andreasson (2010a) compared the divergent implementation methods of indigenisation policies for completing the economic, political, and cultural transformation in South Africa and Zimbabwe respectively. He claimed that the transformation in South Africa had been a greater project than the restricted transformation in Zimbabwe, which has been only targeted "redistribution of ownership and control of public institutions" (Andreasson, 2010a, p. 425).

One must first understand the colonial context out of which these countries have emerged in order to examine the SBRs during the economic transformation period. Colonialism in southern Africa had its origins in the seventeenth century, and more recently South Africa and Zimbabwe were ruled as white settler colonies during most of the twentieth century (Youe, 2018; Andreasson, 2015; 2010a; Martin, 2013a; Good, 1976). They both belong to the same southern African subsystem of settler colonial rule built on the extractive industries, particularly mining and agricultural activities, which were the key constituents of the political economy of the region (for the southern African subsystem, *see* Andreasson, 2010b; Arrighi *et al.*, 2010; Farley, 2008; Amin *et al.*, 1987; Shaw, 1974; Denoon *et al.*, 1972; Bowman, 1968). South Africa was colonised first by Dutch settlers from the mid-seventeenth century and then colonised by British from the early nineteenth century to 1910. The nonwhite majority populations, primarily the region's Africans of South Africa, therefore experienced white settler rule respectively from 1910 to 1961 by Union of South Africa and the Republic of South Africa under the apartheid regime, which began in 1948 when the National Party (NP) were elected to power, from 1961 to 1994.[4]

Likewise, after identifying the rich mineral deposits around the Zambezi River, explorers in Africa aroused the interest of British merchants such as Cecil Rhodes, and colonisation of other parts of southern Africa was launched at the end of the nineteenth century. As a result, the indigenous African peoples of what became Rhodesia (and, following independence, Zimbabwe) became subjects of British colonial rule from 1888 to 1980. In Zimbabwe, white minority rule was ended by an anticolonial insurrection which took place from 1965 to 1979.[5] South Africa became an independent nation free from British dominion in 1910 (Farley, 2008, p. 10). However, white settlers (Afrikaners and Britons) in South Africa established a white minority regime and, in response, black South Africans founded the South African Native National Congress (SANNC) in 1912.[6] Afterward, the Afrikaner nationalist and far-right NP declared a policy of apartheid when it gained power in the 1948 elections. Eventually, apartheid rule in South Africa ended in 1994, and therefore white settler regimes disappeared in southern Africa before the end of the twentieth century.[7] These similar colonial pasts of two southern African countries revealed similar problems after the end of white minority rule and the period of apartheid. For example, land redistribution, creating opportunities for nonwhites in the economy, which is a major part of the transformation of the economy, reducing the negative effects of unequal education, health and job opportunities among the races have been major problems for these two cases, but the Harare and Pretoria governments responded to these problems in different ways.

When the white minority regimes were disappearing in southern Africa, they left behind relatively stable industries, especially in South Africa (*see* Fine & Rustomjee, 1996) and Rhodesia (*see* Shumba, 2018; Dashwood,

2000). During the 1980s, Zimbabwe was not only one of the most promising economies in Africa, but also its inherited economy was more sophisticated than those of most other sub-Saharan African countries (Dashwood, 2000, p. 23; Hawkins. 2004, p. 33). In Zimbabwe, however, the Rhodesians left a significant foreign debt burden to the Mugabe regime (Bond & Manyanya, 2003, p. 17). Several sub-Saharan African countries adopted the neoliberal economic reforms to overcome this crisis through structural adjustment programmes (SAPs) supported by western donors and international financial institutions (IFIs) in the 1980s and 1990s (Hawthorn, 1993, pp. 330–31).[8] Zimbabwe's Economic Structural Adjustment Programme (ESAP) was launched in 1991 to manage the debt legacy of Rhodesia, as well as answered the pressures of domestic economic groups and IFIs (Andreasson, 2007, p. 285). Bond and others have also argued that ESAP was commenced because of pressure from the IMF and the World Bank (Mamdani, 2008; Raftopoulos & Phimister, 2004; Bond & Manyanya, 2003; Bond, 2001). Zimbabwe has experienced its own financial crisis and hyperinflation despite the implementation of ESAP during the late 1990s as a consequence of both domestic and international incidents.

The posttransition government in Harare consolidated SBRs in the early years of its reign as 'white' capital stayed out of politics (Shumba, 2018). Despite the 1992 drought in Zimbabwe, the government consolidated SBRs in the first half of the 1990s. However, the Zimbabwean dollar collapsed against the American dollar on 14 November 1997 because of the high national debt, increasingly corrupt administration in Harare and pressures from the war veterans and opposition groups, including trade unions and the Movement for Democratic Change (MDC), the opposition party of Zimbabwe. As a result of that collapse, Zimbabwe struggled with a foreign debt crisis at the end of the 1990s (Bond & Manyanya, 2003, p. 38), and the Harare government launched new indigenisation and land redistribution policies. As a consequence, Zimbabwe moved away from Western countries and IFIs, and the government seized the lands of the white population. Indeed, a shift in policy choices of the Mugabe regime deteriorated SBRs and caused a breakdown in Zimbabwe. Specifically, indigenisation policies were decisive in the fracturing of SBRs because of the transfer of capital and lands from the white minority to black majority control. Indigenisation policies stimulated both external and internal disarrays in Zimbabwe. Consequently, the indigenisation of the mining industry and agricultural activities and land redistribution policies caused a breakdown between Harare and Western countries, donors, and IFIs in Zimbabwe during the late 1990s and the early 2000s.

In South Africa, the apartheid regime left behind an uneven economic structure which had suffered considerably from external economic sanctions and internal conflict. By comparison with ESAP, the Growth, Employment, and Redistribution policy (GEAR) was launched in South Africa in 1996. Indeed South Africa did not adopt the neoliberal reforms in the same way as most other sub-Saharan African countries. Before GEAR, South Africa had initiated a social-democratic programme in 1994, the Reconstruction and Development Programme (RDP), to overcome the inherited uneven economic structure. So South Africa would arguably not have any neoliberal reforms without the pressure from IFIs during the postapartheid era, and GEAR was a neoliberal homegrown project (*see* Andreasson, 2003; 2001; Carmody, 2002; Bond 2000; Williams & Taylor, 2000). So South Africa developed GEAR as a homegrown project to enable the neoliberal transformation of the country's economy from 1996 to the early 2000s. Western countries and IFIs also asked the ANC to pursue liberalisation policies during the transition period. Indeed, South Africa did not have an entirely liberal and open economic structure in the postapartheid era.

The postapartheid regime in Pretoria did not want to cause any deterioration of the SBRs by making rigid policy choices, and the government had restored the longstanding disagreements between the core capital and South Africa as a result of the economic and military sanctions by the Western core countries against the NP government from the early 1960s to the end of the apartheid regime. Additionally, the ANC government sought to empower the various groups such as blacks, other minorities, and women who had been excluded from economic activities in South Africa during apartheid. Thereby, the BEE policy did not cause the fracturing of the SBRs in South Africa during the early 2000s as the ANC government let mining conglomerates move their headquarters overseas and their assets to foreign stock exchanges. However, after the BEE policy was introduced, tensions arose between old white indigenous capital and the ANC government during the Jacob Zuma government. In contrast with Zimbabwe's indigenisation policy, South Africa's white domestic and foreign corporations were not aggressively marginalised or even threatened with outright expulsion from the country because the ANC government had implemented BEE policy gradually.

In spite of some notable similarities between South Africa and Zimbabwe, there are also some significant differences in the external and internal capabilities of these two states. MWS theory is appropriate for explaining these differences between the two cases of this study as it provides a useful tool for comparing the two countries rather than rival theories such as the Dependency Theory (*see* Frank, 2009 [1967]; Cardoso, 1979; 1977; Emmanuel, 1972; Rodney, 1972; Dos Santos, 1970; Prebisch, 1959; Baran, 1957; Prebisch, 1950) or the Modernization Theory (*see* Wagner, 1993; Jacquette, 1982; Tipps, 1973; Bernstein, 1971; Black, 1966; Rostow, 1962; Rostow, 1960). MWS theory provides a framework for understanding both the nature of the global system and the limits of the regional and global influences of the states. Wallerstein (2006, p. 29) explained the capabilities and differences of robust and weak states:

> The role of each state is very different *vis-à-vis* productive processes depending on the mix of core-peripheral processes within it. The strong states, which contain a disproportionate share of core-like processes, tend to emphasize their role of protecting the quasi-monopolies of the core-like processes. The very weak states, which contain a disproportionate share of peripheral production processes, are usually unable to do very much to affect the axial division of labor, and in effect are largely forced to accept the lot that has been given them.

Jackson and Rosberg (1982) argued that weak state institutions and organisations in sub-Saharan Africa generate widespread political instability. Therefore, peripheral states are more vulnerable than semiperipheral states in terms of political instability and control over the division of labour (Wallerstein, 2011b). This comparative analysis proceeds from the fact that South Africa and Zimbabwe are located in the semiperiphery and periphery of the MWS respectively. Because of their different economic structures, South Africa and Zimbabwe are located in different positions in the MWS, and this has a significant bearing on their respective SBRs—that is, whether they are likely to consolidate or fracture over time.

South Africa and Zimbabwe devised different strategies for managing SBRs and with rather varying results in terms of the evolution of their respective SBNs because of their differing economic and political powers in respect of the MWS. Indeed, Pretoria and Harare searched for similar solutions (liberalisation and indigenisation policies) to overcome the problems of the distribution of capital and land during the transition and posttransition periods (Andreasson, 2011; 2010a). Zimbabwe, following the 2000s breakdown, shifted away from the West and towards China, the most noteworthy rising power of the Global South (Alao, 2014; Breslin, 2013; Youde, 2007). In comparison, South Africa also approached China, but not like Zimbabwe (Tella, 2017; Alden & Wu, 2016; Garcia & Bond, 2015; Qobo & Dube, 2015; Alden & Schoeman, 2015; 2013; Bond, 2013a; Carmody, 2013). Pretoria established more balanced relations with China and did not break away from Western countries or IFIs because of its BEE policies as did Zimbabwe with its indigenisation policy (Alden & Wu, 2016; Qobo & Dube, 2015; Alden & Schoeman, 2015; 2013; Bond, 2013a).

The variety of foreign trade products is another visible difference between South Africa and Zimbabwe in terms of their respective positions in the MWS (Andreasson, 2010a). In this respect, as a semiperipheral country, South Africa mainly exports not only raw materials such as gold and diamonds but also manufactured goods (Wallerstein, 2011b). In contrast, the majority of Zimbabwe's exports are raw materials such as tobacco and minerals (Wallerstein, 2011b). South Africa therefore does not follow the general path of African countries' raw material-based export trends, and this makes it unique in the continent (Tella, 2017; Alden & Schoeman, 2015; Martin, 2013a). Moreover, South Africa has become one of the most powerful economies in sub-Saharan Africa, along with Nigeria (Andreasson, 2015).

In addition to this economic aspect, South Africa established more balanced diplomatic ties than Zimbabwe with China as a consequence of its semiperipheral position in the MWS. China-Zimbabwe relations have a longer history than China-South Africa relations in terms of military assistance. For example, China not only assisted weapons and military equipment to the military force of ZANU but also trained some of the guerrilla leaders of Zimbabwe in China during the Independence War (1965–1979) against the Rhodesian regime (Alao, 2014, p. 6). However, following the independence China-Zimbabwe relations had been stagnant for twenty to twenty-five years until the ZANU-PF government moved away from Western investors following the economic sanctions and implemented Look East policy during the early 2000s (Alao, 2014; Chun, 2014; Bourne, 2011; Youde, 2007). Also, Beijing had changed in Chinese foreign policy towards economic expansion particularly in Africa (Alao, 2014, p. 8). Despite this close relationship between the two countries, Zimbabwe has always been dependent on Beijing and received financial support from China for rescuing the economy.

On the other hand, the pivotal position of South Africa in the continent, particularly in southern Africa, opens up more opportunities for the country in terms of foreign affairs. Indeed, the pivotal role of South Africa makes it a prominent actor in diplomatic issues. For instance, South Africa's inclusion in the group of BRIC countries—Brazil, Russia, India, and China—in 2011 was a sign of the country's significance not only in the continent but also in the world. As a result of these more balanced relations, South Africa has much more leverage and freedom of action than a peripheral country such as Zimbabwe (*see* Andreasson, 2011; Qobo, 2010; Le Pere & Shelton, 2007). It is therefore the argument of this study that the manoeuvrability of South Africa's foreign and domestic policy shifts is related to its semiperipheral position in the MWS. In the same way, Zimbabwe's fragility during major policy shifts regarding foreign and domestic capital is also related to its peripheral position in the MWS.

AN OVERVIEW OF KEY TIME PERIODS AND METHODS

The timeline for the examination of SBRs in these two posttransition societies is from the achievement of independence in Zimbabwe (1980) and the transition from apartheid in South Africa (early 1990s with the official transition being the 1994 elections) respectively, with a particular emphasis on SBRs in the era of liberal reforms in both countries from the 1990s onwards. In particular, the study focuses on how two southern African countries in different locations in the MWS had engaged in these alternating processes of implementing policies of liberalisation and indigenisation in their mining industries before and during the increasing Chinese economic and political presence in the region and affected the consolidation or fracturing of SBRs. The state-based categorisation of the global system in MWS theory is helpful for understanding a general trend of moving away from the western core towards a Chinese-centric semiperiphery in terms of the dominant external influences on South Africa and Zimbabwe. Thus, the domestic effects of policy choices relating to the mining industries will be explored with the help of the MWS theory.

I examine the variations in the SBRs regarding establishing positions in the MWS combined with understanding how the making and the relevance of policy in the respective mining sectors of South Africa and Zimbabwe have been affected by the rise of China and its impact on southern Africa. To facilitate the comparative case study of South Africa and Zimbabwe, I drew on existing secondary sources of data complemented by primary data gathered from my own interviews to measure the arguments and discussions set out above. In the course of my field research, I interviewed relevant actors in the business and, more widely, where relevant, in consultancies, academia, and IFIs to learn the firsthand views of these expert actors as they relate to my study of SBRs in South Africa and Zimbabwe. I also analysed South African and Zimbabwean government, business, and related documents, such as those produced by IFIs and the Chinese state, to identify the nature of liberalisation and indigenisation policies, Sino-South African and Sino-Zimbabwean bilateral economic and political relations, and the reaction of the mining sector to the government's policy choices. Moreover, I make comparisons between these two cases regarding their bilateral economic and political relations with China. I therefore examine the effects of China's presence in South Africa and Zimbabwe during the 2000s and 2010s in each country's mining sector.

OUTLINE OF THE BOOK

This book contains four chapters: the introduction is related to the framing and research design, the historical background, the key periods, and methodology and the theoretical approach of this study. It explains the main argument of the book and what its assumptions are. Also, the introduction suggested research questions of the book and shows what the history says about the respective policy choices of South Africa and Zimbabwe regarding their mining industries under the majority rules. The introduction discussed why the MWS theory is a suitable framework for explaining the SBRs in Africa. It also demonstrated what the role of China is in both countries during the twenty-first century before discussing what makes South Africa unique in its region. Lastly, the introduction showed what the periods and methods of the book are.

Following this introduction, the four key assumptions which constitute the explanatory framework of this study are analysed in four separate chapters. In chapter 1, I analyse the cases of South Africa and Zimbabwe according to the theoretical approaches of the MWS and locate them in the semiperiphery and the periphery respectively. This chapter explains the MWS theory, its components, changing nature during the twenty-first century, and the five aspects of the international division of labour; namely, capital accumulation, unequal exchange, commodity chains, core-periphery dichotomy, and a semiperiphery are the theoretical base of the book. Locating South Africa in the semiperiphery and Zimbabwe in the periphery with the help of traditional measurement methods of the MWS literature are other subjects of the first chapter.

In chapter 2, I analyse the policy choices of Pretoria and Harare on the mining industries of South Africa and Zimbabwe. I examine the liberalisation and indigenisation of the mining industries in South Africa and Zimbabwe during the postapartheid and postcolonial periods respectively; moreover, explaining the history and the current structure of the mining industry for colonial powers, minority rules, majority rules, and international businesses. The chapter compares GEAR and ESAP as liberal policies and BEE and IEE as indigenisation policies in both countries. Empowering the black majorities of South Africa and Zimbabwe have been the key target of those indigenisation policies. The chapter analyses domestic institutions and powerful groups regarding the mining sector with the help of the political settlements framework in both countries.

I also analyse both China's economic and political presence and its relative absence in the respective mining industries of South Africa and Zimbabwe with the help of the MWS perspective in chapter 3. The chapter answers the question of how Beijing's approach is different to South Africa and

Zimbabwe as they represent divergent positions in the MWS and economic opportunities for Chinese state-owned or private mining companies. China's partnership with South Africa is also decisive for the more equal approach of Beijing than the natural resources-oriented approach to the rest of Africa, including Zimbabwe. The chapter discusses whether or not China's presence in Africa, especially in South Africa and Zimbabwe creates a dependency.

In chapter 4, I seek to complete the puzzle through an examination of the combined effects of the initial arguments of the book, namely, location in the MWS and mining policy choices, and the Chinese absence or presence on the consolidation or fracturing of the SBRs of South Africa and Zimbabwe respectively, which is the ultimate goal of this book project. Therefore, the chapter answers the question of how SBRs developed in South Africa and Zimbabwe across the relevant periods of liberalisation and indigenisation. The chapter defines the concepts of consolidation and fracturing of SBRs and the measurement of SBRs in both cases. The chapter analyses the effects of BEE and IEE on the domestic and international mining sectors during the twenty-first century.

Finally, in the conclusion, I not only summarise the findings of the study but also illustrate the extent to which I have been able to answer my ultimate question on the consolidation or fracturing of the SBRs in South Africa and Zimbabwe by means of the study which I have designed for that purpose. I make some recommendations for future research on SBRs in posttransition communities, and discuss what the book's limitations are. The principal aims of this research are to contribute to the political economy of southern Africa, China-Africa relations, and the MWS literature set.

NOTES

1. This book is derived from my dissertation at Queen's University of Belfast, and the dissertation was funded by the Ministry of National Education of Turkey between 2016 and 2020 with the title "State-Business Relations in the Modern World-System: A Comparative Study of South Africa and Zimbabwe." I have rewritten my dissertation for a broader scholarly audience, and transformed into a monograph with major modifications, reductions, or additions to all chapters.

2. Southall (2012, p. 4) argued that "the democratic settlement was simultaneously based on the confirmation of the capitalist basis of accumulation and the consolidation of corporate power."

3. Although the unequal exchange between the core and the periphery of the MWS concept was adopted during the 1970s, the roots of the unequal international trade term or 'unequal exchange' could be found in ECLA schools works from the 1950s (Wallerstein, 2004, pp. 11–12). The unequal exchange concept has also been used in the environmental studies literature during the last decade with the ecological unequal

exchange subconcept (*see* Frey *et al.*, 2018; Foster & Holleman, 2014; Hornborg, 2012; 2009; Jorgenson, 2010; Hornborg *et al.*, 2007; Rice, 2007).

4. For detailed information on South African history, *see* Pretorius (2014); Clark & Worger (2011); Berger (2009); Thompson (2001); Davenport & Saunders (2000); Ross (1999).

5. For detailed information on the Zimbabwean colonial past and the anticolonial insurrection, *see* Schmidt (2013); Bourne (2011); Raftopoulos & Mlambo (2009); Zvobgo (2009); Scarnecchia (2008); Meredith (2003).

6. The SANNC was renamed in 1923 as the ANC. The majority population of African people allied themselves during the 1940s. Africans-Blacks, Coloureds, and Indians united in the ANC against increased attacks on the rights of black people and the rise of extreme Afrikaner nationalism.

7. Angola and Mozambique gained independence from Portugal during the 1970s. After the collapse of Portugal's colonies, white minority regimes also ended in Zimbabwe (1980), Namibia (1990), and South Africa (1994).

8. Zimbabwe was not the only state which struggled with foreign debt in sub-Saharan Africa during the 1980s. The 1980s foreign debt crisis not only led to hyperinflation, but also prevented the problems of underdevelopment in sub-Saharan Africa from being solved.

Chapter 1

Location in the Modern World-System

INTRODUCTION

There are several studies in the literature on SBRs in developing countries and emerging economies (Cali *et al.*, 2011; Jilberto & Hogenboom, 2007; Maxfield & Schneider, 1997; Haggard & Kaufman, 1992; Evans, 1992). However, divergent positions in the MWS and their effects on SBRs context remain a debatable issue. In order to make the argument about the different outcomes of SBRs in South Africa and Zimbabwe, the position of each country in the international division of labour must be explicitly determined. This chapter, therefore, examines not only how South Africa and Zimbabwe are located in the semiperiphery and periphery of the MWS respectively, but also the effects of these different locations on their SBRs.

In addition to locating both countries in the MWS, this chapter also examines the changing nature of the MWS from the 2000s onwards to understand the roles of both countries in this new order under the solidarity of the Global South. Also, this section discusses the existing measurement methods for defining the position of individual countries in the MWS. Positioning South Africa and Zimbabwe in the MWS is essential for this research since the classification of cases is a prerequisite for subsequent comparison. Therefore, as a comparative case study, this chapter aims to evaluate whether these countries can be located in different paths of the world-system according to the definitions of each in MWS theory.

THEORETICAL FRAMEWORK: THE PRINCIPAL FEATURES OF THE MODERN WORLD-SYSTEM

In order to understand how I developed the main assumptions of this study, the theoretical framework of the study, which is the MWS theory, must be clearly determined. This section, therefore, explains why the MWS is a suitable theoretical framework for developing assumptions for this study, rather than rival theories such as the Dependency Theory (*see* Frank, 2009; Cardoso, 1979; 1977; Emmanuel, 1972; Rodney, 1972; Dos Santos, 1970; Prebisch, 1959; Baran, 1957; Prebisch, 1950) or the Modernization Theory (*see* Wagner, 1993; Jacquette, 1982; Tipps, 1973; Bernstein, 1971; Black, 1966; Rostow, 1962; Rostow, 1960). This section separates the economic and political zones of the MWS derived from the work of key contributors to MWS theory (such as Babones & Chase-Dunn, 2012; Wallerstein, 2011a; 2006; 1989; 1980; 1979a; 1975; 1974a; 1974b; Gowan, 2004; Goldfrank, 2000; Chase-Dunn & Hall, 1997; Chase-Dunn & Grimes, 1995; Arrighi & Drangel, 1986; Hopkins & Wallerstein, 1982; 1980; Petras, 1981; Chase-Dunn & Rubinson, 1977). This section also explains the purpose, essential characteristics, and theoretical contributions of MWS theory, for instance, the core-periphery dichotomy, the concept of semiperiphery, unequal exchange, and world-economy. The roots of MWS theory can be found within the *Annales* School (Burke, 2013 [1990]; Dosse, 1994; Huppert, 1982; Forster, 1978; Stoianovich, 1978), Marxism (Evans, 1975; Kay, 1975; Lenin, 1963; Marx, 1849) and Fernand Braudel's *longue durée* approach (Lee, 2013; Wallerstein, 2004; Braudel, 1958).

Immanuel Wallerstein's MWS is the main theoretical framework of this study. This section explains the reasons for selecting the MWS as the theoretical framework and gives a brief overview of the MWS literature. Wallerstein (2014; 1989; 1980; 1974) analysed and explored the capitalist world-economy from the sixteenth century to the twentieth century in his four-volume study. In this current study, I used Wallerstein's model for illustrating and analysing the contrasts and similarities between the mining industries of South Africa and Zimbabwe, which are components of noncore areas of the MWS during transition periods from minority rule to majority rule.

Wallerstein (1975, pp.16–17) criticised the developmentalist model's mechanical and Euro-centric approach and claimed that the problems of the system could be solved by the leadership of hegemonic countries. In contrast to the developmentalist model, he believed that the world-system perspective was a dialectical and not a development model and that it should support the leadership of hegemonic powers and not be Euro-centric. Goldfrank (2000, p. 150) defined the MWS 'method' as a combination of "continental historicism, 'Third World' radicalism, and Marxism." According to Babones (2015,

p. 3–4), as a 'heterodox Marxian approach' the MWS analysis distinguished from 'orthodox Marxian approach' in two significant manners:

> First, it backdates the origin of the current capitalist system from the 1800s to the 1500s. Second, it equates capitalism with the primacy of production for monetary exchange, from which labor relations emerge as a consequence—turning on its head the orthodox Marxian account of the emergence of capitalism as an economic system. World-systems analysis is thus first and foremost a framework for interpreting the modern world of the last 500 years as a social system driven by market exchange.

Petras (1981, p. 148) argued that the selection of the capitalist world-economy as the primary unit of analysis was "the real innovation" of the MWS approach as opposed to the dependency school. The MWS is, therefore, able to answer the scramble for southern African mineral resources along with the development of the capitalist world-economy during the last five hundred years.

The MWS theory was not developed to explain only international relations between states and actors (Chase-Dunn & Hall 1997, p. 2). Instead, it was designed to analyse "the history of national societies and global patterns of development in the modern age," which comprise local, national, regional, interstate, transnational, and global relations in its holistic structure (Chase-Dunn & Hall, 1997, p. 2). Thus the nationalisation of the Marange diamond field and the missing US$13 billion in Zimbabwe (*see* Maguwu, 2016; Saunders & Nyamunda, 2016; Maguwu, 2013; Towriss, 2013) and the massacre at the Marikana mining site, where thirty-four Lonmin platinum mineworkers were killed by the South African police during the 2014 platinum strike, in South Africa (*see* Bond, 2018; 2014; Alexander, 2013) were recent local examples of state intervention in the problems related to the mining industries of noncore resource-rich countries.

Moreover, BEE and IEE in South Africa and Zimbabwe respectively are the national issues related to both the MWS theory and political economy literature. The pivotal position of South Africa in southern Africa not only represents regional relations but also demonstrates the interstate relations between the cases of this study. Thus, investigating the chronic problems of the settler rule, which was a very exceptional model of political economy in southern Africa, is a part of the context in which this study analyses SBRs in South Africa and Zimbabwe. Petras (1981, p. 148) pointed out that the originality of the MWS theory derives from the selection of the capitalist world economy as the primary unit of analysis. He stated that "all phenomena are to be explained in terms of their consequence for both the whole of the system and its parts." The MWS theory can, therefore, explain these specific issues in South Africa and Zimbabwe and their effects on SBRs from the local to the global levels.

This section also aims to show the differences between peripheral and semiperipheral areas of the MWS. These differences will generate a basis for comparing South Africa and Zimbabwe regarding their respective locations in the MWS. It also demonstrates the importance of the division of the MWS into three zones or strata (core/semiperiphery/periphery) instead of the binary division of the world-economy as conceived of by Dependency Theory (core-periphery). Furthermore, this section discusses the strong states and the world-economy relations with the help of Chase-Dunn and Rubinson's (1977) question, "Why is state strength so important to economic production in the world-system?" This section also explains the main function of the concept of a semiperiphery to regenerate the vicious cycle of the unequal exchange and capital accumulation from the periphery to the core through the semiperiphery.

There are three possible scenarios for world-systems, namely, to become a world-economy, a world-empire or a socialist world government, which is the only alternative for the other two types of world-systems. Hence, the MWS is the product of the current capitalist world-economy which is the basic type of world-system. Additionally, the MWS theory suggests that "a world-economy . . . is an 'economic' unit, while a world-empire is a 'political' unit in which one political centre dominates the entire world system" (Gowan, 2004, p. 483). On the other hand, Goldfrank (2000, p. 167) hypothesised that the nature of world-economies is the opposite of that of world-empires because world-economies constitutively "are integrated through the market rather than by a single political center." He, therefore, drew attention to multiple economic and political regions in world-economies:

> In this type of social system, two or more distinct economic and cultural regions are interdependent with respect to necessities such as food, fuel and protection, *and* two or more polities compete for domination without a single center's emerging quasi-permanently.

That said, Wallerstein (2004, p. 57) argued that the only alternative to the world-system is a socialist world government. The MWS is a world-economy which has been dominated by respectively the Netherlands, the United Kingdom, and the United States from the seventeenth century to the twenty-first century. Former hegemonies (such as the Netherlands and the United Kingdom) in the MWS had moved down from their respective hegemonic positions but not from the core during the last four centuries.[1] Moreover, world-empire and hegemony are two quite different ways in which states might realise dominance in the MWS (Wallerstein, 2004, p. 57).

The international division of labour and political action, which includes the interstate system, are the two most essential constituent elements of the MWS (Wallerstein, 2011a; 2004; 1974a). The various economic zones of the capitalist world-economy—namely the core, the semiperiphery, and the periphery—comprise an international division of labour through their specific economic roles, different class structures, and different modes of labour control (Wallerstein, 2011b, p. 162). On the other hand, interstate competition constitutes political action among the most centralised core, semiperipheral, and peripheral states. Hopkins, Wallerstein *et al.* (1982, p. 43) explained the emergence of the MWS through the mutual reproduction of the European state system and the international division of labour from the core-like to the periphery-like areas.

> The progressive formation of these polities as stronger and weaker states in relation to one another in the emerging European (later, international) state-system went hand in hand with the cyclically evolving division of labor between the increasingly "core" areas of the world-system and the increasingly "peripheral" areas. And the world-economy became basically structured as an increasingly interrelated system of strong "core" and weak "peripheral" states, in which inter-state relations—and hence patterns of state-formation and, in that setting, the formation of nationally-organized "societies"—are continually shaped and in turn continually shape the deepening and expanding world-scale division and integration of production.

Based on their distinction between the political and the economic spheres of the MWS, this section discusses the fundamental features of the international division of labour and the interstate system respectively.

Chase-Dunn and Rubinson claimed that "the differences in strength of state structures are partially a result of the division of labor" (1977, p. 456). Hence, there is a specific link between the division of labour and the variation in the strength of state formations in the MWS, which I shall explain below. The peripheral areas, therefore, have more vulnerable state structures than the core areas. Additionally, Wallerstein (1974b, p. 403) argued that "the strengthening of the state-machineries in core areas has as its direct counterpart the decline of the state-machineries in peripheral areas." So, for instance, during the colonial era in Africa, the powerful state apparatus of European nations weakened local authority in colonial countries. However, at the same time and in the similar peripheral areas of the world-system, white minority regimes in South Africa and Zimbabwe strengthened their authority and means of state control. Strengthening state power in peripheral areas might escalate upward mobility in terms of ranking in the MWS for a peripheral country. For example, Mustafa Kemal Ataturk, the founder of modern Turkey, constructed more powerful state machinery than the previous one and the newly independent Turkey consequently rose into the semiperiphery of the MWS (Akçalı & Korkut, 2015; Worth & Moore, 2009; Onis & Aysan, 2000) from its former peripheral position during the final decades of the Ottoman Empire (Islamogu-Inan, 2004; Kasaba, 1988; Pamuk, 1987; Wallerstein, 1979b). Similarly, strengthening the state machinery in China under the communist regime elevated the country's position into the semiperiphery of the MWS (Robinson, 2011; Li, 2008; 2005).

The main structure of the international division of labour has five aspects: capital accumulation, unequal exchange, commodity chains, core-periphery dichotomy, and a semiperiphery. The core-periphery dichotomy and semiperiphery aspects have a primary role in this current study as they explain the crucial differences between the two cases of this study, South Africa and Zimbabwe. In addition to the concepts of a core-periphery dichotomy and a semiperiphery, this section examines the concepts of capital accumulation, unequal exchange, and commodity chains in the international division of labour.

The first aspect of the international division of labour is the endless accumulation of capital and its reproduced connection with the interstate system. States, interstate systems, and the periodic hegemonic powers construct the capitalist world-economy, which includes the international division of labour. Wallerstein (2004), however, stated that a capitalist state fundamentally gives priority to the endless accumulation of capital with the help of the political and cultural dominance of hegemonic core powers. At the end of this process, capitalists still try to escape the dominance of core states (Wallerstein, 2004, p. 59).

Endless accumulation of capital maintains the dominance of the core countries over noncore areas. Similarly, semiperipheral countries dominate the peripheral areas of the MWS through the endless accumulation of capital. Apart from states, the transnational capitalist class (TCC) is among the most important actors for maintaining the existent accumulation system. Therefore, according to Sklair (2002; 2001; 2000; 1997), there are four main fractions of the TCC:

i. The corporate fraction (stakeholders)
ii. The state fraction (global bureaucrats and politicians)
iii. The technical fraction (globalizing professionals)
iv. The consumerist fraction (merchants and media)

In a peripheral or semiperipheral country, the governing elites could join the state fraction of TCC with the help of their statesmen status. However, joining the remaining three fractions might be a challenge for the political and economic elites of a noncore country. In addition to Sklair, Clelland (2012, p. 198) explained who collects the surplus value as a part of this endless capital accumulation and how it is used and expropriated:

> The capitalist world-system is structured to ensure the concentration of surplus into the hands of capitalists and state elites (in the form of profit, rents, interest, and taxes). On the one hand, these groups are motivated to expand the surplus in order to broaden their consumption of luxury goods. On the other hand, the key to the continuation of the world-system is reinvestment of surplus into expanded reproduction of the system, that is, accumulation. In addition, capitalists share part of the surplus with those who perform the functions of capital, the managerial-professional class, and even with sections of the working class. Finally, capitalists may surrender "surplus opportunity" by passing on hidden surplus in the form of lower prices to commodity buyers.

The second aspect, that of 'unequal exchange,' was borrowed from Dependency theorists. Petras (1981, p. 149) considered that

> The central theme of the world systems approach is the proposition that core regions exploit peripheral regions through various mechanisms of unequal exchange . . . It is further hypothesized that the transfer of value from one region of the world capitalist economy to another is a form of primary accumulation that is necessary to the maintenance of monopoly forms of capitalism in the core. As a means of extracting surplus, unequal exchange is not only different from the extended reproduction of capital that is characteristic of the core, but it is the principal contradiction of the modern capitalist world.

Williams (1985, p. 47) explained that unequal exchange is when "there is evidence that exchange, or trade, tends to benefit rich countries while impoverishing poor ones." Unequal trade is not a new model of the unfair income distribution but of unequal exchange, which induces global polarity and is different from the earlier versions, such as mutually beneficial trade and structurally biased trade (Smith & Toye, 1979 cited in Williams, 1985). She also distinguished the unequal exchange model from earlier studies of trade and argued that the type of traded products (such as manufactured goods and raw materials) are less substantial than the wages paid to the individuals who are producing specific products (Williams, 1985, p. 48). For instance, when Zimbabwe produces tobacco, the crucial point at issue is the amount of money salaried to Zimbabwean farmers to produce tobacco, not the fact that it is an agricultural commodity (a modified example from Williams, 1985, p. 48).

MWS analysis provides a broad range of perspectives for this current study. For example, Bergesen (1990) showed that the MWS theory has a similar approach to Realist and Neorealist schools of the International Relations discipline. These schools assume that the international state system is a product of the struggle for power between sovereign states in a condition of international hierarchy (Bergesen, 1990, p. 67). On the other hand, the MWS theory hypothesises that the core-periphery division of labour is a production of unequal exchange processes between underdeveloped and developed states or zones (Bergesen, 1990, p. 67). In this current study, the explanations of the unequal exchange process of the MWS theory for analysing respective SBRs in South Africa and Zimbabwe from a structural perspective are used. SBR theories predominantly position themselves apart from business or the state apparatus (for SBR theories, *see* Evans, 1997; Haggard *et al.*, 1997). Conversely, this current study seeks to analyse SBRs in the capitalist world-system from a structural perspective, namely the MWS theory.

The third aspect of the division of labour answers the question, 'What is the mode of production in the MWS?' by means of the concept of commodity production. Chase-Dunn and Rubinson (1977, p. 455) adopted the concept of commodity production from Wallerstein and argued that there is only one mode of production in the MWS, which is "commodity production for profit on the world market." These three fundamental aspects of the international division of labour are decisive in shaping the relations between not only the cores and peripheries but also the semiperipheries of the MWS, which I shall explain next.

The fourth aspect of the division of labour is a core-periphery dichotomy in the MWS. The structure of the modern world-system includes 'cores' and 'peripheries.' They are united and reproduced through processes of capital accumulation and unequal exchange (Hopkins, Wallerstein *et al.*, 1982, pp. 42–43). Given the changes which have taken place in the nature of the world-system, manufactured goods and raw materials (Chase-Dunn & Rubinson, 1977, p. 454) might not be the only products for locating a country's position in the MWS today. Some core areas continue to produce manufactured goods, and some peripheral areas are still producing raw materials, but in the last forty years, new types of high-technology products—for example, software production for computers and mobile phones—have been produced in the core and semiperipheral areas of the MWS. Similarly, some of the emerging peripheral countries have raised the number of manufactured products in last forty years; for example, Kenya (food and beverages, and petroleum) and Nigeria (cement, food and beverages, textile, and tobacco) in Africa. In peripheral areas, the vast majority of activity would come into the category of peripheral activity.

Despite this, the main distinction between the core and the periphery is the unequal exchange of sophisticated manufactured goods and unsophisticated manufactured goods, raw materials and agricultural goods in terms of commodity production. The same situation is not a necessity for the core areas. Core states tend to have peripheral activities as well (Wallerstein, 1982, p. 93). The main difference between the core and the peripheral areas is the skill levels of labour and technology (Chase-Dunn & Rubinson, 1977, p. 459).

> Productivity varies according to the ratio of constant capital (plant, raw materials, and machinery) to variable capital (the amount of labor power) incorporated into production, according to the capacity of machinery to transform raw materials, and according to the skill levels of labor.

Chase-Dunn and Rubinson (1977, p. 460) also claimed that the reproduction rate of productivity is more significant than the fall and rise of the level of productivity in the core and the periphery.

Hopkins, Wallerstein *et al.* (1982, p. 61) stated that different kinds of economic zones are placed in the core, the semiperiphery and the periphery of the MWS. However, peripheral areas have a less diversified economic structure than the core and semiperiphery. Therefore, as a semiperipheral country, South Africa exports mainly not only precious stones and metals but also motor vehicles and parts. Despite this diversity in South Africa's export products, Zimbabwe exports mainly raw materials and commodities and this, therefore, determines its peripheral rank in the MWS. Wallerstein (2011b, p. 355) claimed that state structures are weaker in the peripheral areas than in the semiperipheral or core areas of the MWS. Therefore, for example, the Zimbabwean economy is more fragile and unstable than the South African economy because of their respective positions in the MWS.

The fifth aspect of the international division of labour is the concept of a semiperiphery. There are several definitions of the term 'semiperiphery' in the literature. For example, Arrighi and Drangel (1986, pp. 11–12) defined the semiperiphery as a link between the core and the periphery. They also argued that the semiperiphery holds both peripheral and core-related activities. Arrighi also characterised the core and peripheral zones of the MWS as productivity activities and placed semiperipheral areas between these zones.

> The core zone tends to become the locus of the "brain" activities of corporate capital, the peripheral zone tends to become the locus of the "muscle and nerves" activities, and the semiperipheral zone tends to be characterized by a more or less even mix of "brain" and "muscle and nerves" activities (Arrighi, 1985b, p. 275 quoted in Arrighi & Drangel, 1986, p. 57).

Chase-Dunn and Hall (1997, p. 37) explained the semiperiphery concept through five different meanings: i) a mix of core and peripheral forms of organisation; ii) a location between core and peripheral areas; iii) a location among two or more competing core areas; iv) semiperipheral areas might perform mediating activities between core and peripheral regions; v) an area "may be one in which institutional features are in some ways intermediate between those forms found in core and periphery." Sectoral allocation in South Africa is an understandable demonstrator of its semiperipheral position in the MWS. For example, finance, real estate, and business activities in South Africa constitute one-fifth of GDP and are twice as big as the share of mining and quarrying (*see* OECD, 2017). Core and peripheral activities of this type give an intermediate role to South Africa and other semiperipheral countries.

From a historical perspective, the roots of the three structural positions in the world-economy had become stabilised by about 1640 (Wallerstein, 1974b, p. 401).[2] The MWS globalised at the end of the nineteenth century because of the competition between the core states (Chase-Dunn & Rubinson, 1977, p. 466). As a result, peripheral areas were colonised by the core powers during this competition, and in this way territories and populations of Africa were incorporated into the MWS.

This current study also argues that Wallerstein's semiperiphery concept needs to be revised because the gaps between weak and powerful semiperipheral countries have been broadening by the rise of China. Chase-Dunn and Rubinson (1977) analysed the characteristic features of the core, semiperiphery, and periphery and explained the reproduction of the MWS through the unequal exchange, core-like, and periphery-like activities. The principal contribution of that work is the concept of "upwardly and downwardly mobile semiperipheral areas." Despite China's rise in more than three decades (*see* Goodman & Segal, 2013; Golley & Song, 2011; Overholt, 2010; Paus *et al.*, 2009; Alden *et al.*, 2008; Callahan, 2008; Chin & Helleiner, 2008; Deng & Wang, 2004), this current study discusses both China and South Africa as semiperipheral countries. Although China could be called an upwardly mobile semiperipheral country, some argue that China is unlikely to become a superpower and will therefore not join other core countries (Buzan, 2011; Agnew, 2010). The successes of Chinese state-owned companies and China's state-led development model, therefore, show that the neoliberal principles such as privatisation and the liberalisation of economies are not the *sine qua non* of economic growth. Because of this fundamental distinction between China and the core states, China might not rise in the MWS as a core country.

Despite this, others have argued that China will either challenge US hegemony within the system (Mearsheimer, 2006) or "try to gain more leadership" within it (Ikenberry, 2011). On the one hand, therefore, China can become a core country without following the rules of the liberal models of capitalism and democracy (Barma *et al.*, 2007). Indeed, Zhao (2015) suggested that China's rise would be peaceful. On the other hand, Golub (2013) argued that "China is following the path of earlier successful capitalist powers" such as the United Kingdom and the United States "through the exploitation of its internal peripheries," including Africa. As a result, China can either challenge the international leadership of the United States with a systemic conflict or integrate into the existing liberal order, which is the current MWS, with eventual assimilation (Friedberg, 2018; 2005; Barma *et al.*, 2007).

This current study aims to understand why SBRs tend to evolve/transition over time, consolidating or fracturing in South Africa and Zimbabwe in the posttransition and economic transformation periods, through the instrument of theoretical discussion of the Wallerstein's semiperiphery concept. The MWS theory provides a clear categorisation and explanation of the relations between developing countries in terms of why SBRs are fractured or consolidated under specific conditions. The MWS theory is therefore useful for answering the core research question of the study, which is why SBRs fracture or consolidate over time during posttransition periods.

It is my contention that a country's position in the MWS does not on its own decide relations with China. However, a country's position in the MWS might illustrate the degree of influence of China in the noncore areas. I also suggest that a country's position in the MWS does not on its own affect its policy choices, such as liberalisation or indigenisation. Nevertheless, a country's position in the MWS might affect the implementation method of these policy choices. For instance, peripheral countries are more eager to implement more radical policies than gradual ones as a result of their state structures (for the structure of the MWS, *see* Babones, 2005; Arrighi & Drangel, 1986; Chase-Dunn & Rubinson, 1977). As a consequence, the MWS perspective is particularly well suited to understanding the variation of SBRs, namely fracturing or consolidation in posttransition communities.

MEASURING THE LOCATION IN THE MWS: SEMIPERIPHERY AND PERIPHERY

The first aim in this subsection is to explain how I measured the countries' position in the MWS. Measurement of the countries' position in the MWS was based on mainly quantitative data sets to indicate any structural differences between South Africa and Zimbabwe. Wallerstein (2011b, p. 355) suggested that state structures are weak in peripheral areas. External forces are more decisive in the periphery than in the semiperiphery because of the weaker and more vulnerable structure and capabilities of peripheral states and economies. This is, therefore, a fundamental difference between the two cases in this study, which derives directly from each country's position in the MWS.

I located South Africa and Zimbabwe in the MWS through the data sets of international organisations and their databanks, including the United Nations

Development Programme (UNDP), the World Bank, the International Trade Centre, the African Economic Outlook, and the Fragile State Index. The economic growth performance of countries is a significant indicator for determining a country's position in the MWS (*see* Babones, 2000; Arrighi & Drangel, 1986; Snyder & Kick, 1979). The first distinct indicator between semiperipheral and peripheral countries is their Gross Domestic Product (GDP) per capita, which "represents the sum total of goods and services produced within the borders of a country" (Babones, 2000, p. 42). Thus produced goods and services and their sectoral allocation of GDP is another useful indicator for locating countries within the MWS (Chase-Dunn & Rubinson, 1977). Also, the sectoral allocation and vulnerability rates of labour forces are significant in illustrating the structure of the working classes in the MWS. The lower vulnerability of workers and employment means more secure working conditions (*see* UNDP, 2016).

Moreover, determining a country's position in the international division of labour can be based on the character of its exports and imports (Williams, 1985). Export and import indicators include the main trade goods, their proportion of the total trade volume, and the total value of trade volume (for an example of a comparison between South Africa and Zambia in the MWS *see* Andreasson, 2001). The Human Development Index (HDI) of the UNDP is another useful indicator for determining a country's position in the MWS. The HDI includes life expectancy at birth, expected and mean years of schooling, and Gross National Income (GNI) per capita. There are four categories of human development within the HDI: very high, high, medium, and low. Finally, the vulnerability to and resilience against domestic and external pressures might not be a reliable indicator for locating countries in the MWS, but it is nevertheless helpful for comparing a country's fragility in terms of uneven economic development, human rights, and the rule of law, and economic decline (Fragile State Index, 2016).

Table 1.1: Locating countries in the MWS

	Periphery	*Semiperiphery*
GDP per capita	Low-income aggregate	Middle-income aggregate
GDP by sector	Agricultural activities and raw materials	A mix of peripheral and core-like activities (in addition to the peripheral activities, in the semiperiphery core-like activities are available: manufacturing, finance)
Vulnerability rates of labour forces	High	Medium or Low
Export and import goods	Agricultural goods and raw materials	A mix of raw materials and sophisticated manufactured goods
UNDP HDI rank	Low	Medium or High

COMPARING SOUTH AFRICA AND ZIMBABWE IN REGARD TO THEIR POSITION IN THE MWS USING EMPIRICAL DATA

The state-based categorisation of the global system in MWS theory is helpful for understanding a general trend of moving away from the Western core towards a China-centric semiperiphery in terms of the dominant external influences on South Africa and Zimbabwe. This analytical method proposes three diverse types in the MWS: core, semiperiphery, and periphery. Wallerstein (2011b, p. 162) asserted that these are the main bases of the capitalist world-economy:

> [T]he capitalist world-economy was built on a worldwide division of labor in which various zones of this economy (that which we have termed the core, the semiperiphery, and the periphery) were assigned specific economic roles, developed different class structures, used consequently different modes of labor control, and profited unequally from the workings of the system.

Based on this schema, South Africa and Zimbabwe might be considered as examples, respectively, of semiperipheral and peripheral states in the MWS. However, this argument needs to be developed with the help of both quantitative and qualitative data for determining both countries' positions in the MWS. This section therefore compares the different positions of South Africa and Zimbabwe using empirical data on economic performance and development. To do this, I have used GDP per capita; the sectoral allocation of GDP; work, employment, and vulnerability rates; the range of export and import goods; and the HDI rankings of both countries in order to determine their positions.

According to the World Bank (2016), GDP per capita demonstrates that South Africa is in the middle-income aggregate (*see* table 1.2). Before the end of the apartheid regime, South Africa was 3.55 times richer than other middle-income countries in 1990. Under the ANC regime, however, South Africa did not perform as well as other middle-income countries from 1995 to 2015, which demonstrates the demise of the country during the last three decades. South Africa's growth rate fell behind not only the world aggregate but also sub-Saharan Africa between 1980 and 2015, but the GDP per capita was still distinctly middle income in comparison with the rest of the continent.

GDP per capita statistics suggest that Zimbabwe has been between the average amount of low income and middle-income countries from the mid-1980s. However, in the first years of majority rule, Zimbabwe was above the average amount of middle-income countries during the early 1980s. These changes, therefore, indicate that Zimbabwe's economic performance has worsened in

Table 1.2: GDP per capita (current US$)

	1980	*1985*	*1990*	*1995*	*2000*	*2005*	*2010*	*2015*
South Africa	2,920	2,142	3,182	3,973	3,009	5,453	7,392	5,724
Zimbabwe	916	635	837	608	535	443	674	924
Middle income	671	708	896	1,143	1,264	1,957	3,900	4,775
Low Income	..	..	292	227	267	328	519	617
Sub-Saharan Africa	683	470.9	589	577	551	899	1,557	1,558
OECD members	8,861	9,731	17,473	22,674	23,505	30,929	35,657	35,886
World	2,495	2,611	4,262	5,386	5,460	7,247	9,482	10,057

Source: Author created with data from World Bank (2016)

comparison with the middle-income countries from the mid-1980s onwards. Also, Zimbabwe's GDP per capita was larger than the average of sub-Saharan Africa from 1980 to 2000, which was the year when economic sanctions were imposed on Zimbabwe by Western countries and IFIs.

In addition to economic performance, the sectoral allocation of GDP is a useful indicator by which to compare their economic structures (*see* table 1.3). These figures show that wholesale and retail trade and agriculture are the major sectors for the Zimbabwean economy, according to the OECD (2017) figures. However, mining, manufacturing, transport and communication, and finance also contribute to the total GDP of the country. Construction, public administration, and defence and the three utilities are the less important sectors for the Zimbabwean economy. According to the same figures, agriculture, utilities, and construction are the least important sectors in terms of their contribution to the South African GDP. Finance, public administration and defence, wholesale and retail trade are the biggest contributors to the country's GDP.

The major differences between South Africa's and Zimbabwe's sectoral distinction are the agricultural, financial, public administration, and defence sectors. Hence, financial services in South Africa are one-fifth of the GDP but are one-tenth in Zimbabwe. Moreover, agricultural activities constitute 2.5 per cent of the GDP of South Africa, whereas they are 14 per cent of Zimbabwe's. These differences demonstrate that South Africa's GDP is much less dependent on agricultural activities than Zimbabwe's GDP. Also, core-like industries, such as finance, are more important than the peripheral activities in South Africa.

One of the visible outcomes of the sectoral allocation of GDP is the vulnerability rates of labour forces. According to a UNDP Human Development Report (2016), the extent of the vulnerability of Zimbabwean workers (65.5

Table 1.3: GDP by sector (percentage of GDP at current prices)

	South Africa	*Zimbabwe*
Agriculture, forestry, fishing, and hunting	2.5	14.0
Mining and quarrying	8.4	9.5
Manufacturing	13.3	11.9
Electricity, gas, and water	3.7	4.5
Construction	4.1	3.5
Wholesale and retail trade	14.8	15.8
Transport, storage, and communication	10.0	12.1
Finance, real estate, and business services	20.5	11.9
Public administration and defence	17.0	3.6
Other services	5.7	13.1
GDP at basic prices/factor cost	100.0	100.0

Source: Author created with data from OECD (2017)

per cent) is far greater than that of South African workers (9.3 per cent). There are also huge gaps between South Africa and Zimbabwe regarding the division of labour. Only 4.6 per cent of South African workers are in agricultural activities, which might be an outcome of using sophisticated farming vehicles and tools for the South African agricultural activities, with 71.9 per cent employed in services. By contrast, 65.8 per cent of Zimbabweans workers are in agricultural activities, and 25 per cent of them work in services. These differences indicate that South Africa's division of labour is much less dependent on agricultural activities than Zimbabwe's. Consequently, these statistics show that Zimbabwe's division of labour is of a decidedly more peripheral-like nature than South Africa's.

Export and import profiles provide additional information about core-like and periphery-like industrial activities in South Africa and Zimbabwe respectively. According to the International Trade Centre (2015), the top ten export goods of South Africa include not only agricultural and mineral raw materials but also manufactured products, such as motor vehicles and parts, industrial machinery, and electrical machinery. For instance, machinery and equipment for mining, which includes machinery for mining, mineral processing and related infrastructure investment, is amongst the most significant category for South Africa's manufactured exports to other southern African countries (Arndt & Roberts, 2018, p. 11).

By contrast, Zimbabwe's top ten export goods are entirely comprised of agricultural and mineral raw materials, including tobacco and precious metals, and its total value of exports (US$2.7 billion) is nearly twenty-five times smaller than South Africa's (US$69.6 billion). Hence, both countries' exports demonstrate the balance of their existing core-like and periphery-like industrial activities. Ultimately, peripheral Zimbabwe's export products are much less diversified than those of semiperipheral South Africa, further reinforcing the divide between the two, as is also indicated by other economic and development indicators. The import profiles of both countries show some similarities, particularly for the major import goods such as oil and mineral fuels and industrial machinery. Nevertheless, the total amount of imported goods reveals a huge gap between the two countries. The total value of imports to South Africa (US$79.5 billion) is more than thirteen times Zimbabwe's total imports (US$6 billion).

The UNDP's HDI indicates the level of development across countries by a combined measure of life expectancy at birth, expected years of schooling, and GNI per capita (*see* table 1.4). According to the UNDP's Human Development Report (2015), South Africa is ranked 116th (of 188 countries) with an HDI of 0.666, which is lower than expected because of the very low life expectancy compared with other semiperipheral countries and is located in the Medium Human Development (third tier) HDI rank. Both the expected years of schooling and the mean years of schooling averages of South Africa are above the averages of sub-Saharan African countries and the world.

On the other hand, Zimbabwe is located in the Low Human Development (fourth tier) HDI rank with an HDI of 0.509 and is ranked 155th. South Africa and Zimbabwe have similar life expectancies at birth with a slight difference, respectively 57.4 and 57.5. The main reason for the relatively low life expectancy at birth in southern African countries is the number of HIV/AIDS-related deaths among younger people. Both the expected years of schooling and the mean years of schooling averages of Zimbabwe are above the average of sub-Saharan Africa, but not the world. Nevertheless, South Africa shows a better performance than Zimbabwe on expected years of schooling, mean years of schooling, and GNI per capita, the latter in particular, which is 7.5 times higher than in Zimbabwe.

Ultimately, each country's vulnerability to and resilience against domestic and external pressures is useful as an indicator of differences between them even though it is not part of a strict definition of classifying their positions in the MWS.[3] According to the 2016 rankings by the Fragile State Index, Zimbabwe receives a 'high alert warning' rank (the sixteenth worst of 188), whereas South Africa receives a 'warning' level rank in the 108th place (Fragile State Index, 2016). This report illustrates the vulnerability of countries to instability on a scale of eleven degrees, ranging from *Very High Alert* to *Very Sustainable*.[4] In sum, South Africa is more stable than Zimbabwe, according to the Fragile State Index.

Finally, it can be concluded that South Africa is in the semiperiphery of the MWS because of both core-like and peripheral activities according to the data sets discussed above, and according to the same figures, Zimbabwe is in the periphery of the MWS since there are no significant core-like activities alongside the dominant peripheral activities.

Table 1.4: Human Development Index, 2014

HDI Rank	*Country*	*Human Development Index*	*Life Expectancy at Birth*	*Expected Years of Schooling*	*Mean Years of Schooling*	*GNI Per Capita*	*GNI Per Capita Rank Minus HDI Rank*
		Value	(years)	(years)	(years)	(2011 PPP $)	
		2014	2014	2014	2014	2014	
Very High Human Development							
1	Norway	0.944	81.6	17.5	12.6	64,992	5
30	Estonia	0.861	76.8	16.5	12.5	25,214	14
High Human Development							
60	Panama	0.780	72.6	13.3	9.3	18,192	1
90	China	0.727	75.8	13.1	7.5	12,547	-7
Medium Human Development							
116	South Africa	0.666	57.4	13.6	9.9	12,122	-29
120	Kyrgyzstan	0.655	70.6	12.5	10.6	3,044	29
Low Human Development							
155	Zimbabwe	0.509	57.5	10.9	7.3	1,615	13
188	Niger	0.348	61.4	5.4	1.5	908	-5
Selected Regions							
	Sub-Saharan Africa	0.518	58.5	9.6	5.2	3,363	—
	OECD	0.880	80.2	15.8	11.5	37,658	—
	World	0.711	71.5	12.2	7.9	14,301	—

Source: Author created with data from UNDP (2015)

LOCATING SOUTH AFRICA IN THE SEMIPERIPHERY OF THE MWS

On the one hand, South Africa emerged in the twentieth century as the continent's most industrialised and diversified economy. It is a semiperipheral country with a core-like production process which has also become a strategic regional trading and financial centre in Africa (McGowan & Ahwireng-Obeng, 1998, p. 176).[5] For example, McGowan (1993, p. 36) described South Africa as

> a classical semiperipheral society because of exporting raw and semiprocessed minerals and agricultural products to the core and importing from these societies machinery, mining and transportation equipment, computers, aircraft and office machinery parts . . .

South Africa is therefore a semiperipheral centre not only for "the collection of surplus for transmission to the core and for the administration of the core" but for investments in the peripheral areas in the rest of the continent (McGowan & Ahwireng-Obeng, 1998, p. 176). In the same manner, the semiperipheral position of South Africa poses unequal relations towards both the core and peripheral areas of the MWS. Whereas the core countries gain an advantage with the help of the established underdeveloping relationships, peripheral ones in southern Africa or more broadly in sub-Saharan Africa have experienced similar unequal relationships with South Africa (Martin, 2013a, p. 180; 2013b, p. 167).

Three circumstances generated the promotion of South Africa within the international system to a 'regional manager' in Africa during the post-apartheid period: the lack of a regional manager in Africa; the existence of substantive power and the perceptions of the international community on this power; and former President Thabo Mbeki's efforts on the leadership of South Africa in the continent and creating partnerships with Western powers (Alden & Schoeman, 2015, p. 244). South Africa's idealistic position, including human rights and peacebuilding activities, regarding foreign policy, has strengthened its pivotal position within the continent (Qobo & Dube, 2015, p. 146). Business in South Africa has enjoyed this kind of influential foreign policy since South African corporates can reach every part of the continent with the help of the country's good reputation. Nevertheless, South Africa experienced a shift from liberal internationalism towards non-Western countries during the Zuma administration, and the ANC-led government ignored domestic business and favoured new investors, such as Chinese state-owned or private firms (Qobo & Dube, 2015, p. 145).

Despite the country's highly influential characteristic in foreign affairs, as a result of unresolved posttransition divisions relating to race, inequality, and underdevelopment, South Africa is located in the semiperipheral area of the MWS as is China. For example, South Africa`s developmental and infrastructural problems such as HIV/AIDS, lack of clean water, and poverty still have to be solved (Seekings, 2013, pp. 316–17). During the apartheid era, nonwhite citizens of South Africa were extremely marginalised in terms of economic, social, and political rights and access. As a result, the colonial-style oppression of the apartheid era caused huge inequalities between the white and nonwhite populations of South Africa.

As a semiperipheral country, South Africa is one of the most dominant and influential powers in Africa because it has a more stable and industrialised economy than most other Africa countries. In the postapartheid era, the South African economy was the biggest economy in Africa and had no rivals. Today, however, Nigeria, as the largest economy in the continent, is the biggest rival of South Africa on the African continent (Alden & Schoeman, 2015, p. 244). However, the existing dominance of South Africa over the continent has not yet been surpassed by another actor within Africa (Martin, 2013b, p. 10). Moreover, South Africa is less fragile and less vulnerable to external economic or political pressures and has the ability to exploit the natural resources of other, peripheral, southern African countries.

South Africa's multifaceted trade relations with the rest of the continent are a visible source of the semiperipheral position of the country. Carmody (2013, p. 51), for example, explained South Africa's diverse range of trade relations with the rest of Africa in four dimensions; as either complementary, competitive, consumptive, or extractive: i) if both parties benefit from the trade it is a complementary relation; ii) if imported goods generate direct competition with the target country's domestic industry it is a competitive relation; iii) if manufactured goods are imported for nonproductive purposes, such as luxuries, it is a consumptive relation; and iv) if "minerals are mined for processing by South African companies and the profits remitted to South Africa," it is an extractive relation (Carmody, 2013, p. 53). These four different trade relation types are helpful for indicating South Africa's numerous options within the rest of the African continent.

The corporate power of South Africa is another semiperipheral dimension of the country. The majority of the listed companies in the JSE have been investing in the rest of the continent for decades (Carmody, 2013, p. 50). In addition to the mining industry of South Africa (for example, Anglo Platinum, De Beers, and Impala Platinum), consumer goods and services, finance, media, and telecommunication companies (for instance, MTN Group, Old Mutual, SABC, SAB Miller, Standard Bank, and Telkom) also have investments and activities in the rest of Africa and other parts of the world despite the heavy presence of European and Chinese firms. Therefore other investors from outside the continent are a bigger threat for South African investments because they might bring competition, and this would restrict the activities of South African corporates.

The economic activities and investments of large South African corporates, such as the MTN Group, Shoprite Holdings Ltd., Vodacom, Woolworths, Anglo American, De Beers, and others, illustrate its 'subimperialist role' in the rest of Africa thanks to both its historical legacy and its recent inclusion in the BRICS alliance (Garcia, 2017a; 2017b; Garcia & Bond, 2015; Alden & Schoeman, 2013; Bond, 2013a; Taylor, 2011). Amisi *et al.* (2015) suggested that the BRICS countries loot Africa's resources like a second 'Scramble for Africa' through the activities of their large corporations on the continent (on the Scramble for Africa *see* also Moyo & Yeros, 2015; Burgess & Beilstein, 2013; Martin, 2013a; Carmody, 2011; Alden *et al.*, 2008; Lee, 2006). The pivotal position of South Africa's economy in sub-Saharan Africa is emphasised by the presence of the headquarters of the large retail, mobile phone, banking, and mining corporations in Sandton, more broadly Johannesburg (Reddy, 2015; Farley, 2008). So as a finance, trade, services, extraction, and manufacturing centre, Johannesburg can be considered a second-tier city after first-tier economic hubs such as London, New York, and Tokyo (McGowan & Obeng, 1998, p. 176).

The majority government has maintained the semiperipheral position of the country through FDIs within Africa. In this regard, the Industrial Development Corporation (IDC) is vital for South African corporates' investments in the rest of the African continent (Carmody, 2013, p. 50). The IDC was set up to promote industrial development and to foster economic growth under the ownership of the South African government as a state-owned development finance institution. Contributing to the economic empowerment of all South Africans and the creation of balanced and sustainable economic growth for other African countries are the major missions of the IDC, which reproduces the pivotal role of South Africa within the continent. According to its most recent Annual Report (Industrial Development Corporation, 2019), the IDC created 23,348 jobs in 2018 and invested R11 billion, which was 13 per cent of the total portfolio of the institution, in seventeen sub-Saharan African countries.

In spite of this regional advantage, two of the biggest investors in Africa, China and India, do not need to use South Africa as a gateway for their investments in the rest of Africa (Cheru & Obi, 2010). Indeed, although South Africa has the majority of the largest corporates in Africa as domestic drivers of the African economy, other African countries have experienced accelerating growth from 2002 onwards (Alden & Schoeman, 2015; Tang & Pigato, 2015; Akyuz, 2012). The high economic growth rates of the African economies have not yet produced the expected outcome of reducing the dependencies, and the continent as a whole remains on the periphery of the MWS (Taylor, 2016a; 2014, Garcia & Bond, 2015; Carmody, 2013; 2012).

South Africa also has an ability to establish more balanced bilateral relations with other semiperipheral countries such as Brazil, China, and India than other African countries under favour of the role of South Africa within the BRICS group and the IBSA Dialogue Forum (*see* Taylor, 2014; Bond, 2013a; Carmody, 2013; 2012; Stephen, 2012; Andreasson, 2011; Taylor, 2009; Alden & Viera, 2005). However, South Africa's leadership roles in international groupings, such as the G20, the United Nations Security Council (UNSC), and BRICS, constitute 'symbolic representativity' and create problems for Pretoria's ongoing foreign policy dilemmas (Alden & Schoeman, 2015). As a result, South Africa's increasing roles in international blocs and groupings unsurprisingly reproduce its pivotal position in Africa. However, South Africa is not powerful like other BRICS countries, although it has played a pivotal regional role for decades (Qobo & Dube, 2015, p. 156).

The subimperial role of South Africa was created during the white-settler rule (Martin, 2013a, p. 163). Martin (2013a, p. 181) believes that 'subimperialist' analyses of South Africa's role in the world-economy have been valuable for the last fifty years. Still, he argues that they ignore "the on-going struggle to create a new world order":

> Whether one looks at the future of reserve currencies, international financial institutions, migrant labour and capital flows, entrepreneurial and firm forms, post-structural adjustment policies, or the new international divisions of labour emanating from 'emerging' states, it is in Asia that innovation is taking place and not Europe or the United States.

The economic reason behind the emergence of the BRICS countries during the twenty-first century was "high commodity prices and low wages" (Garcia, 2017a), which enhanced the increased growth of BRICS countries since a huge amount of global investment is attracted by the alliance. Nevertheless, these improvements in economic growth have not yet provided equal development from below to above among the BRICS countries and other emerging powers. The BRICS countries have benefitted from "the structural context of neo-liberal globalization" to transform and develop their economies, in terms of transnationalisation and openings, with the help of "the governance framework of transnational regulation" (Stephen, 2014).

Another core-like aspect of South Africa is the successful transition to democracy in the postapartheid era. According to the 2016 Freedom House report on democratic institutions, South Africa was rated a 'free' democratic country (Freedom House, 2016, p. 23). In addition, South Africa was also rated 'partly free' and 'free' respectively on press and internet freedom issues (Freedom House, 2016, p. 23). Nevertheless, despite the positive aspects of being a semiperipheral country, South Africa has some significant weaknesses in terms of sustainable development goals, notably its persistently high levels of income inequality (Carmody, 2002, p. 272) and inadequate access to clean water and sanitation.

South Africa is therefore a conventional example of a semiperipheral state, a category which includes a range of countries with some different attributes and challenges, such as Brazil, China, India, Malaysia, Russia, and South Korea. Schubert and Sooryamoorthy (2009) argued that, for instance, "South Africa is a semiperipheral region, a centre for the periphery, and a periphery for the centre." Also, South Africa has during the twentieth century established a dominant position in Africa—and particularly in southern Africa (McGowan, 1993, p. 36)—as exemplified by its high levels of industrialisation and diversification. Although the South African economy is not powerful like the economies of other BRICS countries, it has better institution scores in terms of macro-economic fundamentals, the quality of its financial institutions and its business sophistication levels (Qobo & Dube, 2015, p. 156). This creates a secure environment for the existing businesses, as well as for foreign investors in South Africa rather than the majority of the African continent.

LOCATING ZIMBABWE IN THE PERIPHERY OF THE MWS

On the other hand, Zimbabwe exhibits all the key features of a peripheral state in the MWS. For instance, Zimbabwe is not only highly dependent on natural resources ranging from cash crops such as tobacco to minerals but also does not use these resources on behalf of Zimbabwean citizens. Wallerstein (2006, pp. 17–18) argued that "the ultimate result of an exchange between core and peripheral products was a flow of surplus-value (meaning here a large part of the real profits from multiple local productions) to those states that had a large number of core-like processes." Thus, Zimbabwe has a considerable and cheap labour force and does not block surplus value flows to the semiperiphery and core, as is characteristic of peripheral states in the MWS.[6]

However, Zimbabwe has not been like other sub-Saharan African countries all the time. Zimbabwe was more developed than the rest of the continent, except for South Africa, during the early days of majority rule (Simpson & Hawkins, 2018, p. 3; Dashwood, 2000, p. 23; Hawkins. 2004, p. 33). The relatively sophisticated domestic industry of Zimbabwe was a result of minority rule just as it was in South Africa (Simpson & Hawkins, 2018, p. 3). Indeed Zimbabwe was not a mono-economy like other sub-Saharan

African counterparts until the 1990s and therefore, according to Simpson and Hawkins (2018, p. 3),

> it boasted a diversified economy driven primarily by large-scale commercial agriculture, underpinned by sub-Saharan Africa's third largest manufacturing sector—after South Africa and Nigeria—a small, but diverse and profitable mining industry, and the region's second most sophisticated financial and banking sector after South Africa.

Nevertheless, the mismanagement during majority rule and the debt burden of the former period of minority rule accelerated the peripheralisation of the country during the 1990s (Bond & Manyanya, 2003, p. 17). The declining number of varieties of manufactured, extracted, or agricultural goods also fuelled the peripheralisation of Zimbabwe through ESAP (Nyabereka, 2017, p. 8). As a result, the existing mining industry diminished and has become completely reliant on the government. Also, manufacturing might still be important for the Zimbabwean economy, but the country is not an important actor in the continent as it was in the past.

Zimbabwe is located on the periphery of the MWS and therefore has a less powerful state structure than those in South Africa and other semiperipheral countries. Simpson and Hawkins (2018), for example, recently analysed the state structure of Zimbabwe and suggested that the country shows similarities with fragile states. As this chapter has shown, Zimbabwe is among the fragile states with a *High Alert* warning on the Fragile State Index (2016). Following the economic crisis in 1997, Zimbabwe has experienced subsequent political, social, and financial crises during the last two decades. Indeed, Fast-Track Land Reform Program and Western economic sanctions have fuelled the deterioration of the socioeconomic and political situation in Zimbabwe between 2000 and 2008, resulting in state fragility (Musekiwa, 2016, p. 91). Simpson and Hawkins (2018, p. 19) suggested that if a country has experienced political deadlocks, declining legitimacy of state institutions, low-level civil unrest, and deteriorating economic and social indicators, it can be labelled a fragile state. They also identified four indicators of deterioration in economic and social conditions:

i. High and worsening levels of poverty;
ii. Low economic growth rates;
iii. Poor health and education outcomes; and
iv. Severe deficits in terms of human rights and governance indicators (Simpson & Hawkins, 2018, p. 20).

Zimbabwe has experienced all four of these steps during the last two decades and beforehand, and shortcomings such as these strengthen the country's position in the periphery of the MWS.

Maunganidze (2016, pp. 50–56) also stated that "the absence of control and accountability over state institutions and resource distribution" caused the country's economic decline and hyperinflation from the late 1990s, deterioration of health and food security, migration for survival or brain drain, and political polarisation under one-party rule. Moreover, the type of political regime is considered a significant factor of fragility, including not only the elections and replacements of leaders but also the inclusivity of the public to the political process (Valling & Moreno-Torres cited in Olowu & Chaine, 2016, p. 3). Therefore, despite the resilience of the regime, the controversial elections under the majority rule and the replacement of Mugabe with a coup in 2017 have been the visible examples of fragility in the policy realm.

Furthermore, Zimbabwe has valuable mineral deposits but has not developed an effective domestic industry to extract them, unlike South Africa. Because of this, Zimbabwe's extractive mining industry relies heavily on foreign mining corporations or companies. Zimbabwe is also a less influential actor in southern Africa than South Africa is because it is not in a dominant position in terms of foreign trade and diplomacy. Zimbabwe's peripheral position in the MWS leads to a higher vulnerability to exploitation of its raw materials by semiperipheral and core-countries, and Harare is less likely to be able to establish equal relations with semiperipheral countries such as South Africa and China.

Also, the Zimbabwean people have had little ability to influence their government's policy choices, which concern them, because of the authoritarian nature of the ZANU-PF government and regime led until November 2017 by President Robert Mugabe. Some liberation parties in southern Africa, which fought with colonial rulers for a long time and violently, such as Zimbabwe, Angola, and Mozambique, have maintained their administration as a political hegemony. In contrast, other liberation struggles against white settler colonialists, such as in Namibia and South Africa, have followed a different path and they respect civil rights (Chesseman, 2013, p. 14). In the Freedom House report referred to above, Zimbabwe was rated 'partly free' in terms of democratic freedom (Freedom House, 2016, p. 24) and was rated 'not free' and 'partly free' respectively on press and internet freedom issues. These figures show that South Africa has more democratic institutions than Zimbabwe regarding democracy, the internet, and press freedom. In other words, as a semiperipheral country, South Africa has more core-like ruling bodies than peripheral Zimbabwe regarding democracy.

The weak state structures in peripheral areas of the MWS have some inevitable outcomes (Wallerstein, 2011b, p. 355). External forces are therefore more decisive in the periphery than in the semiperiphery because of the weaker and more vulnerable structure and capabilities of peripheral states and economies (Herbst, 2014 [2000]). This is a fundamental difference between the two cases in this study, which derives directly from each country's position in the MWS. According to MWS theory, Zimbabwe is peripheral because of its underdeveloped economy and class structure. Zimbabwe's peripheral position is not a distinction like South Africa's position in the rest of the continent as the majority of the countries are located in the periphery of the MWS. Inevitably this does not produce more extraordinary debate about the restricted manoeuvrability of the peripheral countries. To conclude, Zimbabwe is highly dependent on the industrial technology and capital of countries and corporations in the core and the semiperiphery.

THE CHANGING NATURE OF THE MWS AND ITS EFFECTS ON THE COUNTRIES' POSITIONS

Before I conclude the chapter, I discuss in this section the changing nature of the MWS. Golub (2013) said that "the systemic restructuring" had been started by East Asian countries during the 1950s and 1960s. Japan was the pioneer of this restructuring and Newly Industrialised Countries (NICs) of North-East Asia (such as South Korea and Taiwan), the Association of Southeast Asian Nations (ASEAN) countries (such as Malaysia, Singapore), and China have followed in Japan's footsteps from the 1970s onwards. This systemic change in the Global South has affected the foreign policy decisions of South Africa and Zimbabwe into the twenty-first century. So changes in the global economy have reconfigured the MWS, specifically the rise of the Global South during the twenty-first century, and South Africa has been the most significant country for this change in Africa (Garcia, 2017a; Garcia & Bond, 2015). South-South cooperation, which is "a new Southern multilateralism of the emerging regional powers," goes hand-in-hand with the rise of non-Western powers, such as the India-Brazil-South Africa Dialogue Forum (IBSA) and the BRICS group (Stephen, 2012). On the other hand, following the Western economic sanctions imposed during the early 2000s, Zimbabwe has moved away from the core towards the semiperiphery with its 'Look East' policy from 2002 onwards.

Moyo and Yeros (2015) defined the south as peripheries, semiperipheries, and 'emerging' peripheries. The nonemerging old semiperipheries have been seen as safety zones for the international system or the core. On the other hand, 'emerging' semiperipheries are able to challenge the US hegemony within the

MWS. Conversely, Bond (2015) argued that the emergent BRICS countries lubricate the neoliberal regime process globally. Bond (2015) described the BRICS countries as subimperial powers in their regions. Therefore, South Africa lubricates the neoliberalism in southern Africa, and Brazil is doing the same thing in South America thanks to their subimperial positions in the international system. Indeed, the term 'subimperial' was coined during the Cold War era to mean that subimperialist states maintain and extend US imperialism around the globe (Garcia & Bond, 2015). Luce (2015) explained that subimperialism is the highest stage of dependent capitalism. Unequal and troubled relations between the BRICS countries are the critical weaknesses of the alliance (Bond, 2018). For example, China's economic dominance over South Africa reproduces South Africa's economic dominance over other southern African countries, including Zimbabwe.

China is the most dominant power among the BRICS countries in terms of political, economic, diplomatic, and military influences (Hung, 2017). Hung (2017) stated that there are two possible scenarios for the future of the MWS: the first is "a semiperiphery transformative takeover of the system" and the other is the second round of US hegemony. He believed that China is the only candidate for this "transformative takeover" among the BRICS countries because of its dynamism and assertiveness (Hung, 2017). However, the United States can maintain its hegemonic position in the MWS because of its economic, political, and military power (Hung, 2017). Moreover, China's dominance has been maintained by the establishment of the New Development Bank in 2015, which is headquartered in China (Carmody, 2017). Although South Africa is part of this alliance, the country's inclusion in BRICS has not yet produced better outcomes in terms of economic development. Despite this, the emerging presence of BRICS might be more beneficial than the neoliberal SAPs for peripheral countries of the continent, such as Zimbabwe (Nyabereka, 2017). On the other hand, Garcia (2017a, p. 39) argued that the economic activities of BRICS countries has been concentrated on natural and energy-related resources, a cheap labour force, and consumer markets in the peripheral areas of the MWS, like sub-Saharan Africa, and that therefore these activities do not foster economic growth in countries such as Zimbabwe.

Consequently, the changing nature of the MWS does not have any considerable effect on the respective positions of South Africa and Zimbabwe as they maintain their inherited status from periods of minority rule. These constant development trajectories of both countries retain their business environment over time.

CONCLUSION

Comparing South Africa and Zimbabwe in terms of their respective positions in the MWS has revealed the sharp differences between them. These differences affect their business environments and the relationship between the state and business. The World Bank (2019) developed a method for measuring a country's business environment, namely Ease of Doing Business, through ten topics related to local laws, trade opportunities, infrastructure, and financial security (*see* table 1.5). World Bank (2019) data show that "high ease of doing business ranking means the regulatory environment is more conducive to the starting and operation a local firm." The majority of sub-Saharan African countries are ranked in the bottom half of 190 countries in the world. Only six countries, Mauritius, Rwanda, Kenya, South Africa, Botswana, and Zambia, of the forty-eight sub-Saharan African countries are ranked in the top half of the list. These figures show that starting or conducting business in sub-Saharan Africa is not attractive to either foreign or domestic investors. Despite these low rankings, oil-rich and mineral-rich countries of sub-Saharan Africa are still worth doing business with as they are highly profitable industries.

South Africa is ranked fourth and Zimbabwe 28th in sub-Saharan Africa. Inevitably, the respective BEE and IEE laws affect the rankings of South Africa and Zimbabwe; however, these statistics reveal the contrasts between them in terms of the business environment. South Africa has better rankings than Zimbabwe because of the ease of doing business. The largest gaps

Table 1.5: Ease of doing business rankings of South Africa and Zimbabwe within sub-Saharan Africa (and the world)

	South Africa within sub-Saharan Africa (within the world)	*Zimbabwe within sub-Saharan Africa (within the world)*
Ease of Doing Business Rank	4 (82)	28 (155)
Starting a Business	25 (134)	41 (176)
Dealing with Construction Permits	13 (96)	41 (176)
Getting Electricity	9 (109)	31 (166)
Registering Property	10 (106)	13 (109)
Getting Credit	9 (73)	14 (85)
Protecting Minority Investors	4 (23)	9 (95)
Paying Taxes	5 (46)	24 (145)
Trading across Borders	24 (143)	29 (157)
Enforcing Contracts	18 (115)	38 (168)
Resolving Insolvency	4 (66)	35 (159)

Source: Author created with data from World Bank (2019)

between the two countries are dealing with construction permits, getting electricity, paying taxes, starting a business, and enforcing contracts. Both countries are preferred destinations for doing business in terms of registering property, getting credit, and protecting minority rights. South Africa might be a preferred destination for doing business because of lower trading across borders and starting business rankings. Nevertheless, South Africa's rankings reveal that the country has a more preferable business environment than Zimbabwe.

Both countries' respective positions in the MWS are decisive for producing different outcomes regarding their SBRs, either fracturing or consolidation. As this chapter has suggested, the fragile state structures in the periphery cause a fragile relationship between the government and business in posttransition communities. The lack of sophisticated domestic industry is another outcome of a country's peripheral position. Thus peripheral countries are more dependent on foreign investors and technology to foster economic growth. On the other hand, semiperipheral countries are not as fragile as peripheral countries in terms of their state structure. The existing relatively sophisticated domestic industry brings an advantage to semiperipheral countries for stabilising their SBRs. This makes semiperipheral countries less dependent on foreign investors, but for domestic business. However, the discussion in this chapter suggests that competition with a more powerful semiperipheral country, such as China, does not foster economic growth in a semiperipheral country, such as South Africa. Also, the inclusion of a more semiperipheral power in domestic industry might cause a breakdown between the government and the existing business.

NOTES

1. Both the realist school and the systemic school have used the concept of hegemony to define the most powerful state in the interstate system and they consider the United Kingdom and the United States to be respective hegemonic powers. Thus, the realist school has developed the concept hegemony under the name of hegemonic stability theory (*see* Keohane, 2005; Webb & Krasner, 1989; Gilpin, 1987; 1981), which claims that "international economic openness and stability is most likely when there is a single dominantly state" (Webb & Krasner, 1989, p. 183).

2. At the same time, European settlements in Cape began when the MWS emerged after the Peace of Westphalia in Europe.

3. I hope that presenting measures such as this will provide an updated and more sophisticated measure of location in the MWS.

4. Twelve respective classifications, including *Uneven Economic Development*, *Human Rights & Rule of Law*, and *Economic Decline*, formulate this report.

5. There are some notable studies on South Africa's semiperipheral position in the MWS; see Andreasson (2013; 2011); Martin (2013a; 2013b); Schubert & Sooryamoorthy (2009); Ahwireng-Obeng & McGowan (1998); McGowan & Ahwireng-Obeng (1998); McGowan (1993); Shaw (1978); Wallerstein (1976).

6. See these significant works which emphasise the underdevelopment of Zimbabwe: Willems (2011); Chinguno (2010); Bond & Manyanya (2003); Wanmali & Islam (1997); Weiner (1991); Jansen (1990); Smith (1982).

Chapter 2

The Economic Transformation of the Mining Industries of South Africa and Zimbabwe

From Liberalisation to Indigenisation Policies

INTRODUCTION

In order to enable a discussion about the different outcomes of SBRs in South Africa and Zimbabwe, the shifts in the policy choices made by the Pretoria and Harare governments must be debated frankly, since they have been decisive elements for the business environment in both countries. In this chapter, I examine the type of policy choice characterising the approach to regulating the mining industries in South Africa and Zimbabwe. In this study, I argue that the respective semiperipheral and peripheral positions of South Africa and Zimbabwe in the MWS, which I discussed in the previous chapter, and the policy choices of their governments on their mining industries have affected these countries' SBRs to consolidate or to fracture. Examining the liberalisation and indigenisation of the respective mining industries in South Africa and Zimbabwe is therefore crucial to explaining the SBRs in both countries.

South Africa and Zimbabwe moved from some degree of isolation to liberalisation and indigenisation successively (*see* figure 2.1). Under the thumb of a minority regime, South Africa experienced economic sanctions during the latter decades of apartheid. The apartheid regime was threatened by a student revolt in Soweto in 1976, but the widespread riots and societal upheaval were suppressed, and the situation was stable for the subsequent decade. During the mid-1980s, however, the apartheid regime was in disorder because of international sanctions, intensifying capital flight and creating a floundering economy (Martin, 2013b, p. 143). Rhodesia went through a period of isolation during the Unilateral Declaration of Independence (UDI) between 1965 and 1979. As a consequence, with the end of white minority rule in Zimbabwe (1980) and South Africa (1994), both countries liberalised their economies from the late 1980s and mid-1990s respectively, including their mining industries, in accordance with the financial institutions of the core (on the neoliberal transition in South Africa, *see* Carmody, 2002; Bond, 2000; Williams & Taylor, 2000; Fine & Rustomjee, 1996; and on the neoliberal transition in Zimbabwe, *see* Bond & Manyanya, 2003; Dashwood, 2000; Raftopoulos, 1996).

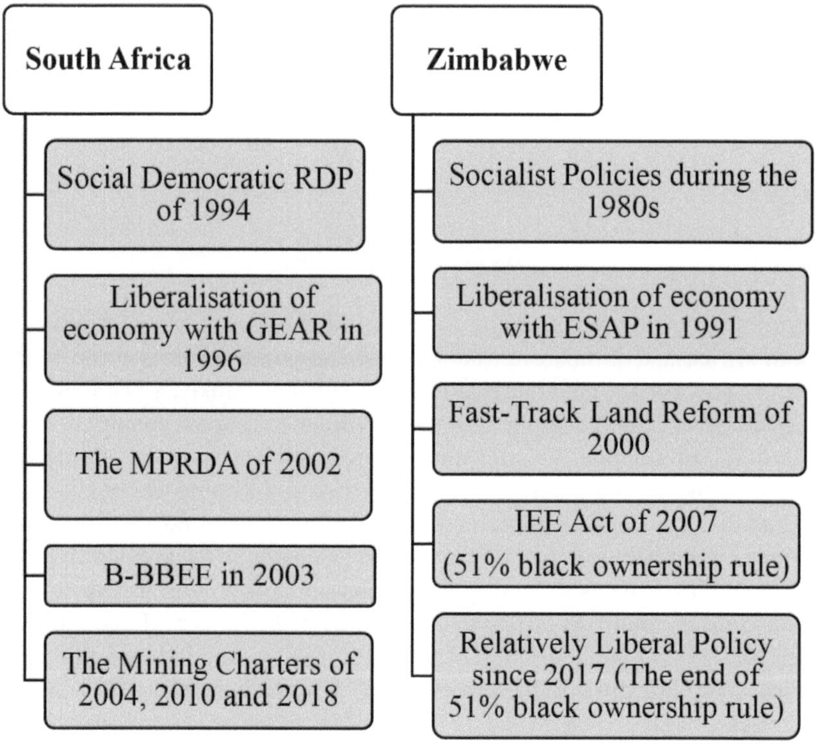

Figure 2.1. The Policy Choices of South Africa and Zimbabwe.

Another common policy choice has been indigenisation in order to empower the black majorities in South Africa and Zimbabwe, but not in the same manner in practical terms for both countries. Even though both countries had pursued liberalisation policies during the 1990s, the ANC and the ZANU-PF shifted their liberalisation policies to indigenisation policies during the 2000s ostensibly to benefit their disadvantaged citizens—that is, the black majorities (Andreasson, 2010a). The settler colonies of southern Africa and the apartheid regime in South Africa marginalised mainly the black[1] indigenous people and promoted the white minorities. In order to complete the economic transformation in South Africa and Zimbabwe, both black-majority governments implemented indigenisation policies because they did not achieve the expected outcomes from the liberalisation policies.

Although both governments sought to indigenise their economies by their respective policy choices from the early 2000s, the BEE in South Africa and the indigenisation of land and the economy in Zimbabwe were formulated for different reasons. On the one hand, the ANC government wanted to empower the economically disadvantaged black majority with the BEE policy, so the BEE was introduced to broaden development and participation in the economy for the black majority in South Africa. On the other hand, the ZANU-PF government implemented more oppressive indigenisation policies, namely the Fast-Track Land Reform in 2000 and the IEE Act of 2007, which involved seizing the lands of whites and compelling the private mining companies to indigenise 51 per cent of their ownership in order to keep the party in power (Raftapoulos & Phimister, 2004, pp. 368–69). The Fast-Track Land Reform led to violence caused by attacks by Zimbabwean War Veterans on white farmers and caused an upheaval in the country, including the economic meltdown of the 2000s (Farley, 2008, pp. 21–22; Muzondidya, 2007; Moyo & Yeros, 2005; Hammar *et al.*, 2003). This policy transformed Zimbabwe into a more autocratic country under the presidency of Mugabe.

The respective policy choices on the mining industries of South Africa and Zimbabwe have had a significant impact on their SBRs during the last three decades. Examining these policy choices is therefore an important step to understanding the relationship between the respective governments and their mining industries. In this chapter, I analyse the respective policy choices of South Africa and Zimbabwe regarding their mining industries, and show the major problems and concerns around these specific policy choices from a critical perspective and with the support of empirical evidence. Lastly, I offer political settlements approach for understanding divergent fates of South Africa and Zimbabwe in terms of their policy choices.

MEASURING THE POLICY CHOICES: LIBERALISATION AND INDIGENISATION

I measured government policy choices in the context of each country's respective mining industries, characterised as a policy either of liberalisation or of indigenisation, by using the qualitative data. I measured the general characteristics of these policy choices, and how they differ in this section (*see* table 2.1). Policies of liberalisation have been adopted in developing countries; for Africa, in particular, the starting point was the annual report of the IMF (1980) on accelerated growth, but the most important publication was the World Bank's report *Accelerated Growth in Sub-Saharan Africa: An Agenda for Action* in 1981.

The liberalisation policies were intended to increase "the role of [the] market mechanism" and reduce "existing barriers to international trade and capital movements" by means of export-driven and antistatist practices (Edwards, 1984). Governments also reduced their support for state-owned enterprises in order to promote private enterprises in every sector (Smith & Harvey, 2008; Jilberto & Hogenboom, 2007). Multinational companies, therefore, ended up dominating economic transformation by means of privatisation, particularly in the least developed countries, because the domestic companies did not have the necessary capital. For example, the majority of sub-Saharan African countries experienced this type of economic transformation through SAPs informed or directed by the IMF and the World Bank during the 1980s and 1990s (Mkandawire & Soludo, 2003; Pedersen & McCormick, 1999;

Table 2.1: The comparison of liberalisation and indigenisation policies

	Liberalisation	*Indigenisation*
General Features of Policies	Export-driven Private capital Antistatist Private foreign ownership (multinational companies) Rapid trade liberalisation	Empowerment of disadvantaged groups Promoting disadvantaged groups' entrepreneurship An attempt to create an indigenised capitalist class Creating more jobs for the disadvantaged indigenous people
Application of Policies	Neoliberal structural adjustment programmes for SSA countries during the 1980s and 1990s Zimbabwe started a national SAP, namely ESAP, for responding to external pressures from the IMF and Western donors in 1991 South Africa launched a homegrown neoliberal programme, namely GEAR in 1996	Gradual indigenisation (e.g. 30% ownership rule in South Africa) BEE (started in the late 1990s) B-BBEE (became law in 2003) Rapid indigenisation (e.g., 51% ownership rule in Zimbabwe) Fast-Track Land Reform was launched in 2000 (previously willing seller, willing buyer) Harare government applied the indigenisation policies following the Western sanctions from the early 2000s. IEE Act of 2007 became law in 2008 51% ownership rule of IEE was relaxed in 2018

Carmody, 1998; Maclean *et al.*, 1997; Hawthorn, 1993). Both Zimbabwe and South Africa pursued the neoliberal economic programmes in the 1990s, namely ESAP and GEAR respectively.

These specific neoliberal economic policies were complements of economic transformation processes in South Africa and Zimbabwe, as the first phase of economic transformation with the liberalisation of domestic economies through relaxing the restricted rights for nonwhite majority in South Africa and Zimbabwe were launched during the political transition periods 1994 and 1980 respectively. Following the implementation of these liberal economic policies, majority governments in South Africa and Zimbabwe launched respective indigenisation policies to complete economic transformation (Andreasson, 2010a). Indigenisation policies are not completely against the liberalisation of the economy; for example, BEE was called a neoliberal project during the early 2000s (Andreasson, 2010a, p. 430). However, indigenisation policies restrict ownership rules in terms of race or nationality of investors, which causes a clash with neoliberal economic policies.

By contrast, during the 1970s, some of the postcolonial and postminority-rule countries, such as Malaysia[2] and Nigeria respectively, implemented indigenisation policies with the purpose of promoting the state-led empowerment of disadvantaged groups against previously advantaged groups (Zvoushe, 2017; Andreasson, 2010a; 2007; Murombo, 2010; Raftopoulos & Compagnon, 2003). Hence governments implemented economic indigenisation policies by promoting entrepreneurship among disadvantaged groups in order to combat high levels of unemployment and economic marginalisation (Cargill, 2010). Economic indigenisation policies were, therefore, one attempt to generate an indigenous capitalist class in former settler colonies (Bowman, 2019).

From the late 1990s onwards, both South Africa and Zimbabwe pursued such policies of indigenisation for redressing colonial imbalances. On the one hand, South Africa launched BEE in the late 1990s, and ultimately these policies became known as Broad-Based BEE (B-BBEE) in 2003. For regulating the mining industry, the ANC government implemented the First Mining Charter in 2004, which included a gradual indigenisation policy in terms of ownership rule. In doing so, the intended black-empowered ownership rule in the mining industry increased from 15 per cent to 26 per cent gradually from 2004 to 2010 with the Second Mining Charter (Leon, 2012, p. 17). The ownership rule target became 30 per cent in 2018 with the Third Mining Charter.

On the other hand, Zimbabwe implemented a 'Look East' policy in response to Western economic sanctions in the early 2000s. After that, the ZANU-PF government implemented extreme indigenisation rules in the mining industry with Zimbabwe's IEE Act of 2007, which became law in 2008 and required 51 per cent black-empowered ownership rule (Raftapoulos &

Phimister, 2004, pp. 368–69). These policies produced what might be characterised as more gradual and extreme indigenisation policies, respectively, in South Africa and Zimbabwe (*see* Andreasson, 2010a). Despite this, following the coup in Harare in 2017, the new President Emmerson Mnangagwa relaxed the 51 per cent black-empowered ownership rule to attract more foreign investors with the motto 'Zimbabwe is open for business' (Dzirutwe, 2018a).

THE SIGNIFICANCE OF THE MINING INDUSTRIES OF SOUTH AFRICA AND ZIMBABWE FOR COLONIAL POWERS AND CONTEMPORARY FOREIGN ACTORS

The legacy of the Second Boer War (1899–1902) shaped independent southern Africa's political and economic landscape, including the nature of the Union in 1910, as the British-controlled colonies and Boer Republics fought for control of the precious gold and diamond resources. Britons then colonised substantial parts of southern Africa, including South Africa and Zimbabwe, to control and monopolise the lucrative mining resources after the discovery of diamonds and gold during the second half of the nineteenth century in southern Africa (Burgess & Beilstein, 2013, p. 123; Love, 2005, p. 33).

Monopolisation of the mining industries in southern Africa was popular among all of the settler colonies and white minority governments through the South African-origin multi-national giant corporates such as De Beers and Anglo American, established by Cecil Rhodes and Ernest Oppenheimer respectively (Love, 2005; Fine & Rustomjee, 1996). These South African-origin mining companies dominated not only the South African mining industry but also the Rhodesian one, because the white-settler population of Rhodesia had focused on agricultural and other industrial activities. For example, De Beers and Anglo American were historically the most active mining corporates during the Rhodesian era and extracted diamonds and platinum respectively from Zimbabwean soil.

Mining industries have been an attractive sector for not only colonial powers or white minority rules but also the black majority rules of South Africa and Zimbabwe respectively. Beyond these two countries, colonial powers used the mining sector as a multiplier or accelerator of development or economic growth in colonies (Katzenellenbogen, 1975, p. 361 cited in Hilson *et al.*, 2019, p. 345; Murombo, 2013, p. 33). Acemoglu *et al.* (2001, p. 1370) claimed that colonizers benefited from the resource-rich colonies by transferring the resources of "extractive states" to Europe. The most extreme case was the Congo Free State under the rule of Leopold II of Belgium (Acemoglu *et al.*, 2001, p. 1375). Settler colonies also benefited from the cheap labour force of South Africa and Zimbabwe for extracting mining through "extractive institutions" (Acemoglu & Robinson, 2017, p. 82). According to Kanyenze *et al.* (2016, p. 5) ruling elites created extractive colonial institutions for benefitting themselves and inequalities in the colony increased as a result. The Rhodesian government implemented cost minimization and profit maximization strategies on the mining companies (Makambe, 1994, p. 82). Thus, the abuse and exploitation of the African labour force was "a dominant phenomenon" for Zimbabwe's colonial economy (Makambe, 1994).

The mining sector had also been useful for constructing or expanding the colony's railways and harbours around the mining sites (Hilson *et al.*, 2019, p. 349). Therefore, growth in the mining sector means growth in the infrastructure of colonies (Hilson *et al.*, 2019, p. 350). But this economic growth and transformation was restricted around the mining sites and did not benefit all of the regions or populations in a colony. For instance, the discovery of gold near Johannesburg in 1886 triggered the first phase of rapid economic and social transformation in South Africa (Demissie, 1998, p. 447). As a result of the rapid industrialisation of the Rand region, the expansion of the mining sector created a labour market around Johannesburg (Demissie, 1998, p. 447).

The raising number of miners created a new problem in the mining sector in South Africa. The cost of British or Afrikaner white miners was higher than that of African miners for extracting deep gold mining in Johannesburg during the early twentieth century (Demissie, 1998, p. 449). This approach might have some similarities with modern mining extraction processes. African-origin miners are cheaper than even Chinese mineworkers, who have more costs for the Chinese-owned mining firms in Africa. Therefore, reducing costs make the mining industry more profitable for Chinese or other foreign mining firms in Africa. Similar to today's conditions, the mining industry in South Africa was a source of migration from other African communities during the early twentieth century and beyond (Demissie, 1998, p. 452). Similar to colonial powers or white minority rules, respective black majority governments in South Africa and Zimbabwe have prioritised the mining sector for the countries' development and economic growth through indigenisation policies (Murombo, 2013, p. 39).

Some researchers believe that China has a role of coloniser in Africa for gathering natural resources or they believe that the Chinese presence in Africa has caused the "new scramble for Africa" (*see* Taylor, 2014; West, 2014; Burgess & Beilstein, 2013; Carmody, 2013; Campbell *et al.*, 2012; Carmody, 2011; Nwoke, 2007; Rogers, 2007; Lee, 2006; Ramo, 2004) and some others not (*see* Brautigam, 2009; Ampiah & Naidu, 2008; Campbell, 2008; Dollar, 2008; Le Pere, 2007; Marks, 2007; Naidu, 2007). West (2014) claimed that Sino-African relations are not equal, and that China does not pursue different policies when it is compared with Western activities. Burgess and Beilstein (2013, p. 123) criticised Chinese state-owned mining companies and argued that they "have proven to be less productive than privately owned firms." They believed that the Chinese presence in Africa had caused the "new scramble for Africa" and was sometimes harmful to African and Western interests (Burgess & Beilstein, 2013, p. 124). Alden (2007) discussed China's foreign policy towards Africa in terms of three different roles, development partner, economic competitor, and coloniser. He suggested that China is a partner and a competitor for Africa, but that the coloniser role is "spurious and overblown."

Taylor (2014, p. 137) thought that the Chinese presence is harmful to African industries and stated that "recent economic growth in Africa is based on trade in resources, not production." Industrialisation and commodity production might, therefore, produce a developed Africa, instead of depending on the exporting of resources. Taylor (2014, p. 142) believed that "without serious and credible policies, the diversification of dependency towards the BRICS and other emerging powers may lead to negative outcomes for Africa." China's role in Africa in the twenty-first century is uncertain, unlike the role of European colonial powers in Africa during the colonial period. Therefore, Beijing has had a development and economic growth agenda through gathering natural resources of Africa, but Beijing has also offered new opportunities and new cooperation within the Global South and a development model for African countries.

The mining resources of southern Africa were integrated into the world-economy through colonial rule. Bretton Woods Institutions, which were "the largest foreign financier to several regional colonies" had historically supported the settler-colonies of southern Africa (Bond, 2000, p. 157). Although the MWS literature has categorised countries and regions peripheral or core the production processes were core-like or peripheral-like at the beginning (Wallerstein, 2006, p. 17). Therefore, the production processes decide the location of a country in the MWS at once. The existence of core-like activities in South Africa had escalated the country's position within the MWS. On the other hand, Rhodesia's core-like activities were restricted and following the end of minority rule the country's position decreased swiftly within the MWS. The reproduction of the capitalist world-economy is provided by mining activities in the periphery, which supply the surplus value flows from peripheral areas to the core. Gellert (2012, p. 404) pointed out the significance of the extraction for the MWS:

> Extraction is fundamental to the structure and history of the world-system. As early world-systems analysis explained, extraction provides the basic raw materials for production and consumption, and in the capitalist world-system, these raw materials are transformed into commodities with exchange values.

> Declining terms of trade and persistent unequal exchange render extractive peripheries underdeveloped and ecologically impoverished.

Some of the settler-colonial powers, such as Algeria, Kenya, Rhodesia, and South Africa had a relative advantage over Third World countries as they avoid relegation to the periphery of the MWS (Good, 1976, p. 597). The cooperation between the core colonial powers and settler colonies prevented this relegation. Although the class formation of settler colonies was less sophisticated than the core countries, they were more sophisticated than other postcolonial communities within the MWS.

> They [settler colonies] thereby avoid relegation to the periphery of the world system as perpetual suppliers of raw materials, and as providers of dependent domestic markets for the manufactures of the metropole. In the process, the colon state assumes an ambivalent position in relation to imperialism in that it co-operates with the metropole, providing a secure and cheap occupation of a strategic area in return for political support and military (Good, 1976, p. 597).

South Africa was exceptional in terms of class formations under the settler rules thanks to independently capitalist development. Rhodesia was also exceptional, but with a less sophisticated industry (Good, 1976, p. 609):

> Capitalist agriculture has both produced and reduced the peasantry to property-less conditions, and industrialisation has brought the growth of massive working-class formations, whose emiseration has remained steady if not increased, and which is unincorporated into the ruling system.

So the settler colonies such as Rhodesia and South Africa had mixed production types and products of both core and peripheral areas of the MWS. They were lubricating the unequal exchange between the periphery and the core countries through the capitalist mode of production per the MWS theory (*see* Garcia, 2017a; Bond, 2013a).

South Africa has sustained domestic industrialisation and development under not only the white segregationist (1910–1948) and apartheid (1948–1994) regimes but also the postapartheid regime from the early twentieth century onwards because of the country's semiperipheral position in the MWS. During the late 1960s and early 1970s, South Africa's white citizens enjoyed an economic boom despite the imbalance between Afrikaners and British elites. The apartheid regime fulfilled the NP's 1948 election promises, and the whites benefitted from the solid economic growth (Martin, 2013b, p. 143).

When Western sanctions came to increasingly isolate the southern African economies from 1965 to 1979 under the Rhodesia's UDI and during the 1980s under the apartheid regime in South Africa, these regimes attempted to create a relatively independent regional market within the capitalist world-economy. Nevertheless, the mining industries of South Africa and Zimbabwe were still dependent on global markets, as they needed to sell their products not only in local markets but also in the global market. The isolated regimes in South Africa and Zimbabwe were also dependent on global finance for investment, as their industrial activities needed capital-intensive operations. Gold prices hiked up during the 1970s; the price of gold increased to over US$150 per ounce in 1975 and US$600 per ounce in 1980 as a result of the economic crisis related to the abandoning of the dollar-gold standard by the United States in 1971 (Martin, 2013b, p. 146). Also, the petrol crisis of the 1970s fuelled economic growth in South Africa as the demand for low-wage, cheap coal exports as an alternative energy source increased. However, the continuing economic stagnation in the world during the 1980s negatively affected South Africa's economic growth because the price of gold decreased sharply to US$400 per ounce (Martin, 2013b, p. 146). As a result of this economic recession, the South African mining houses sought to expand their activities abroad because they needed to find new resources and markets in order to become more profitable (Taylor, 2016b; Bond, 2000).

South Africa's top mineral resources are gold, diamonds, platinum group minerals, coal, chromium, manganese ore, and iron ore. Pivotal mining companies in South Africa are De Beers, Cullinan, and Venetia in diamonds; AngloGold Ashanti, Gold Fields, and Sibanye in gold; Exxaro, Glencore (which originated in Switzerland), and South32 (which originated in Australia) in coal; Anglo American Kumba in iron ore; and Anglo American, Implats, and Lonmin (which originated in the UK) in the platinum group minerals. The South African mining houses have operated in the rest of Africa's resource-rich countries for a long time.

Even though the importance of the mining industry for South Africa has decreased over time, it comprised 8 per cent of the South African economy in terms of overall GDP in 2017 (Menon, 2018, also *see* figure 2.2). After the implementation of the Mineral and Petroleum Resources Development Act (MPRDA) and the Mining Charter in 2002 and 2004 respectively, the South African mining industry did not benefit from the Commodity Boom in the 2000s like Zimbabwe did, but remained stagnant as the transformation had just started (Baxter, 2009). In addition, the mining growth rate was calculated to be 3.7 per cent in 2017, which contributed R312 billion to GDP (Chamber of Mines of South Africa, 2018a, p. 8).

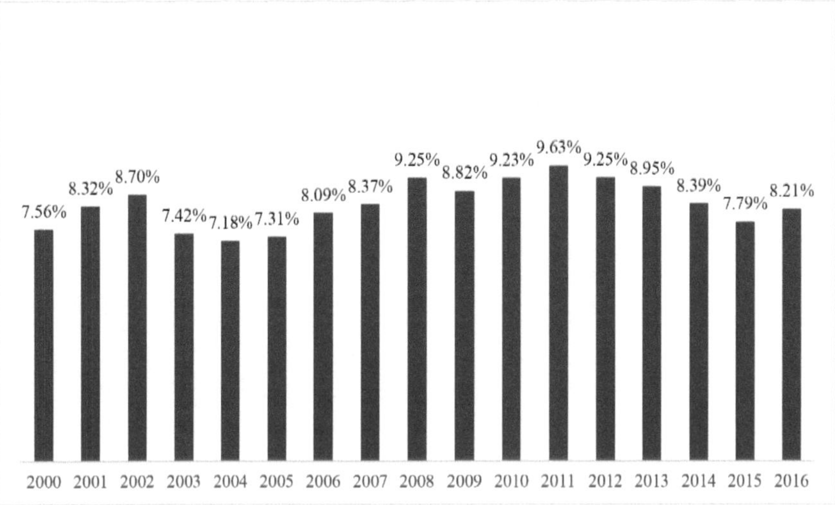

Figure 2.2. The Contribution of Mining and Quarrying to the GDP in South Africa, Value Added (%of GDP). Source: Author created with data from African Development Bank Group (2018); Statistics South Africa (2015, p. 10).

Zimbabwe's top mineral resources are gold, platinum, palladium, and nickel. Key mining companies in Zimbabwe are ASA (formerly Mwana), Blanket, Duration, Metallon mainly in gold; Murowa, DTZ-OZGEO in diamonds; Amplats (Anglo American), Mimosa (Implats), RioZim (formerly Rio Tinto), and Zimplats (Implats) mainly in platinum; Hwanga Colliery in coal; and Premier African Minerals in lithium (Zimbabwe National Statistics Agency, 2018, p. 32).

The mining contribution to GDP in Zimbabwe increased considerably from the postsanctions period (the early 2000s) to the International Economic Crisis of 2007–2008. In addition to the global changes and interventions, changes in the government's policies towards agricultural activities and mining extraction were another reason for these fluctuations during the last two decades (*see* figure 2.3). Following the Western economic sanctions in the mid-2000s, the mining industries had contributed to the country's GDP since the Zimbabwean agricultural activities and other sectors collapsed. However, after the implementation of the IEE, along with the negative effects of the 2008 International Economic Crisis and Western sanctions, foreign investors took their money out of Zimbabwe. In addition, the resource nationalisation policies of the Harare government caused greater vulnerability and instability in the mining industry in subsequent years.

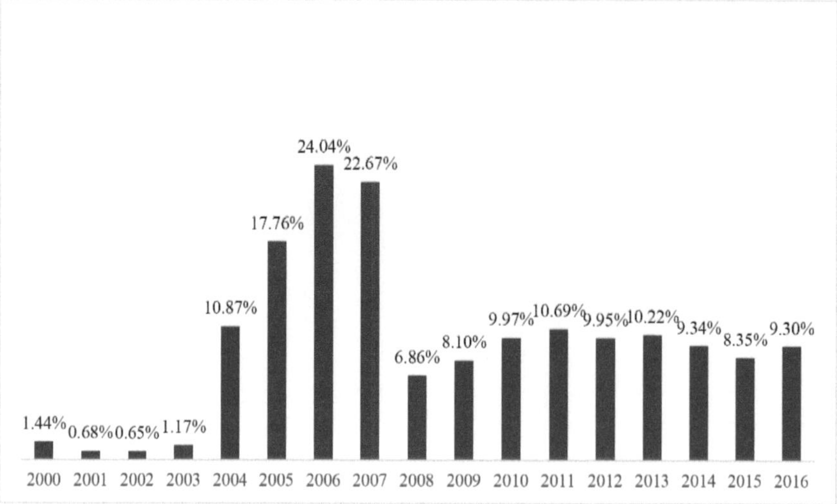

Figure 2.3. The Contribution of Mining and Quarrying to the GDP in Zimbabwe, Value Added (%of GDP). Source: Author created with data from African Development Bank Group (2018).

In particular, during the commodity boom in the 2000s, mining activities in Zimbabwe contributed more than in other years as the economy of Zimbabwe was highly dependent on raw material production. On the other hand, the contribution of the mining production in South Africa had less effect than in Zimbabwe because South Africa's economic structure has been more sophisticated and diversified than Zimbabwe's. Also, the Zimbabwean mining industry has depended more on foreign investors than the South African mining industry, which has depended on domestic investments. In addition, the International Financial Crisis of 2007–2008 had a greater influence on the Zimbabwean economy and the contribution of mining activities plummeted from 22.67 per cent to 6.86 per cent from 2007 to 2008 as peripheral economies are more affected by an external crisis than semiperipheral ones. The implementation of the IEE might also have had a negative effect on the contribution of mining production to the country's GDP. Consequently, the implementation of the indigenisation policy in the mining industry affected Zimbabwe's more vulnerable and inconsistent economy and SBRs.

In this section, I have examined the importance of the mining industries and their contributions to the economies of South Africa and Zimbabwe during the white minority and black majority rules after overviewing the mineral profiles of both countries. I shall now analyse the first phase of their economic transformation policies, which was the liberalisation of the economy in both countries under majority rule.

IMPLEMENTING LIBERALISATION POLICIES IN THE MINING INDUSTRIES OF SOUTH AFRICA AND ZIMBABWE

Both countries experienced isolation from the world-economy under white minority rule, as well as segregationist policies against the black majorities. In order to transform political and economic landscapes, political transition and economic transformation are necessary steps for postminority rule. Both Harare and Pretoria achieved the political transition, which also meant democratisation (*see* Andreasson, 2007; Louw, 2004), to some extent, but not yet economic transformation. Economic transformation has two phases, economic liberalisation and indigenisation policies, in South Africa and Zimbabwe.

The first phase of economic transformation meant liberalisation for South Africa and Zimbabwe during the 1990s, but with different methods and consequences for both countries (Andreasson, 2007, p. 278). Liberalisation policies in South Africa and Zimbabwe were adopted in accordance with the IMF and the World Bank requirements through the principles of the Washington Consensus, although Pretoria developed its own neoliberal project GEAR (for the Washington Consensus *see* Gore, 2000; Stiglitz, 1998; Williamson, 1993; 1990 and for SAPs in Africa *see* Herbst, 1990; World Bank, 1981; IMF, 1980). The standards of the Washington Consensus and the 'structural adjustment' set by the IMF and the World Bank included government budget cuts, increased fees for the use of public services, the privatisation of state enterprises on behalf of self-employed entrepreneurs, the removal of the control of the state apparatus over the market and currency, the relaxation of import tariffs and the promotion of exports (Bond, 2013b, p. 119). Both the ANC and the ZANU-PF had leftist or socialist roots and stance during their resistances against white minority rules. Despite this, the neoliberal turn of South Africa and Zimbabwe was an output of the capitalist MWS and its exploitative nature asymmetrically from the core to the peripheral areas:

> in order to sustain the exploitative nature of economic exchange, the core countries must expend their political capital and impose structural constrains upon the political-economic arrangements of peripheral and semiperipheral countries (Chase-Dunn and Grimes 1995). Such arrangements may come in the form of bilateral economic agreements or as multilateral organizations (e.g., the International Monetary Fund). Hence, economic and political processes are

> never separate, and political capital is used as a resource to reinforce neocolonial global economic exploitation. (Balaev, 2012, p. 224)

Thereby, not only Harare shifted its 'socialist' policies to neoliberal ones, but also Pretoria replaced its social democratic RDP with neoliberal GEAR during the 1990s. The mining companies in South Africa and Zimbabwe therefore welcomed the liberalisation of the economy after the years of isolation under white minority regimes.

The Neoliberal Turn of South Africa

South Africa's mineral resources were exploited by foreign and domestic white capital after the discovery of diamonds in 1867 and gold in 1886. The soils of the black majority population of South Africa and their natural resources had been controlled by the white minorities since the discovery of the gold in the Witwatersrand region and diamonds in Kimberley even before the Union of South Africa, which was founded in 1910. Hence, the black majority, Indians, and coloureds were excluded from the ownership and management positions in the mining industry and instead became the labour force because the white minority of South Africa continued to exploit these resources until the end of the apartheid regime in 1994. However, the independent South African regime partially delinked the economy from the global economy, especially under the apartheid regime. After introducing the apartheid regime, which was a more organised and expansive fortification of former segregationist policies, in 1948 the NP monopolised the significant mining resources in South Africa for the sake of perpetuating white minority rule and partially delinked from the capitalist world-economy (Bond, 2000, p. 20). The NP relatively isolated the South African economy in response to the Western economic sanctions during the last two decades of the apartheid regime.

Towards the end of the Cold War, the ANC received support from Western powers against the apartheid regime. Western countries and the ANC created bilateral relations during South Africa's transition period in the late 1980s and early 1990s. During the last two decades of the apartheid era, South Africa's GDP growth declined dramatically from the 1970s to 1993 (McGowan, 1993, pp. 38–39). Because of the resistance against apartheid, the regime failed at the end of the 1980s, and a transition process started. Limited liberalisation policies had actually been launched by the apartheid regime in South Africa during the 1980s but not to the same degree as the turn to neoliberalism in the 1990s (Louw, 2004; Fine & Rustomjee, 1996, p. 105). Despite the restricted liberalisation policies of the apartheid regime during the 1980s, Western powers demanded a democratic transition in South Africa. In the decades leading up to the political transition to majority rule in South Africa, its mining industry was unable to attract foreign investments because of the civil unrest and the economic sanctions (Maponga & Maxwell, 2001, p. 15). Following the end of apartheid, the ANC government adopted economic liberalisation policies, which was welcomed by the mining industry, in accordance with the IMF and the World Bank guidelines, during the mid-1990s. The support given by the mining industry to this economic liberalisation was significant for the majority rule because the mining/energy sector of South Africa has been the "core quarter of the economy" since the late nineteenth century (Bond, 2000, p. 18).

The ANC discarded its commitment to socialism and abandoned nationalisation policies in order to apply liberalisation policies. The dispute over this transition was the application of the 'pro-market' GEAR in 1996, instead of the 'social democratically inclined' RDP (Southall, 2012, p. 1; Louw, 2004, pp. 196–97). The RDP represented a slight continuity of the state-interventionist, developmentalist, and socialist policies of the ANC through the redistribution of wealth "from the (white) rich to the (black) poor" (Louw, 2004, p. 196). Williams and Taylor (2000, p. 34) considered that even though GEAR had some new policies compared with the RDP, it was also a continuation of the RDP despite the ANC policymakers claiming that GEAR had a vision of a more equal and progressive order than the RDP. They also argued strongly that the neoliberal policies had exacerbated inequality and increased the wealth of a rich minority in South Africa (Williams & Taylor, 2000, p. 37). The ANC's turn to neoliberalism was led by the then deputy president of South Africa Thabo Mbeki during the late 1990s. Moving away from the social democratic RDP to the neoliberal GEAR was Mbeki's idea (Louw, 2004, p. 185). In order to attract more foreign investment to South Africa through fiscal discipline, the implementation of the 'good financial governance' policy of the IMF was the main feature of GEAR (Louw, 2004, p. 185).

Following the end of apartheid, the ANC government liberalised the South African economy through the homegrown project GEAR with the help of neoliberal reforms during the mid-1990s (Louw, 2004; Andreasson, 2003; 2001; Carmody, 2002; Bond 2000; Williams & Taylor, 2000). The IMF and the World Bank were not important determinants of the implementation of a macroeconomic policy; instead, it was a homegrown structural adjustment policy (Bond, 2000, p. 189). Implementing GEAR was also an attempt to tackle the fall of the South African rand during the late 1990s (Carmody, 2002, p. 258). Patrick Bond (2000) named this process 'elite transition' in his analysis of the democratic and economic transition in South Africa. The elite transition was the result of the fracturing of the pre-1994 regime within political and economic lines (Southall, 2012, p. 4). Thus, the newly elected ANC government attempted to create a middle class and an entrepreneurial class, in other words, a "patriotic bourgeoisie" among the black majority (Andreasson, 2007; 2006; Louw, 2004; Bond, 2000). Because of this transition, the newborn ANC government pursued the liberalisation of the mining industry for domestic and foreign private corporations with the help of Nelson Mandela's Deputy President Mbeki (Louw, 2004).

The application of the economic liberalisation policy in South Africa resulted in the majority government abandoning the policy of nationalising the banks, mines, and monopoly capital (Martin, 2013b; Bond, 2013b; Louw, 2004). The ANC government not only had to repay a US$25 billion apartheid-era debt but also legalised the formal independence of the central bank (Bond, 2013b, p. 121). South Africa also benefitted from IMF funding, which included US$850 million loans for implementing the principles of the Washington Consensus and joining the General Agreements of Tariff and Trade (GATT) (Bond, 2013b, p. 121).

The neoliberal policies actually exacerbated inequality and raised the wealth of the rich minority in South Africa by relaxing exchange control and raising interest rates (Bond, 2013b, p. 121). The failed targets of GEAR proposed that "it would increase annual growth by an average of 4.2 per cent, create 1.35 million jobs by 2000, boost exports by an average of 8.4 per cent per year and—perhaps crucially—improve social structure" (Taylor, 2016b, p. 32). Bond (2000, p. 42) described it as "the shrinkage of the national and especially provincial civil services mandated by Gear began with 100,000 civil service job cuts from 1994 to 1999." As a result, South Africa became one of the world's most unequal economies (Williams & Taylor, 2000, p. 37). In fact, the ANC's business-friendly liberalisation policies caused the labour and communist or socialist parties within the Tripartite Alliance[3] to be ignored, as they had expected to follow sociodemocratic policies such as the RDP. Consequently, South Africa's turn to neoliberalisation caused friction between the ANC and its allies COSATU and SACP (Williams & Taylor, 2000, p. 37).

On the other hand, large-scale Anglophone and Afrikaner investors had to globalise their activities by the 1990s as their significant activities remained domestic; the proportion was 93 per cent (Carmody, 2002, p. 262). One of the most visible outcomes of the neoliberal GEAR in business, particularly in the mining industry, was the relaxation of South Africa-based corporates, including the significant mining houses, through the deisolation of the economy. Local and foreign companies became active in South Africa during the first years of the postapartheid period as a result of the liberal economic transition. As a consequence of GEAR, some of the white-owned mining corporates moved their financial headquarters from Johannesburg to London and thus reintegrated themselves in the world-economy (Martin, 2013a, p. 175; Louw, 2004, pp. 197–98; Carmody, 2002, p. 263; Bond, 2000, p. 26). The domestic mining houses, including Anglo American, BHP Billiton, and De Beers, were now able to enjoy South Africa's turn to neoliberalism as they found a chance to move their assets to the London Stock Exchange (LSE) in the late 1990s and early 2000s. Consequently, President Mandela was criticised for liberalising too much and allowing the biggest South African companies to leave the Johannesburg Stock Exchange (JSE) and go to London or elsewhere overseas (Interviewee 5, 2017). Despite this criticism, the relationship between the mining industry and the ANC government developed considerably, and black political and white business elites enjoyed the economic transformation of the country during South Africa's shift to neoliberalism.

The ANC transformed the economic structure of South Africa to the benefit of the black elite rather than the South African black majority (Taylor, 2016b). Bond (2018) described the economic liberalisation period as the "transition from racial to class apartheid" because it worsened the inequality, doubled the unemployment rates and deindustrialised the economy in South Africa. These decisions accelerated the assimilation of the ANC leaders and their policies during the political transition period. Following this elite transition in South Africa, Pretoria introduced what became known as the policy of BEE because of the failure of GEAR during the early 2000s (Bond, 2000). One of the aims of the BEE was to achieve the indigenisation of the mining industry in South Africa.

However, BEE was not the only solution for the ANC government under Zuma presidency. South Africa adopted a policy of a developmental state during the early Zuma reign. It was an ANC policy that received significant attention from the South African political economy literature (Mothabi, 2016; Ayee, 2013; Gumede, 2011; Tshishonga & de Vries, 2011; Turok, 2010; Lodge, 2009). The developmental state policy targets promoting and achieving economic growth through a strong state as an accelerator of development, such as health, education, and infrastructure (Tshishonga & de Vries, 2011, p. 60, 62). The African governments considered the developmental state an alternative to the Washington Consensus during the 2000s and beyond (Turok, 2010, p. 497). Hence, a developmental state is the opposite of a neoliberal state because it prioritises making progress through a strong (hard) state over making money through a loose (soft) state (Tshishonga & de Vries, 2011, p. 61). Following the financial crisis of 2007–2008, the importance of the state increased, and the developmental state became a reasonable alternative for the neoliberal state (Turok, 2010, p. 497). Botswana and Mauritius, for example, have become well-known successful examples of developmentalist states in Africa (Kanyenze *et al.*, 2016, p. 14).

The ANC adopted the developmental state policy to the country's national development plan and there were lots of references in official state documents to this policy (Ayee, 2013, p. 262). President Zuma proposed that the South

African state 'would invest more in education, health and social infrastructure' in his State of the Nation Address in 2009 (Tshishonga & de Vries, 2011, p. 61). Moreover, the ANC has suggested the developmental state policy in the 'National Democratic Revolution paradigm,' the 2009 general elections manifesto and South African National Development Plan 2030 (Ayee, 2013, p. 262). The developmental state approach was not an unfamiliar strategy for the ANC even before 2009. The adoption of the developmental state principles in the postapartheid period was a solution for tackling the legacies of the apartheid, such as poverty, inequality, and unemployment, through the state economic intervention (Mothabi, 2016, p. 99; Tshishonga & de Vries, 2011, p. 59). However, South Africa's economic strategy or policy choices did not reflect the ANC's intention to adopt the principles of a developmental state during the postapartheid era. Thus, the respective ANC governments applied a homegrown neoliberal policy during the early postapartheid era (*see* Andreasson, 2003; 2001; Carmody, 2002; Bond 2000; Williams & Taylor, 2000) and adopting developmental state principles has been slow during the Zuma reign (Mothabi, 2016, p. 99). In this section, I have analysed the reasons for and consequences of South Africa's turn to neoliberalism under majority rule, as well as its effects on the mining industry.

Implementing ESAP as a Liberalisation Policy in Zimbabwe

The Rhodesian white-settler regime declared unilateral independence from the United Kingdom in 1965, and the economy of Rhodesia was isolated from the world-economy. Following UDI, Rhodesia's black majority launched an anticolonial insurrection against Ian Smith's government. After gaining independence from white minority rule in 1980, Zimbabwe's isolation from the world-economy ended. In fact, even though President Mugabe had pursued socialist policies during the 1980s, he did not touch business in Zimbabwe (Interviewee 7, 2018). So in spite of the socialist inclinations of the ZANU-PF government, the mining industry was liberalised during the late 1980s and early 1990s by the implementation of neoliberal policies (Bond & Manyanya, 2003; Dashwood, 2000).

Following the end of colonial rule, Zimbabwe was one of the major rising powers in Africa, particularly in southern Africa. Zimbabwe's new regime inherited one of the most developed economies in sub-Saharan Africa but with a huge foreign debt burden (Brett, 2005, p. 92; Hawkins, 2004). Also, MacLean (2002, p. 520) stated that Zimbabwe's economic situation was positive in 1980 because of the "country's well established export-agriculture industry and its relatively strong manufacturing and minerals sectors." The new postcolonial regimes of southern Africa struggled with the negative economic legacies of settler-rule, such as the Rhodesian debt in Zimbabwe (Bond, 2000, p. 158). The neoliberal transformation in Africa was imposed by Western donors and the Bretton Woods Institutions, including the IMF and the World Bank, during the 1980s for reducing the debts by means of privatisation and antistatist policies (Bond, 2000; Carmody, 1998; Hawthorn, 1993).

African countries therefore implemented SAPs to liberalise their economies. Economic liberalisation involved lessening the role of government through privatisation and export-led economy policies in Africa. In addition, Zimbabwe pursued liberalisation policies during the late 1980s and 1990s, like other developing African countries. Hence, Zimbabwe's ESAP was introduced by Harare in 1991in cooperation with the World Bank and the IMF (Mamdani, 2008; Raftopoulos & Phimister, 2004; Bond & Manyanya, 2003; Bond, 2001). During this liberalisation period, the mining sector became an emerging industry for Zimbabwe's economy in the 1990s (Saunders, 2016, p. 18). The mining industry had been an essential element of the Zimbabwean economy as it was a target for foreign investment and a source of state revenue (Saunders & Caramento, 2017, p. 2). Thus, the new mining investors in the country were based in core countries such as Australia, Canada, and the United Kingdom. For instance, Australian-based mining companies BHP and Delta Gold or Canadian-based Casmyn Corporation and Trillion Resources or British Rio Tinto were the most important investors (BusinessMap, 2001 cited in Shumba, 2018, p. 102). This shows that the implementation of liberalisation policies in Zimbabwe was beneficial for the core foreign investors in the mining industry during the 1990s.

Although the mining industry enjoyed the economic liberalisation policies of the majority government, ESAP was arguably counterproductive, facilitating rather than reducing elite corruption and producing a deterioration of ordinary Zimbabweans' living standards (Saunders, 2009, p. 69). Zimbabwe became more dependent on a narrow band of productive resources in the mining, agriculture, and manufacturing sectors (Nyabereka, 2017). Thus, ESAP subjected Zimbabwe to being poorly integrated into the global economy during the early 1990s, which accelerated the peripheralization of the country. The risk of this accelerated peripheralization was also a risk to maintaining the cooperation between the government and the domestic mining industry. Even so, it was still an opportunity for foreign mining investors because of the reducing exchange value of the local currency, which meant lower costs for extractive activities and lower wages for domestic labour forces. The rapid liberalisation of Zimbabwe in the 1990s by the neoliberal SAPs caused deindustrialization, increasing the volatility and vulnerability of the markets and worsening problems of poverty and marginalisation (Andreasson, 2010b, p. 133). Additionally, Carmody and Taylor (2003, pp. 55–56) asserted that ESAP caused deindustrialization of the Zimbabwean economy and resulted in foreign economic competition in Zimbabwe. In this period, foreign and domestic capital enjoyed these privatisation and economic liberalisation policy choices of the government.

ZANU-PF government introduced ESAP to tackle the debt burden of the Rhodesian regime; however, foreign debt to GDP ratio has increased during the 1990s. Foreign debt percentage of GDP in Zimbabwe before ESAP was 45 per cent and 46 per cent during the first and second half of the 1980s respectively (RBZ Annual Report, 2004 cited in Makochekanwa *et al.*, 2012, p. 8). Following the implementation of ESAP this ratio has increased to 65 per cent and 69 per cent during the first and second half of the 1990s respectively. Bond and Manyanya (2003) claimed that the Zimbabwean economy collapsed in 1997 because of the significant amount of foreign debt. They also stated that senior economists from the MDC, the main opposition party in Zimbabwe, believed that this was not enough to explain the reasons of the economic crisis and insisted on seeing "the debt problem as merely one of malgovernance" (Carmody & Taylor, 2003, pp. 55–56). The IMF similarly interpreted the economic collapse of Zimbabwe as a result of 'inadequate' macro-economic and structural policies, as well as the "lack of liberalisation and fiscal and monetary discipline" (IMF, 2004, pp, 2–4 cited in Andreasson, 2007, p. 288). Thus, actors other than the ZANU-PF blamed the financial mismanagement of the government despite the implementation of ESAP.

After the mid-1990s, popular support for the ZANU-PF government declined because of the deepening economic crisis (MacLean, 2002, p. 521). As a result, ESAP failed within a five-year period and caused an economic crisis in Zimbabwe. Dashwood (2000) argued strongly that the failure of Zimbabwe's liberalisation strategy was not caused by pressure from IFIs, but by the Zimbabwean ruling elite. Conversely, for instance, Bond and Manyanya (2003) asserted that "ESAP . . . was designed by the World Bank and IMF and aimed to quickly deregulate and indebt an economy seen as overprotected and inefficient." The economic crisis in 1997 and Zimbabwe's involvement in the Congo Wars[4] in 1998, despite Western powers' objections, led to an internal crisis during the 2000s along with the Fast-Track Land Invasion policy (MacLean, 2002, pp. 521–22).

As a result, the ZANU-PF government's policy mistakes and violations led to the suppression of the press, an attempt to bring about undemocratic constitutional change, unpopular financial privileges for war veterans, the invasion of white-owned land, implicit support for the violent war veterans' land invasions, and the unpopular military involvement in the conflict in the Democratic Republic of Congo (DRC) (MacLean, 2002, pp. 521–22). Western countries and IFIs withdrew their support from the Harare regime, and this caused an economic breakdown. Ultimately, following the violent suppression of the domestic political opposition and the land invasions,

Western powers and IFIs imposed economic sanctions on Zimbabwe during the early 2000s.

In conclusion, on the one hand, following the period of isolation from 1965 to 1979, the majority government in Zimbabwe liberalised the economy step by step. Mugabe shifted Harare's socialist policies to liberalisation policies from the late 1980s by the implementation of ESAP in 1991 and became a more business-friendly president, including to the mining industry. During this period, the implementation of antistatist and proprivatisation policies was beneficial for foreign investors in Zimbabwe's mining industry. However, the lack of domestic capital and investment developed into a significant problem during the 2000s, and the ZANU-PF government searched for new solutions with the Fast-Track Land Programme and the IEE Act.

On the other hand, Mandela switched South Africa's first sociodemocratic policy, namely the RDP, to a probusiness policy, GEAR, in 1996. The implementation of neoliberal policies created more opportunities for the sophisticated domestic mining industry of South Africa. The mining industry therefore welcomed the deisolation of the economy from the rest of the world and enjoyed the relaxation of outward investments from South Africa. Thus the big mining houses moved not only their financial headquarters to core countries such as the United Kingdom but also their assets to core stock exchanges such as the LSE. Despite this positive linkage between the white domestic mining industry and the ANC government, demands for economic transformation from the black majority and party-linked entrepreneurs increased.

So for both countries, the legacies of the white-minority regimes had been erased politically, but the economic effects were still influential during the liberalisation periods. Both the Harare and the Pretoria governments decided to implement indigenisation and economic empowerment policies to tackle the historical disadvantages in their mining industries.

THE INDIGENISATION OF SOUTH AFRICA AND ZIMBABWE FROM THE EARLY 2000S ONWARDS

The Indigenisation of South Africa's Mineral Resources

The implementation of the MPRDA and the Mining Charter in 2002 and 2004 respectively represented the formal beginnings of the BEE in South Africa's mining industry. The apartheid era was cautious about a liberal policy, especially for the black indigenised population of South Africa. The Native Land Act 27 of 1913 considered the mineral rights of indigenous communities as unimportant (Cawood & Minnitt, 1998). White-owned private mining companies and parastatals played an important role in the industry during the segregation and apartheid periods. The first ANC government shifted it to a liberal policy and established that mineral rights could be owned by both the state and private individuals and companies, including the black indigenised South Africans, through the Restitution of Land Rights Act 22 of 1994 (Cawood & Minnitt, 1998). Nevertheless, the implementation of the MPRDA in 2002 helped the state to become the custodian of the mineral and petroleum rights on behalf of all the people of South Africa.

When the first Mining Charter came into force in 2004, the policy shifted away from liberalisation and became a nonliberal policy since the Historically Disadvantaged South Africans (HDSAs) were unable to compete with the white-dominated old private companies because of the segregationist policies and laws. The ANC government therefore implemented the BEE policy to benefit HDSAs. In 2003, the B-BBEE Act stated that the indigenisation or the BEE policy meant "the economic empowerment of all black people including women, workers, youth, people with disabilities and people living in rural areas through diverse but integrated socio-economic strategies." The Act also stated that "'black people' is a generic term which means Africans, Coloureds and Indians." In this current study, 'black' is used in the same manner to refer to South African economic empowerment. The main target of the B-BBEE Act was to redress the disadvantages of white-minority rule in economic and social privileges, which included preference in employment, skills development, ownership, management, socioeconomic development, and privileged procurement, on behalf of the black majority of the country.

The first Mining Charter of 2004 was intended to deracialise by 15 per cent by 2009 and 26 per cent by 2014 the ownership structures of the mining companies, in other words, empowering black ownership in the mining companies to increase to these levels (Leon, 2012, p. 17). In fact, the empowerment of black ownership focused on not just HDSAs such as blacks, coloureds, and Indians, but also women, young people, the disabled, and rural communities. If the mining companies did not deracialise their ownership structure, they would not be granted mining licences. The second and third Mining Charters respectively sought 26 per cent and 30 per cent ownership of the industry by HDSAs including black-owned companies, entrepreneurs, employees, and community trusts. In 2016, the proportion of the industry owned by HDSAs was 39 per cent, which was significantly above the Charter target of 26 per cent (Chamber of Mines of South Africa, 2018a, p. 30).

The actors of the mining industry (Interviewee 1, 2017; Interviewee 2, 2017; Interviewee 4, 2017) believed that the government had done the right thing as it was a necessary and good policy approach not only to reverse the bad legacy of apartheid but also to ensure stability in the mining industry since increasing numbers of black South Africans would now have a stake in the economy. In addition to the political battle, policy shifts such as the Mining Charter and the MPRDA were necessary for the industry if the economic battle against apartheid legacy was to be won (Interviewee 4, 2017). In fact, the mining industry primarily took care of the acquired mining rights and stakes within the South African economy based on a pragmatic approach.

The negotiations with the government of South Africa had been mainly conducted by the Minerals Council South Africa[5] from the beginning of the postapartheid period to the implementation of the suspended third Mining Charter in 2017. The members of Minerals Council South Africa, which represented about 90 per cent of South Africa's mineral production, provided 464,667 direct jobs, supported approximately 4.5 million dependants, and their employees earned annually R126 billion in 2017 (Chamber of Mines of South Africa, 2018a). These figures show the influence and the dominance of the Minerals Council in South Africa's mining industry. Although the Minerals Council has been the principal representative of the South African mining companies, the suspended third Mining Charter of 2017 was not discussed or negotiated with it during President Zuma's government (Interviewee 6, 2018; Interviewee 1, 2017; Interviewee 3, 2017; Interviewee 4, 2017).

Mining transformation has been one of the most important targets of the mining industry in South Africa as it would address the legacies of the past and contribute to politics, practices, and outcomes which would reflect the true demographics of South Africa (Chamber of Mines of South Africa, 2018a, p. 30). Interviewee 1 (2017), also stated that the transformation of the mining industry was a necessary step to achieving economic transformation (with complete political transition), but it was a total failure in terms of policy shifts in South Africa. On the other hand, Interviewee 2 (2017), said that the government had a right to deracialise the South African economy. In addition, the mining industry had supported governments to carry out this economic transformation with only a few exceptions. Additionally, Interviewee 2 (2017) supported the transformation process enormously and said that the BEE had had a positive impact on posttransition divisions. Even so, he argued that there were also some positive developments on that issue even before 1994 and the first Mining Charter of 2004. Ownership, procurement, and employment equity were the three significant topics for the transformation of mining in the Mining Charter.

The first and second Mining Charters were successful attempts to transform the industry because they were negotiated, even though during the implementation of the first version of the suspended third Mining Charter of 2017 there was no negotiation between the government and the industry and this nonnegotiated plan caused instability in the mining industry (Interviewee 4, 2017). In addition, Interviewee 6 (2018), a mining lawyer who was also the global cochairman of a global law firm, raised concern over the unresolved discussions and negotiations around the suspended third Mining Charter of 2017 and BEE laws, which put South Africa in the wrong direction and took a hard line with the mining industry. The Council's CEO Roger Baxter identified one of the key roles of the organisation as "to facilitate interaction among mining employers to examine policy issues and other matters of mutual concern to crystallise and define desirable industry standpoints" (Chamber of Mines of South Africa, 2018a, p. 3). He also argued that the Council "acts as a principal advocate for mining in South Africa to government" (Chamber of Mines of South Africa, 2018a, p. 3). Despite this role of the Minerals Council, the South African government and DMR ignored the Council and attempted to establish and impose the suspended third Mining Charter of 2017. However, the renewed negotiations under the new government in Pretoria brought a renewed third Mining Charter in 2018 under the leadership of Cyril Ramaphosa.

Ramaphosa was elected the President of the party at the ANC National Conference on 18 December 2017 by 51.9 per cent of the votes against Nkosazana Dlamini-Zuma, who had served different ministries from 1994 onwards.[6] Two months after his election as the new president of the ANC, Ramaphosa became the new president of South Africa on 15 February 2018, following Zuma's resignation. The reactions to the new president from the mining industry were mainly positive. For example, the deputy chairman of Anglo American South Africa, Norman Mbazima, reacted positively to the election of Ramaphosa as the president of the ANC (Seccombe, 2018a). He believed that the new ANC leader could be an ideal leader for the mining industry:

> It is very helpful if the president of the country understands your industry. . . . Nevertheless, we will not be talking to Cyril, he will have a team, and they should similarly be people who know the industry, who understand it and know the economy, who we can discuss details with . . .

According to some of my interviewees, as representatives of the mining industry (Interviewee 1, 2017; Interviewee 3, 2017; Interviewee 4, 2017), Ramaphosa and his cabinet might create a business-friendly environment for the industry.[7] In addition, the CEO of the Minerals Council talked positively about Ramaphosa's presidency and said that he brought "a new sense of hope" to the country, particularly to the mining industry (*AFP*, 2018). The positive reactions from the mining industry were fruitful for the amendments to the suspended third Mining Charter of 2017.

The first challenge to the third Mining Charter was the ownership rule. It was to increase by 30 per cent from 26 per cent black ownership within a five-year period after the third Mining Charter became law in 2018. The mining companies therefore had to transfer 30 per cent of their assets to the HDSA investors, which comprised 20 per cent to black entrepreneurs, 5 per cent to employees, and 5 per cent to communities around the mine sites. However, when a black empowered shareholder sold her/his assets to someone who was not an HDSA investor, the mining company had to find another black entrepreneur to sell its assets in order to retain the mining licence. Thus, reempowerment was another concern for the BEE as some black empowered owners sold their shares, and the companies had to reempower. The executive head of a nonprecious metal corporate, Interviewee 4 (2017), suggested that they needed to put a mechanism in place to ensure that if a black empowered owner wanted to sell, then they needed to ensure that he/she sold to a black partner. Increasing the amount of empowered ownership might cause more problems for the companies because of the re-empowerment issue.

> So now when we move to the 30% [BEE ownership] that they are proposing or that they are imposing, you are not just moving from 26% to 30%. If your BEE partners had sold 15%, you need to top up to get to 30%. Therefore, you are not moving from 26 to 30, instead of adding 4% you must add 15%. You need to facilitate when you are funding it, [which] costs a lot for companies to do that as well.

Thus, reempowerment was a major issue for corporates because if they were to lose their BEE partners, they needed to find new BEE investors to replace them. However, after the fruitful negotiations, the "once-empowered, always empowered" principle became law with the third Mining Charter of 2018.

Another aspect of the ownership challenge was that the third Mining Charter of 2018 required that 1 per cent of a company's net profit after tax (NPAT) must be paid as dividends to BEE partners. Interviewee 4 (2017) thought that this was not a fair rule for the other shareholders of a company, as she believed that this rule disadvantaged the nonempowered partners:

> We must pay 1% of that [NPAT] to the BEE partners, however, you are disadvantaging other shareholders within the company. How do we pay for one party and not pay to other parties? We should only pay people through profit-sharing of dividends and that kind of thing.

However, this rule also was changed with the implementation of the third Mining Charter of 2018. Mining companies in South Africa have to allocate 1 per cent of their NPAT for community development if they want to maintain their social licence to operate. According to the Minerals Council's survey, twenty-five of twenty-eight mining companies in South Africa spent more than 1 per cent of their NPAT on community development in 2016. The industry's whole NPAT for 2016 amounted to R34 billion, of which 1 per cent was

R339 million. However, the industry's total spends on community development amounted to R1.14 billion in 2016, which was three times larger than the amount stipulated by the second Mining Charter of 2010 (Chamber of Mines of South Africa, 2018a, p. 32). Whereas the second Mining Charter of 2010 required that the mining companies spent 5 per cent of their annual revenue on human resources development (HRD) in 2016, the mining industry actually spent 5.5 per cent (Chamber of Mines of South Africa, 2018a, p. 28).

Procurement was just as important as ownership for the industry and for HDSAs because it involved R11.1 billion for HDSA companies for capital goods, R61.0 billion for HDSA services, and R40.7 billion for HDSA suppliers who sold consumables to the mining industry in 2016 (Chamber of Mines of South Africa, 2018a, p. 31). The industry exceeded the Mining Charter targets for capital goods, services, and consumables provided by HDSAs in 2016 (*see* table 2.2).

Despite these figures, according to Interviewee 4 (2017), the other concern was the procurement rule that a company needed to procure, for example, 80 per cent of services supplied by companies owned and controlled by HDSAs. However, this was not sustainable for the mining industry since there was not enough equipment and goods of the right quality manufactured in South Africa. The third Mining Charter of 2018 requires at least 70 per cent of the mining-goods procurement budget must be spent on manufactured goods in South Africa. Also, the latest Charter demands at least 80 per cent of the money spent on services must be South African companies. According to Bond (2000), this procurement problem has started under the apartheid regime. During the 1950s and 1960s, the South African economy had become more dependent on mineral extraction activities and energy-related industry development. The economy had become more dependent on the production of luxury goods as the government "encouraged luxury consumer goods producers to locate in South Africa" by offering protective tariffs. On the other hand, the government discouraged capital goods producers (such as machinery) by imposing tariff barriers of 2 per cent for machinery and 15 per cent for luxury consumer goods. As a result, this transformation of the economy "left South

Table 2.2: The proportion of procurement

	Procurement target of the second Mining Charter of 2010	*The proportion of procurement from HDSA entities within the South African mining industries*
Capital goods	40%	69%
Services	70%	75%
Consumables	50%	68%

Source: Author created with data from Chamber of Mines of South Africa, 2018a, p. 31.

Africa with an even greater dependence upon imported machines" (Bond, 2000, p. 20).

The other challenge in the third Mining Charter of 2018 was employment equity. The inclusivity of HDSAs in skilled and management positions was denied under the white minority government until the late 1980s. One of my interviewees explained that:

> Of course, to change what was in the industry until the early 1990s . . . it was in the industry, as I said whites had all of the best jobs. There were not many black people with the ability to own shares in the economy because the entire apartheid system was designed to prevent people from acquiring wealth. (Interviewee 2, 2017)

Following the end of apartheid, the transformation of the mining industry started to include black miners in skilled and management positions. In 2004, the percentage of skilled HDSAs was nearly 20 per cent. After the introduction of the first Mining Charter in 2004, the inclusion of HDSAs into skilled and management positions within the mining industry soared to between 40 per cent and 75 per cent, depending on the category (Chamber of Mines of South Africa, 2018a, p. 30). The second Mining Charter of 2010 set a target of 40 per cent HDSAs in all reporting categories by 2014 (*see* table 2.3). According to the third Mining Charter of 2018, at least 50 per cent of directors and 50 per cent of top management must be black.

However, even though these figures demonstrate that the mining industry almost met the conditions of the Mining Charter, the employment equity transformation still did not completely reflect the South African demography:

> In skilled positions, any management positions about more than 50% today are black people whereas in the early 1990s it was more or less 0% maybe 1%. Of course, that means if you compare the 50% with the demography of the country, that means it is still not equal because 90% of the population is black. (Interviewee 2, 2017)

Table 2.3: Employment equity transformation

	2014	*2016*
Top management	50.4%	49.3%
Senior management	41.9%	48.3%
Middle management	50.9%	49.8%
Junior management	54%	58%
Core and critical skills positions	75.5%	84.4%

Source: Author created with data from Chamber of Mines of South Africa, 2018a, p. 31.

There has therefore been a significant change in the nature of the industry from the end of apartheid onwards, and the positive developments in terms of the employment equity transition from the enforcement of the MPRDA and the first Mining Charter in 2002 and 2004 prepared the ground for future improvements. The ANC had created a black patriotic bourgeoisie in the mining industry through these policies, and the relationship with the existing white-dominated domestic industry changed considerably. The South African mining industry enjoyed the turn to neoliberalism until the early 2000s when the emerging problems with new rules in the economy affected the nature of the relations.

Interviewee 1 (2017) supported the rules on workforce transformation and believed that the mining companies could live with them. Nevertheless, for him, the main problem was the insufficient numbers of black women in managerial positions. Interviewee 1 (2017) also believed that empowering black individuals in terms of education and skill training was also workable:

> Some of them are unworkable but generally, I think the targets which the government has set in terms of empowering the black individual, in terms of training black individuals, in terms of investing in education and skills training, are feasible.

However, Interviewee 3 (2017), the managing director of a private consulting firm,[8] contradicted this view and claimed that it would take time as the majority of blacks are not well educated. It is therefore the government's responsibility to solve this problem and not the mining industry's:

> The ideal black shareholder is somebody who is in the industry you are in; in the sector you are in . . . and interested in who wants to be an owner who wants to work in the company . . . Perfect! However, there are not many people around because of the numbers of black people with the education; skills and experience needed to be at that position are relatively small. That is great but takes time. In addition, education comes through as very poor. Universities are still OK, but the high school level is poor in general. There are some very good schools in and around. However, the average person in this country gets a below-par education.

According to the HDI of the UNDP (2016), expected years of schooling and mean years of schooling of South Africa are below the average of the OECD countries and above the average of sub-Saharan Africa. However, the quality of primary education in South Africa is even below the average of measured sub-Saharan African countries according to the Global Competitiveness Index 2017–2018 of the World Economic Forum (2017).

The inclusion of women in the mining industry has been an important issue for South Africa as the apartheid regime segregated not only the races but also the genders (Interviewee 2, 2017). The gender issue was something which needed to be addressed by the BEE regulations, and it was mentioned in both the MPRDA and the Mining Charter. In particular, women have historically been ignored since the formation of the mining industry of South Africa (Interviewee 4, 2017). Following the introduction of the MPRDA in 2002 and the first Mining Charter in 2004, the numbers of women in the mining industries rose considerably. Before the introduction of the MPRDA, the number of women in the industry was approximately 11,400, but this figure increased significantly to more than 53,000 in 2017, which represented 12 per cent of the mining labour force (Chamber of Mines of South Africa, 2018a, p. 29). According to the 2017 figures, women represented 15 per cent of top management, 16 per cent of senior management, 22 per cent of professionally qualified employees, and 18 per cent of employees in the skilled and technical areas in South Africa's mining industries (Chamber of Mines of South Africa, 2018a, p. 29). In fact, promoting black women to managerial positions is a hard step for mining companies as there are not enough well-trained, skilled, and educated women in South Africa, and the extractive industries globally tend to be substantially male-dominated (Interviewee 4, 2017). There is therefore competition among the BEE requiring mining companies in South Africa to employ rare highly educated and qualified black South Africans, particularly women.

There are some controversies about the achievement of BEE policy in South Africa. The mining industry argues that the problem of selling BEE shares should be solved by the government (Interviewee 6, 2018; Interviewee 1, 2017; Interviewee 3, 2017; Interviewee 4, 2017), and that if a black company wants to sell its stakes, it must sell to another black company. This means that a company would be 'once empowered, always empowered.' However, black-empowered mining owners generally sell their shares to make more profit and look for more short-term opportunities in other sectors than the mining industry, which is a long-term investment. These activities therefore cause serious problems for the mining companies as they need to empower again by finding another black investor (Interviewee 1, 2017; Interviewee 3, 2017; Interviewee 4, 2017; Interviewee 5, 2017). Interviewee 1 (2017) stated that the reempowerment of BEE stakes is a huge burden for the mining companies.

Uncertainty is another major concern for the mining industries. Policy shifts are bad for business as they cause uncertainty for investors and create volatility in any case (Interviewee 6, 2018; Interviewee 3, 2017), so they slow down investment and business and can potentially stop them. Moreover, the BEE unsettles people as it has changed too much and will continue to change in the future. It costs too much for employers and the government did not consult them about changes in the Mining Charter (Interviewee 3, 2017). Although the indigenisation policy of South Africa in the mining industry has been gradual, it has still created uncertainties in the market. In fact, the ANC government has changed it three times in fifteen years, and this has been the source of uncertainties for the new investors and stakeholders.

According to the Chamber of Mines, 28 per cent of the mining industry has been indigenised until 2017, but other sources claimed that nearly a decade ago black people in South Africa controlled only 8.9 per cent of the mining industry in 2009 when the target was 15 per cent (Leon, 2012, p. 17):

> the current BEE policy is based on the view that empowerment means giving millions of rands worth of shares to a few individuals, while they leave the overwhelming black majority as disempowered as ever. Instead of making a rich elite minority even richer, BEE should benefit the workers, including the unemployed and poor communities. (['BEE Policies Should Be Replaced—Cosatu,' Miningmx, 18 August 2010] cited in Leon, 2012, p. 18)

In addition to the concerns of the mining industry, COSATU, in 2010, called for the revision of the BEE itself and raised their concerns. Interviewee 1 told me his concerns about the rapid changes in government policy, commenting that "when the second Mining Charter of 2010 was adopted, the government told the industry this was the final amendment in the Mining Charter, but from 2017, the government has been trying to change it again" (Interviewee 1, 2017).

Because mining ownership in the world has changed in the last thirty to forty years in South Africa, both the BEE and this global trend ended family ownership in the mining industries (Interviewee 2, 2017). The financial crisis of 2007–2008 had a catastrophic effect on the mining industry of South Africa (Bond, 2018; Sorensen, 2011; Baxter, 2009). As a consequence of the crisis, mineral prices fell drastically between 2011 and 2016. Inevitably, the South African economy was unable to take full advantage of the commodity boom during the 2000s, and the South African rand-US dollar exchange rate fell from R6.3 per US dollar in 2011 to R17.9 per US dollar in early 2016 (Bond, 2018). The biggest South Africa-based mining houses such as Anglo American, Anglovaal, and BHP Billiton fled from South Africa as they did not see their futures there (Interviewee 3, 2017):

> They were South African companies when they started. They have nothing in South Africa now. You look at BHP . . . They split into South32. They do not have any other assets in Africa. In addition, it is not just South Africa, but it is [the whole of] Africa. Moreover, it is all because of the political risk and inefficiencies and the problems in Africa in general.

Because of this transformation in the ownership of the mining industry, the number of black-owned mining companies increased along with the BEE policies. For example, African Rainbow Minerals took over some of Anglovaal's operations in 2003 as a black-empowered company (Wild & Cohen, 2013). Sudden policy changes affected the stability and predictability in economic policy-making in South Africa, and this prevented attracting more FDIs and promoting the business (Baxter, 2009, p. 115).

Corruption is one of the biggest problems for South Africa's mining companies, especially in the black-owned companies, as the government turns a blind eye to such activities (Interviewee 5, 2017). According to Transparency International's (2019) Corruption Perception Index, South Africa was at 73rd place among 180 countries with a low score in 2018. For instance, former President Zuma was forced to resign over corruption allegations and his close links with the Indian-born billionaire Gupta family (*see* more on 'state capture' in South Africa: Renwick, 2018; Basson & Toit, 2017; Myburgh, 2017). South African police raided the luxury home of the Gupta family four hours before Zuma's resignation (Macharia & Cropley, 2018). Eventually, the corruption allegations and the ANC-linked promotion in entrepreneurship became decisive elements in the political economy of South Africa.

In addition, ANC-linked South African black individuals benefited from the BEE policies, which affected the mineral industry (Leon, 2012). For example, Ramaphosa was the former deputy president of South Africa (2014–2018), the former National Union of Mineworkers (NUM) and ANC Secretary-General before he became an eminent businessman in South Africa, and he is one of the richest black businesspeople in South Africa thanks to the BEE policies and has chaired the Shanduka Group (a company which he founded), Bidvest, and MTN.

Also, Patrice Motsepe is the founder and chairman of African Rainbow Minerals, which is an empowered leading mining company. After Mandela was elected president of the New South Africa in 1994, Motsepe's rise began, and he became a mining magnate. He became a billionaire in 2008 and was the first black African businessman on the Forbes billionaires list (Wild & Cohen, 2013). In addition, before the former Gauteng Premier and government minister Tokyo Sexwale became a billionaire, he was imprisoned under the apartheid regime because of his support for the antiapartheid struggle. Indeed, Andreasson (2015, p. 311) thought that the biggest winners of the BEE policies, such as Ramaphosa, Sexwale, and Motsepe "have all benefited from close connections to, and key roles in, the ruling ANC. These captains of industry symbolise the intersection of political and economic power since the onset of minerals-fuelled industrialisation."

Interviewee 1 (2017) criticised the ANC's economic policies and argued that they were not enough for both the liberalisation and the indigenisation of South Africa's mining industry. Interviewee 1 (2017) believed that transformation had already happened in South Africa. He stated that "there are much better ways than the government thinks. The managers and the workers are black in the mining industries. In addition, nearly 40% of the mining industry shares are owned by black South Africans." Interviewee 2 (2017), however, thought that the Mining Charter had restrictive negative effects on the decline of the mining industry in South Africa and that it had been a good step towards completing the economic transition:

> I think that it was a necessary and good policy approach to take for the government because one of the important functions that the new government in South Africa had to carry out was to reverse the neglects of apartheid, which was obviously very pronounced in the mining sector and in the entire economy.

Apart from the controversies around the Mining Charter and its effects on the mining industry, electricity prices, unstable labour environment, and accommodation problems (such as the two-wives phenomenon) are also other minor issues for the mining industry in South Africa (Interviewee 4, 2017).

Despite the criticisms of the third Mining Charter of 2018 from the mining industry, the alleged corruption, and elite empowerment, South Africa's mining corporates are still highly sophisticated and active in the rest of the continent because of the country's semiperipheral position in the MWS.

The Indigenisation of Zimbabwe's Mineral Resources

Following independence, the highest priority of the ZANU-PF government was land reform rather than the transformation of the mining industry. In fact, the political economy of colonial Zimbabwe had been largely shaped by mining extraction and agrarian activities, which were dominated by whites (Moyo & Yeros, 2005). However, there were "intensifying inter-capital clashes between white agrarian capital, on the one hand, and mining capital and London-based finance, on the other" (Arrighi, 1973 cited in Moyo and Yeros, 2005, p. 167). Because of these capital clashes, white agrarian capital took the leadership of colonial Zimbabwe (Southern Rhodesia) and became the dominant domestic economic industry.

By the early 2000s, however, mining had become more important for the ZANU-PF government as the agricultural activities collapsed because of the Land Reform in 2000 and then the 2002 drought. In addition, the escalation of the prices of the mineral commodities made mining activities more attractive to the ZANU-PF government. During this period, the profile of the foreign investors in the mining industry changed significantly from the 1990s, as I have already discussed. The main investors of the mining industry were therefore from the neighbouring country, South Africa. In addition to South Africa-based companies, such as Implats and Anglo Platinum, Chinese Sinosteel, British Rio Tinto, and Mwana Africa were other significant investors of Zimbabwean mining industry (BusinessMap SADC FDI Database [Johannesburg] and Media, Mining House, Chamber Reports cited in Saunders & Caramento, 2017, p. 12).

The global reason for that escalation was the famous Commodities Boom during the 2000s. Following the Great Commodities Depression in the 1980s and 1990s, commodity prices rose because of the growing demand from the emerging markets of the Global South, such as the BRIC countries (Schwartz & Creswell, 2015; Hendrix & Noland, 2014). As a result, when mineral prices increased significantly across the world during the early 2000s, the ZANU-PF government realised the importance of the mining industry (Interviewee 7, 2018). Therefore, mining production was also related to this problem and caused a disturbance in Zimbabwe's mining industries. The policy shift of Harare, which was the move away from the Western core countries to the semiperiphery or the Global South in foreign policy, affected the mining industry, and South Africans and Chinese became the biggest investors during the 2000s.

The ever-increasing importance of the mining industry in Zimbabwe affected the government's policy choices. The ensuing years were therefore marked by not only the economic collapse of Zimbabwe but also the government's extreme indigenisation laws. President Mugabe signed the IEE Act of 2007 into law in 2008 despite resistance from the main opposition party, the MDC. In this act, indigenisation "means a deliberate involvement of indigenous Zimbabweans in the economic activities of the country, to which hitherto they had no access, so as to ensure the equitable ownership of the nation's resources." Thus, it seems that the BEE policies, the MPRDA and the Mining Charter of South Africa and the IEE of Zimbabwe were on the same side against the legacies of their former white-minority regimes. This act also defines what an indigenous Zimbabwean is:

> "Indigenous Zimbabwean" means any person who, before the 18th April, 1980, was disadvantaged by unfair discrimination on the grounds of his or her race, and any descendant of such person, and includes any company, association, syndicate or partnership of which indigenous Zimbabweans form the majority of the members or hold the controlling interest. (Republic of Zimbabwe, 2008)

President Mugabe implemented the indigenisation policy not only to enable his regime to survive but also to promote a politically linked black bourgeoisie within the ZANU-PF government in order to control the mineral resources and economic activities in the country (Interviewee 7, 2018). Zimbabwe's empowerment and indigenisation policies can be read as a response to the economic sanctions imposed by the European Union and the United States. Unfortunately, according to sources in the Zimbabwe Chamber of Mines, Zimbabwe's economy shrank 54 per cent from 2000 to 2010 in terms of total GDP (Magure, 2012, p. 71).

The indigenisation policy of the ZANU-PF government required that 51 per cent of foreign mining firms must be owned by state-owned enterprises or black Zimbabweans with a net asset value of at least half a million US dollars (Leon, 2012, p. 20). Nevertheless, neither local Zimbabweans nor the government could afford the required capital to comply with the 51 per cent indigenisation rule. Interviewee 7 (2018), who worked as an extractive consultant at the World Bank, told me that four groups in Zimbabwe's mining industry came into existence because of the indigenisation rule. Foreign investors had been the most influential members of this group for the implementation of IEE in Zimbabwe. They had the necessary money and technology to develop the mining industry and create jobs for the local people. In addition, there were small domestic players in the mining industry, but they were still weak and lacked capital. There were also artisanal miners in Zimbabwe who had not been affected by the indigenisation policies. Ultimately, the implementation of the IEE bolstered the politically linked black companies which have been owned by wealthy politicians (Interviewee 7, 2018). Magure (2012, p. 79) stated that:

> Foreign-owned mining companies accused by ZANU PF politicians of seeking to derail the indigenisation programme include Murowa Diamonds, Pan American Minings, Zimplats, Blanket Mine, Mimosa Holdings and Duration Gold Mine.

Indigenisation failed in Zimbabwe largely because the 51 per cent ownership rule had been "disastrous" (Interviewee 7, 2018; Interviewee 3, 2017; Saunders & Caramento, 2017; Magure, 2012). People preferred not to invest in Zimbabwe because there was no chance to manage your own money and make decisions about it (Interviewee 3, 2017); that was another result of the 51 per cent ownership rule. The visible consequences of the extreme indigenisation in the mining industry were that there were no capital, foreign investment, or business activities in the country. The mining industry needed to attract more foreign investors to tackle the twenty-year economic crisis:

> Particularly in the mining industry, the projects are capital intensive, so we are talking about big money. It is impossible for a Zimbabwean to own . . . just about possible exactly for Mugabe, he is very rich . . . for an average Zimbabwean, it is impossible to own 51% of a project because they do not have the capital

> to invest in it. They cannot borrow the money because not very many people would lend money into Zimbabwe. It is a very risky place. (Interviewee 3, 2017)

Magure (2012) also criticised the black economic empowerment, which contained the indigenisation of the mining industry in Zimbabwe, and argued that this policy would not "promote and retain foreign investment." Following the IEE, Zimbabwe either expelled or banned some transnational corporations such as the Australian-British mining firm Rio Tinto in 2015 (Riseborough & Latham, 2015) and the Chinese diamond-extraction company Anjin in 2016 (Kuwaza, 2016).

The ZANU-PF government used the mining industry as an instrument to maintain its ruling power from the mid-2000s to 2017. Because of the indigenisation policies, mining activities in Zimbabwe decreased and became inefficacious for the government, labour, and business (Magure, 2012; Saunders, 2009). There are therefore some contradictions about the influence and contribution of the mining industry to Zimbabwe's economy (Magure, 2012, p. 79).

Elite rent-seeking and resource nationalisation became the main political approaches of the ZANU-PF governments during the 2000s and the 2010s. According to Transparency International's (2019) Corruption Perception Index, Zimbabwe was at 160th place among 180 countries with a very low score in 2018. Peripheral countries of the MWS have experienced elite rent-seeking activities as a consequence of their undemocratic, uncontrolled and nontransparent regime structures. For example, Mugabe allegedly looted US$13 billion from the Marange diamond field in 2013 (Saunders & Nyamunga, 2016; Maguwu, 2013). Government-linked black empowered companies in Zimbabwe are other examples of elite rent-seeking policies. On the other hand, resource nationalisation became a common approach of resource-rich African countries, especially during and after the mining prices boom in the 2000s and early 2010s (Andreasson, 2015; Burgess & Beilstein, 2013; Jackson *et al.*, 2013; Bremmer & Johnston, 2009). So following the implementation of the IEE, the ZANU-PF pursued resource nationalisation policies through the 51 per cent indigenised ownership rule in the private sector, particularly in the mining industry.

Zimbabwe's mining development required a less autocratic approach (Saunders, 2009, p. 84) and needed more capital and more investors. Interviewee 5 (2017) informed me that at the time of Mugabe's resignation, he maintained that his wealth could save Zimbabwe's future:

> They get very interesting now because the question is going to be asked with Mugabe out of power "can he get his money?" because Zimbabwe desperately needs money, hundreds of millions of dollars, to re-float the economy. They can

get it back from Mugabe's wealth off-shore or the cronies around him. Then, they could start really doing some repairs.

Mugabe looted the mines during the postsanctions period and left a completely broken mining system behind him (Interviewee 5, 2017). Hence, the ZANU-PF government allegedly participated in illegal diamond extraction in Marange in 2013, and that might have brought into disrepute any formal mining business growth during the 2000s (Saunders & Nyamunda, 2016; Maguwu, 2013).

After Mugabe's resignation, Emmerson Mnangagwa became the new president of Zimbabwe on 24 November 2017 through a soft coup in Harare. Zimbabweans then went to polls to elect a new president on 30 July 2018. ZANU-PF's candidate Mnangagwa became the first elected president of Zimbabwe after the thirty-seven-year Mugabe era. One of Mnangagwa's top priorities was the amendment of the 51 per cent indigenised ownership rule in the IEE (Dzirutwe, 2018a). The amended Act stipulated that foreign-owned mining companies did not need to empower 51 per cent of their ownership structure except for the country's most valuable mineral resources, namely diamonds and platinum.

Nevertheless, Nico Muller, the CEO of the South African mining corporate Implats, declared that the Zimbabwean government agreed to waive the 51 per cent ownership law in its Zimbabwe operation, namely Zimplats, which is controlled by Impala Platinum (Njini, 2018a). Zimplats has empowered 20 per cent of its assets, selling 10 per cent to the employees and another 10 per cent to communities in Zimbabwe. Muller said in an interview that "The equity stays. Instead of a transfer of ownership, we are achieving that through business development in Zimbabwe. We have agreed on that with the government" (Njini, 2018a). As things stand, the platinum companies in Zimbabwe are not obliged to sell 51 per cent of their assets to local Zimbabweans and the government, so the new president has started his reign with a business-friendly notion (Turak, 2018). For example, Hugh Warner, executive chairman of Prospect Resources, believes that Zimbabwe is open for business as he is content with the new government's attitude towards the foreign mining companies (*BBC World Service*, 2018). Prospect Resources is an Australian mining company which established a lithium mine just outside Harare five years ago, and the company is looking for another investment in the country. As the executive chairman of a small mining company, Warner thinks that the balance sheet is competitive against the large companies in Zimbabwe. Moreover, Neal Froneman, the chief executive of Sibanye-Stillwater, thinks that the political changes in not only South Africa but also Zimbabwe are going in the right direction (Stoddard & Lewis, 2018).

The key question is whether President Mnangagwa can bring the elite rent-seeking and resource nationalisation policies of Harare to an end. These significant issues need management and determination from the newly elected president, together with extreme indigenisation and economic empowerment policies. Hence, the first impressions of the post-Mugabe government have been relatively positive in terms of loosening the extreme indigenisation and economic empowerment policies and opening a new door for foreign investors who have the necessary capital to invest in the Zimbabwean mining industry. The policy choice of the new government might not be completely liberal because of the uncompleted economic transformation, but even so, the Mnangagwa administration might have to search for alternative solutions to the lack of capital and investment in the country's mining industry. During the last two years, Mnangagwa has never closed the country's door to Western core or noncore investors, including Chinese state-owned and private mining firms.

For Zimbabwe, the nonnegotiated 51 per cent indigenised ownership rule had been the biggest problem. As in South Africa, there was no negotiation between the government and the industry. Interviewee 4 (2017) told me that investors do not want to invest in South Africa or Zimbabwe anymore as they prefer to invest in other Southern African Development Community (SADC) countries such as Botswana, the DRC, and Tanzania. Nevertheless, Interviewee 3 (2017) claimed that South Africa is in a better state than Zimbabwe because it did not follow the 51 per cent rule, and there is more money in the hands of the government and black South Africans. Zimbabwe's mining industry has been mainly driven by external actors, whereas in South Africa the mining activities have carried out mainly by domestic companies.

POLITICAL SETTLEMENTS IN SOUTH AFRICA AND ZIMBABWE

This section explains how the political settlements approach is useful for understanding the divergent fates of South Africa and Zimbabwe in terms of their policy choices, power configurations, and institutions. Although the MWS theory offers significant explanations for the international political economy, it does not offer much about domestic policy choices. Therefore, as complementary to the MWS theory, this section needs a domestic-level political economy approach, namely, political settlements, which "promises to move beyond institutionalist approaches and their application to development" (Kelsall & vom Hau, 2020, p. 6). Khan (2017, pp. 638–39) suggests that the increase of political settlements within the literature "as a critique of approaches that ignored the conflictual aspects of institutions and the conflictual nature of the social transformations that development entailed." Moreover, the literature on the political settlements approach provides an alternative to neopatrimonialism, which is based on Weberian ideal state-types and systems of power and new economic approaches, such as new institutional economics, embedded in the neoclassical economic assumptions (Behuria *et al.*, 2017, pp. 524–25; Gray & Whitfield, 2014, p. 2). Indeed, Gray and Whitfield (2014, p. 2) argue that they "do not explicitly engage with capitalism as an analytical concept."

The UK Department for International Development defines the political settlements framework as "the forging of a common understanding, usually between political elites, that their best interests or beliefs are served through acquiescence to a framework for administering political power" (Di John & Putzel, 2009, p. 4). Bell and Pospisil (2017, p. 579) suggest that "in its most 'lay' meaning, the term political settlement connotes relative stability characterised by political and social order." Khan (2010) as the founder of the framework, defines it as "an analytical framework for analysing institutions and governance in developing countries." The political settlements approach also analyses the capitalist transformation of economies in African countries from the 1960s, but Behuria *et al.* (2017, p. 521) argue that the transformation in Africa has been uneven. South African and Zimbabwean capitalist transformations have been problematic, as I analysed in this chapter.

The political settlements framework explains not only why conflicts occur, and states collapse or become fragile, but also how they rehabilitate themselves successfully with suitable policies (Kelsall & vom Hau, 2020, p. 2). A key number of factors might shape a political settlement such as "the relationships between political elites, productive capitalists and broader social groupings" (Mutebi & Hickey, 2013, p. 5). Khan (2010, pp. 7–8) argues that the organisation of the ruling coalition; the quality of entrepreneurs and their power relationship with the ruling coalition are the reasons behind different performances in institutions. Under the white-minority rules, South Africa and Rhodesia had sophisticated institutions for whites. Some of them were transferred to majority rules but Zimbabwe could not protect and develop most of those institutions. South Africa has been relatively successful in this process as it has a fairly dominant position in its region (Khan, 2017, p. 637; Khan, 2010, p. 1). For example, in South Africa, farming, manufacturing, or mining sectors have been sophisticated as they are also legacies of white-minority rule. South Africa and Zimbabwe required a new settlement under the majority rules as they have experienced a long period of settler colony period and the institutions in both countries were incompatible with the requirements of the black majorities. Solving the inequality problem or unequal development depends on governments and businesses and, therefore, in South Africa and Zimbabwe the outcomes have been different (Khan, 2017, p. 640).

The political settlements approach shall be helpful to link the economic transformation and state-business relations with analysing internal dynamics in South Africa and Zimbabwe regarding their respective policy choices of liberalisation and indigenisation. The political settlements approach provides a detailed analysis of the power configuration and institutional outcomes of the South African and Zimbabwean political economies. Khan (2017, p. 637) believes that "the distribution of organizational power" is at the core of the political settlements framework (on the distribution of power *see* Gray & Whitfield, 2014; Khan, 2010). The distribution of power is linked to ZANU-PF in Zimbabwe, but in South Africa, it is linked to the ANC and domestic mining sector and other influential social groups. Indeed, organizational power is a product of holding power, which "is partly based on income and wealth but also on historically rooted capacities of different groups to organize" (Khan, 2010, p. 1; *see also* Khan, 2017, p. 640). According to Behuria *et al.* (2017, p. 512), political settlements can provide "tracing the changing distribution of power between different groups over time, as reflected in struggles over property or rents." Thus, this book traces the changes in the distribution of power from Mugabe to Mnangagwa in Zimbabwe and from Mandela to Ramaphosa in South Africa in terms of SBRs regarding the mining industry.

In both countries, the history of political struggles is decisive for gathering the holding power. Beijing supported the ZANU instead of the Soviet-backed ZAPU during the Rhodesian Bush War and ZANU-PF became the most powerful group after the struggle against the Rhodesian government. The ANC, trade unions, and communists were the historically powerful groups among blacks in South Africa. However, the domestic white-owned mining industry supported the majority rule during the isolation periods of the 1980s and the 1990s mostly for economic reasons. Personalized politics have been visible during the postindependence period in Zimbabwe and under the Zuma presidency in South Africa. Historically, the mining sector, trade unions, the ANC, and communists have the holding power in South Africa. ZANU-PF and Mugabe have generated this historical power from the rebellion against Rhodesian oppression. Political settlements framework also be helpful to define the institutional structures and differences between state and business actors of both countries (Khan, 2017, 2010). Accessing economic resources is another significant dimension of organizational power (Gray & Whitfield, 2014, p. 11). Thus, it has been one of the most important aspects of political settlement in Zimbabwe as it is visible in shifting policies regarding the mining industry. Conversely, in South Africa, trade unions or communists have become significant parties of the political settlement despite they have not had a chance to access economic resources. However, protecting a working but unequal system was the priority of the initial ANC governments during the 1990s.

The political settlements framework, which was defined by (Kelsall & vom Hau, 2020, p. 3) "as an ongoing agreement amongst the most powerful groups of societies," generates two major questions for the domestic political economy of South Africa and Zimbabwe. What are the most powerful groups from both countries in the mining industry? How do governments adopt policies along with those powerful groups? In Zimbabwe, ZANU-PF adopted ESAP in accordance with Western corporates and IFIs, which were powerful groups during the colonial period as well. Mugabe adopted the Look East policy and later IEE in accordance with his close allies in other state institutions and the Beijing government. Mugabe provided some special rights for China's state-owned mining companies and created a new political settlement in Zimbabwe, excluding the domestic or international Western mining sector, trade unions, and the majority of the Zimbabwean population. In South Africa, the ANC adopted GEAR in accordance with domestic white-owned corporates and IFIs. The ANC adopted the BEE policy in accordance with not only black majorities but also white-owned corporates in the mining sector and the BEE policy has become gradual. Mugabe did not care about international or domestic mining companies or other institutions when he was adopting the IEE policy. Although Zuma received too much criticism and faced a trial regarding corruption or 'state capture,' the gradual progress of the BEE policy in South Africa continued during the 2010s. In South Africa, there has been a search for a common understanding between elites, but Zimbabwe has not shifted its policy from liberalisation to indigenisation (*see* Di John & Putzel, 2009, p. 4). Therefore, the major differences between South African and Zimbabwean political settlements reflect their divergent SBRs during the late twentieth and the early twenty-first centuries.

Power configuration is one of the most significant aspects of a political settlement. The configuration of power might be concentrated, dispersed, or balanced. Cohesion among the elites even with a low intraelite conflict is the outcome of a political settlement with a concentrated configuration of power (Kelsall & vom Hau, 2020, p. 17; Kelsall, 2018, p. 11; Gray & Whitfield, 2014, p. 18). The intraelite conflict was low along with elite cohesion during the liberalisation periods in both countries although black majorities were expecting a swift transformation in the economy. Intraelite conflict was high during the Zuma presidency in South Africa between 2009 and 2017 and from the mid-2000s to 2017 in Zimbabwe. South Africa under the Zuma presidency experienced a dispersed configuration of power, which represents a lack of cohesion among elites and high intraelite conflict (Kelsall & vom Hau, 2020, p. 17). There has been a dispute between the Zuma government, the ANC-supported black mining businesspeople, trade unions, domestic white businesses, and the communists in the three-partite alliance during the 2010s. Initially, Mugabe broke down its relations with Western counterparts and mining houses during the mid-2000s but has adopted the Look East policy and created bilateral relations with China. Actually, in Zimbabwe, Mugabe excluded the other domestic or international elites from the policy scene and kept its domestic allies there. The allegedly looting of Marange diamond fields by his allies in the army was the most visible example of this elite cohesion in 2013. The second breakup happened with Chinese mining companies after the implementation of the 51 per cent indigenisation rule in the mining sector, although they had initially been excluded from this rule. This resulted in a dispersed power configuration in Zimbabwe and Mnangagwa dethrone Mugabe. Zimbabwean political settlement was unsustainable under the Mugabe presidency and the South African one under the Zuma presidency.

In addition to power configuration, narrow or broad social foundations are decisive for different typologies of political settlements. Intraelite contention and bargaining include not only domestic or international political or economic elites but also nonelites of a society (Di John & Putzel, 2009, p. 4). ZANU-PF elites, military commanders, and periodically China's state-owned mining companies have more advantages than other groups in Zimbabwe. It is more complicated but the ANC, domestic mining sector (black or white), and trade unions have more advantages in South Africa. Mondliwa and Roberts (2021) argue that the expanding distribution of power in political settlements in South Africa should have included black domestic mining elites. However, they believe that the inclusion of ANC-linked black owners in the mining sector has some negative effects on the development of technology (Mondliwa & Roberts, 2021, p. 330). The domestic mining sector has been integral to the South African political settlements during the postapartheid era, and they have relatively powerful counterparts in Zimbabwe (for the importance of domestic capitalists *see* Gray & Whitfield, 2014, p. 20).

While South African domestic capital has been a powerful and influential actor, weak domestic capital in Zimbabwe has been ignored since the early 2000s by the ZANU-PF governments. Gray and Whitfield (2014, p. 22) define this ignorance as problematic as domestic capital should be an integral part of a successful political settlement. Political settlement is a one-sided process in Zimbabwe and many other African countries for long periods (Behuria *et al.*, 2017, p. 519). Therefore, Zimbabwe has had a narrow social foundation since 2003 along with the implementation of the Look East policy because "the top leadership primarily worries about the cooptation of a small range of particular groups" (Kelsall & vom Hau, 2020, p. 18). There have been fewer groups in Zimbabwe than in South Africa during the last two decades because the country's social foundation has been narrow. For Mugabe after the Look East policy, there were not too many choices. Some close allies in state institutions and China and South Africa were the most powerful groups in that narrow social foundation. This narrow social foundation along with concentrated power provides more independent policy choices, such as the Look East policy, Fast-Track Land Reform, or IEE, for the ZANU-PF or Mugabe; however, the results were not satisfying for solving the legacies of Rhodesia or other problems that arose since 1979. A concentrated power configuration fits with Zimbabwe under the Mnangagwa presidency as well. For example, the adoption of the 'Zimbabwe open for business' policy has been a visible example of a concentrated power configuration recently.

On the other hand, South Africa has a broad social foundation, which includes plenty of powerful groups in the politics and economy of the country (Kelsall & vom Hau, 2020, p. 18; Kelsall, 2018, p. 7). The ANC, NGOs, trade unions (COSATU), and business associations (Minerals Council) have been members of this broad social foundation in South Africa. There have also been some powerful groups in politics, such as Democratic Alliance and the communist parties, even though they were not members of the government. The ANC has often required approval from different powerful groups when applying different policies. But sometimes—for example, under Zuma's presidency—the power configuration became concentrated. According to Goodfellow (2014, p. 313), a political settlement "must be able to generate and sustain a certain level of political stability and economic performance" and, therefore, South Africa has better political stability and economic performance after the implementation of respective indigenisation policies. Kelsall (2018, p. 7) argues that the broader factions have different outcomes for society and that political settlement might be more successful. Thus, relatively successful political settlement in South Africa might have been a result of the main powerful groups representing different political or economic interests within society. The groups are broad-based in South Africa, but the development has been low during the apartheid era. There have been some other reasons for this low development, such as massive inequalities in society or corruption. Balanced power configuration might generate better outcomes for South Africa's SBRs; Kelsall (2018, p. 11) argues that it "may prove to be optimal for development over the longer term . . . the top leadership can make binding decisions but only after consultation processes, negotiation and presumably some concession making." This section compares the political settlements of South Africa and Zimbabwe and suggests that the divergent power configurations and institutions generates differing outcome for both countries.

CONCLUSION

The mining industries of both South Africa and Zimbabwe have been significant for internal and external powers ever since the discovery of diamonds in Kimberley in 1866. As a result, mineral resources became an attractive prospect for colonisers, white settler regimes, and independent or postapartheid nonracial regimes of southern Africa from the last quarter of the nineteenth century (Andreasson, 2015, p. 311). The production of minerals and their contribution to the GDPs of South Africa and Zimbabwe illustrate the key differences between the two countries. In addition, South Africa's active mining corporates in Zimbabwe and the rest of Africa point out another key difference in their respective mining industries. South Africa has a diversified economy, including core and peripheral activities, whereas the Zimbabwean economy is less diversified and characterised by typical peripheral activities including agricultural activities and mineral extraction.

South Africa's economic transformation experience has not been primarily about producing a radical redistribution of wealth as the ANC proposed with the RDP in 1994. However, the first phase of economic transformation in South Africa liberalised the mining industry, and the corporates found a chance to invest overseas without government regulations. On the other hand, implementation of ESAP was a significant step to reducing the effects of the isolation on the business sector. Black political and white economic elites established close links during the liberalisation period in South Africa and Zimbabwe as a consequence of their respective neoliberal policies. However, these links were eventually strained during the indigenisation processes in both countries (Nattrass & Seekings, 2010, p. 8).

The liberalisation policies did not produce the expected outcomes in terms of economic growth and reducing poverty. So to answer pressure from the black majority, the Mugabe administration shifted the liberalisation policy to a nonliberal policy with the implementation of Fast-Track Land Reform and the IEE. As a result of this shift, the relationship between the white economic elites and the majority government broke down. Zimbabwe's indigenisation experience was more about regime survival to strengthen the levers of government over all aspects of the economy. Foreign investors have been significant and more active in the mining industry of Zimbabwe than domestic investors. So the newly elected government unsurprisingly sought to attract more foreign investors to generate a profitable mining industry.

South Africa's indigenisation process was less harmful to the established links between state and private white-dominated capital than was the case in Zimbabwe. The domestic industry has become a more important actor than foreign investors in South Africa's mining industry. South Africa's indigenisation policy created a middle and entrepreneurial class, termed a 'patriotic bourgeoisie,' among the black majority. These new emerging black entrepreneurs of South Africa have joined the existing white domestic mining industry over the last two decades. Although both systems have been prone to corruption and favouritism, it has been more flagrant in Zimbabwe. According to Wallerstein (2011b, p. 348), the strength of the MWS as a world-economy is based on the favouritism of the capitalists by the state apparatus:

> I am not here arguing the classic case of capitalist ideology that capitalism is a system based on the noninterference of the state in economic affairs. Quite the contrary! Capitalism is based on the constant absorption of economic loss by political entities, while economic gain is distributed to "private" hands. What I am arguing rather is that capitalism as an economic mode is based on the fact that the economic factors operate within an arena larger than that which any political entity can totally control. This gives capitalists a freedom of maneuver that is structurally based. It has made possible the constant economic expansion of the world-system, albeit a very skewed distribution of its rewards.

Thus, corruption and favouritism have not been merely specific to South Africa and Zimbabwe, although the extent of it considerably higher than the majority of the rest of the world. In order to understand the effects of these specific policy choices on SBRs in South Africa and Zimbabwe, the increasing Chinese presence in both countries must be analysed. In fact, shifts in both countries' policy choices during the 2000s opened a space for China not only in the economic realm but also in policy.

NOTES

1. Multiracial groups in South Africa (blacks, coloureds, and Indians) were united under nonwhite-led organisations from the 1950s against apartheid. Moreover, the term 'black' covered all of these multiracial groups (Martin, 2013b, p. 151).
2. The indigenisation policy in Malaysia became a role model for South African indigenisation policy, namely B-BBEE (*see* Cargill, 2010; Ponte *et al.*, 2007; Freund, 2007).
3. The Tripartite Alliance is an alliance between the ANC, the Congress of South African Trade Unions (COSATU), and the SACP.
4. MacLean believed that Zimbabwe's involvement in the DRC conflict was "the most odious decision for citizens" (2002, p. 522).
5. The president of Chamber of Mines of South Africa Mxolisi Mgojo announced that the Chamber was renamed Minerals Council South Africa in May 2018, after having been formalised in 1889 (Van Vuuren, 2018a).

6. Nkosazana Dlamini-Zuma was the former wife of previous President Zuma, who had supported her against Ramaphosa at the ANC National Conference (Cohen & Mkokeli, 2017).

7. My interviewees had positive expectations of Ramaphosa before the ANC National Conference on 18 December 2017.

8. This consulting firm is a Johannesburg-based globally active mining engineering consultancy which is active in both South Africa and Zimbabwe.

Chapter 3

The Chinese Presence in South Africa and Zimbabwe

INTRODUCTION

This chapter engages with China's significant presence in South Africa and Zimbabwe from the early 2000s onwards, since the Chinese presence was relatively insignificant before that date. In the previous two chapters, I have already analysed separately the respective semiperipheral and peripheral roles of South Africa and Zimbabwe in the MWS and the policy choices made on their respective mining industries by both countries. It is my argument that the increasing influence of Chinese state-owned and private mining companies has different effects on the SBRs of a semiperipheral and of a peripheral country, namely, in this case, South Africa and Zimbabwe respectively.

The Chinese presence changes the general trajectory and therefore the outcomes of countries' position in the MWS and their respective policy choices. First, Chinese business interests are different in peripheral and semiperipheral countries. Indeed, China has developed bilateral relations with peripheral countries of Africa for more natural resources. In contrast, China's bilateral relationship with semiperipheral countries such as South Africa is not shaped only by the demand for natural resources but also by political partnerships with BRICS and more sophisticated trade and investment relations, including the competition between the two semiperipheral powers. Second, China has more dominance in Zimbabwe's political and economic activities than in South Africa. Third, China's economic and political presence in South Africa and Zimbabwe has different outcomes in terms of power and dependency.

Chinese state-owned and private mining firms have invested in the mining industries of both countries through partnerships with their respective governments. South Africa created bilateral relations with China in 1998 after recognising the Beijing government instead of an independent Taiwan (Alden & Wu, 2016; Grimm *et al.*, 2014; Shelton & Kabemba, 2012; Le Pere & Shelton, 2007; Payne & Veney, 1998). South Africa positioned itself against the core countries as a result of "the country's close relationship with the BRICS countries" (Qobo & Dube, 2015, p. 156). Moreover, although there were already established diplomatic relations between China and Zimbabwe, their bilateral relationships gained momentum with Harare's 'Look East' policy after the imposition of Western economic sanctions during the early 2000s (Alao, 2014; Chun, 2014; Bourne, 2011; Youde, 2007). The trade volume between Zimbabwe and China increased almost twenty times, from US$71.6 million to US$1.3 billion between 1999 and 2015 (National Bureau Statistics of China, 2017). The Sino-South African trade volume also increased dramatically from US$1.7 billion to US$65.2 billion between 1999 and 2013 (National Bureau Statistics of China, 2017). The Chinese presence in South Africa and Zimbabwe has clearly increased during the last two decades and has inevitably affected the development trajectories of both countries.

In this chapter, I examine China's economic presence in the mining industries of South Africa and Zimbabwe during their posttransition periods (Andreasson, 2015; Burgess & Beilstein, 2013; Shelton & Kabemba, 2012; Gonzalez-Vicente, 2011; Shaw *et al.*, 2007). Chinese investments and trade activities might be either beneficial or harmful to business environments. Hence, some have argued that China's economic presence in South Africa, or more broadly across the continent, has created competition with the South African manufacturing industries (Carmody & Taylor, 2010; Schoeman, 2007). Others have argued that China's investments in Zimbabwe have compensated for the lack of money and technology caused by the Western economic sanctions from the early 2000s (Mason, 2017; Burgess & Beilstein, 2013). Before making any conclusions, I shall compare China's effect on the extractive industries of semiperipheral and peripheral South Africa and Zimbabwe, along with their policy choices in regard to these industries.

BILATERAL RELATIONS BETWEEN CHINA AND AFRICA

In order to understand the evolving nature of foreign investments in sub-Saharan Africa during the last two decades, the phenomenon of China's significant presence must be clearly analysed. The increasing amount of state-owned Chinese investments in the resource markets of the African continent has changed the profile of the foreign investors as well as the structure of SBRs. In fact, the overtaking of Western private extractive companies by Chinese state-owned companies in the continent has changed the business environment over the last two decades (Mason, 2017; Burgess & Beilstein, 2013; Carmody & Taylor, 2010; Schoeman, 2007). There has been a significant shift for the continent because China's state-owned companies do not come by themselves; they also bring their infrastructural investments, aid programmes, and cooperation in foreign policy (Taylor, 2014; Halper, 2010; Brautigam, 2009; Ampiah & Naidu, 2008). South Africa and Zimbabwe have also been attractive targets for Chinese state-owned extractive companies because of their rich precious and industrial mineral resources (Besada & O'Bright, 2016; Andreasson, 2015; Alden *et al.*, 2008; Shaw *et al.*, 2007). Also, the implementation of indigenisation policies in both countries has discouraged Western mining corporates and generated space for Chinese investors (Burgess & Beilstein, 2013; Shelton & Kabemba, 2012). Despite this, China's investment and policy patterns towards sub-Saharan African countries are not the same in South Africa (Garcia, 2017a; Tella, 2017; Alden & Schoeman, 2015; 2013; Garcia & Bond, 2015; Qobo & Dube, 2015; Qobo & Soko, 2015; Carmody, 2013).

Sino-African bilateral relations gained momentum in the fields of aid, development, investment, and trade after the first FOCAC summit in Beijing in 2000 (Brautigam, 2009). China's foreign policymakers were looking for a market to sell their manufactured goods and for a raw material source to improve their industrial production, and Africa fitted these criteria (Wang & Elliot, 2014). The China-Africa trade volume in 2016 was US$148 billion, which demonstrates the importance of Africa for China and *vice versa* (*see* figure 3.1). China became the largest trade partner of Africa in 2011 and surpassed the United States with a total volume of US$166 billion, which is "a trade explosion of 160 times over 30 years" (Wang & Elliot, 2014, p. 1014). A year before the first FOCAC summit in 2000, Chinese foreign direct investments (FDIs) in Africa were US$196 million (National Bureau of Statistics of China, 2017). This multiplied ten-fold within sixteen years, and US$1.1 billion in Chinese FDIs was committed to Africa in 2016.

Before the increasing Chinese presence in Africa, China had been a long-standing friend for African countries, particularly during the Cold War. During the independence era for African nations, Beijing had also supported the Non-Aligned Movement (NAM) throughout the continent by providing political, economic, and military aid. Also, the Tazara (Tanzania-Zambia Railroad) is one of the most visible legacies of Maoist China from the Cold War (Wand & Elliot, 2014, p. 1013). During the 1970s, however, Beijing's nonalignment policy ended in Africa with China's intervention in the Angola War. China became an active ally and enemy of different parties in the Angola War during the 1970s and 1980s.

Following the end of the Cold War, China continued to develop bilateral relations with African countries in the early 1990s. Besada and O'Bright

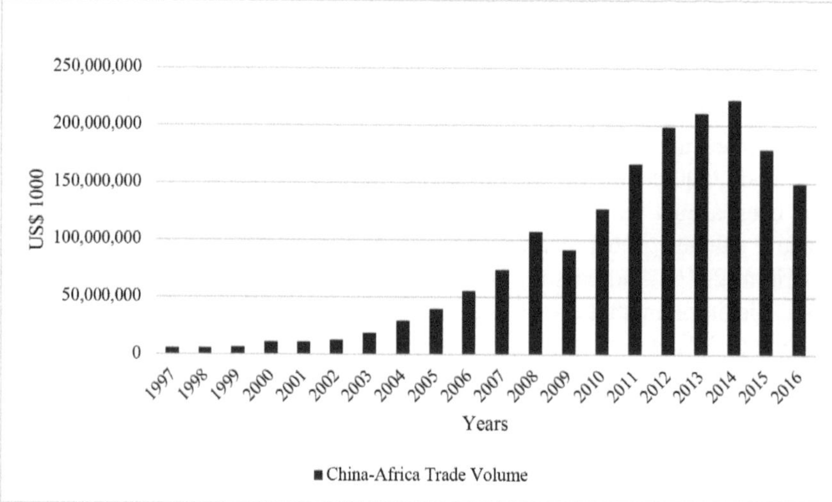

Figure 3.1. China-Africa Trade Volume (1997–2016). Source: Author created with data from National Bureau of Statistics of China (2017).

(2016, pp. 2–3) thought that "the modern Sino-African partnership" was maintained by two notable points in the 1989–1993 period. First, the Chinese Foreign Minister's diplomatic visits to fourteen African capitals between 1989 and 1992, and second, the transformation of China's oil trade trend from exporter to importer in 1993. As a result of these two events, China established bilateral ties with African countries.

The start of the new millennium brought hope to African people because of China's influence on the continent's economies. China's presence gradually increased from the mid-2000s to the present in terms of economic, political, social, and cultural links in Africa. African countries started to develop in the 2000s with the help of Chinese development, investment, and trade activities and the democratic reforms of the 1990s. China's infrastructural investments had importance for providing the basic needs such as transport, health, education, and communication, which were the legacies of the colonial era. Taylor (2014, p. 102) believed that the Chinese presence in Africa was the most significant development for the continent in the post-Cold War era despite the unfair economic data and trade figures between China and Africa which created a new dependency for African countries. China's increasing influence in the continent therefore raised some new questions in the literature: Is China a hegemon or a partner for African countries? (*see* Besada & O'Bright, 2016; Mason, 2016; Tang & Pigato, 2015; Taylor, 2014; 2006; Carmody, 2013; Viera & Alden, 2011; Carmody & Taylor, 2010; Cheru & Obi, 2010; Christensen, 2010; Halper, 2010; Brautigam, 2009; Alden *et al.*,

2008; Ampiah & Naidu, 2008). Does Beijing challenge the American power in Africa and beyond? (*see* Buzan, 2011; Robinson, 2011; Callahan, 2008; Campbell, 2008; Li, 2008; 2005; Schoeman, 2007; Carmody & Owusu, 2007; Mearsheimer, 2006; Deng & Wang, 2004). The current study is designed to demonstrate how China's significant presence, following the combined effects of countries' position in the MWS and their respective policy choices, produces a specific effect on the consolidation or fracturing of SBRs.

The Chinese impact brought both criticisms and positive comments in its wake from both the African and the Western perspectives. On the one hand, optimists have believed that China's presence in Africa is helpful for overcoming the underdevelopment problems which were the legacies of the colonial era (*see* Brautigam, 2009; Ampiah & Naidu, 2008; Campbell 2008; Dollar, 2008; Carmody & Owusu, 2007; Le Pere, 2007; Marks, 2007; Naidu, 2007), so they have assumed that Africa is rising and developing because of the Chinese investments in the continent. Also, Nyabereka (2017) argued that developing countries such as Zimbabwe have benefited more from their relations with BRICS countries than from Bretton Woods institutions. She commented that "growing industry, an improved health care system and better fiscal management" have been the products of intensified relations with BRICS countries (Nyabereka, 2017).

On the other hand, the Sino-African relationship has been criticised for unfair trade arrangements, ignoring the rule of law and good governance, and creating a new dependence for African economies just as in the colonial era (*see* Carmody, 2017; 2013: 2011; Taylor, 2014; West, 2014; Burgess & Beilstein, 2013; Campbell *et al.*, 2012; Nwoke, 2007; Rogers, 2007; Lee, 2006; Ramo, 2004).[1] For instance, Taylor (2014, p. 137) claimed that "recent economic growth in Africa is based on trade in resources, not production." These trade relations might be profitable in the short or medium term, but this is not a sustainable trend because of the limited sources of minerals in the long term. Industrialisation and commodity production might generate a developed Africa instead of dependence on the export of resources (Taylor, 2014, p. 144).

Even though this bilateral relationship has been profitable for the Chinese economy much more than for African countries, they have started to develop again. However, unequal trade relations between China and Africa might create a new dependency for African countries or maintain the continent's dependence on foreign capital. For example, Taylor (2014, p. 107) pointed out that Africa's raw material sources are helpful for maintaining Chinese growth, but also raised an alert that "this is where the dangers of entrenching African dependency loom largest." According to figures published by the International Trade Centre (2018), China imported mainly raw materials and unfinished products from African countries in 2017. Moreover, extracted resources and other minerals dominated China's imported goods from African countries along with agricultural products (International Trade Centre, 2018). On the other side, African countries have mainly imported manufactured products from China such as electrical and technological goods and machinery, vehicles, clothes, footwear, and furniture (International Trade Centre, 2018). Indeed, trade relations of this type prevent investments in the manufacturing sector, and African countries become more dependent on peripheral activities such as agricultural, mineral and petroleum production, and inevitably Chinese money.

Despite these unequal trade relations between African countries and China, Chinese investments in Africa have sometimes created new opportunities for the continent. For example, China's infrastructural projects, technical support, and educational partnership programmes have aided African countries' economic and social development (Gonzalez-Vicente, 2011, p. 69). Also, Chinese investors have invested in the riskier places in Africa, as Chinese companies have a different risk appetite from that of their Western counterparts which are listed on LSE or the New York Stock Exchange (Interviewee 3, 2017). Interviewee 3 (2017) believed that, in theory, Chinese investments are the same as many other foreign investments, but that in reality they do not care too much about business ethics and he argued that "they are quite happy to put money on the table to make things happen and you can do it in Africa." Mining matters for China as China and other industrialised countries go to Africa to share in the resources of the continent (Shelton & Kabemba, 2012). However, Beijing's foreign policy was dictated by an "anti-hegemonic" approach, particularly with regard to African states during the early 2000s (Taylor, 2006). China has therefore not approached African countries as a benevolent and paternalistic actor or a hegemon; instead, Beijing approached them as trade and diplomatic partners (Schoeman, 2007).

Breslin (2013) described China as having four different identities: a developing country, an emerging power, a global power, and a quasisuperpower. First, China is the biggest developing country in the world and the most important economic partner of African countries. This identity of China gives inspiration to developing African, Asian, and Latin American countries. Second, China is an upwardly mobile semiperipheral country in the MWS and can challenge the hegemony of Western core countries, particularly the power of the United States (for China's rise as a semiperipheral country within the MWS, *see* Xing & Christensen, 2012; Downes, 2009; Radice, 2009; Li, 2005). Third, China has dominated world trade for two decades and this gives it a global power identity along with its upwardly mobile semiperipheral position. Fourth, China's military power has also escalated and expanded during the last two decades along with its diplomatic influence within the UNSC and BRICS. China has therefore gained a quasisuperpower identity through its increasing power in military and diplomatic terms.

There are some pessimistic analyses of and inferences from China's economic presence in Africa and the comparison with the Western powers, especially the United States, in the Sino-African relations literature. For example, Gonzalez-Vicente (2011) argued that China has negative effects on African countries. China's trade activities in Africa have unavoidably worsened the resource curse, environmental degradation, and the usage of nonrenewable resources (Gonzalez-Vicente, 2011, p. 66). Chinese manufacturing imports to the continent have negative effects on African industries and many textile companies in Africa consequently stopped their production in the 2000s (Carmody & Owusu, 2007, pp. 510–11). In addition, Burgess and Beilstein (2013) argued that China's presence in Africa was causing a "new scramble for Africa" and was sometimes harmful to African and western interests. Moreover, West (2014) argued that Sino-African relations are not equal, and that China acts no differently compared with the West.

There have also been debates comparing China's role/s in Africa with Western countries' demands from African countries. Some scholars claimed that China has been acting as the Western powers in Africa and that this is harmful to African countries (West, 2014; Gonzalez-Vicente, 2011). Moreover, other scholars have argued that China's noninterference policy is the only major difference with Western countries in Africa (Besada & O'Bright, 2016; Chen *et al.*, 2015; Carmody & Taylor, 2010). Despite the claim of only minor differences, Western countries demand good governance, transparency, and respect for human rights from African countries before they are prepared to make investments and support their developmental progress (Chen *et al.*, 2015). However, political stability is more important than environmental issues, the rule of law, and protecting human rights for the Chinese private and state-led investors in Africa. Carmody and Taylor (2010) argued that the main difference between the American and Chinese foreign policies towards African countries was their different approaches to nondemocratic states. Beijing's noninterference policy makes China a preferable partner than the United States in Africa, which is "a defining feature of flexigemony." In addition, China does not act like Western powers in the political area and does not pursue paternalistic policies towards African countries (Gonzalez-Vicente, 2011, p. 70).

The Sino-African relationship has been under discussion during the last two decades since it represents not only solidarity among the southern hemisphere countries in Africa, Asia, and Latin America but also a challenge to the Western-dominated core powers such as the United States, the IMF, and the World Bank in the continent. Africa is not unified, and African countries do not have a common policy in regard to China. However, Beijing has developed its own foreign policy towards African countries since the beginning of the twenty-first century (Shelton & Kabemba, 2012). China has therefore sometimes been regarded as a coloniser and competitor in the continent despite African leaders commonly having stable relations with it as partner countries (Shelton & Kabemba, 2012).

The Sino-African relationship has decreased the dependence of African countries on previous colonial powers and the core countries of the MWS during the last two decades. As a result, SBRs regarding mining industries in the continent have been reconfigured as a consequence of the increasing Chinese presence through state-owned and private mining companies and investments. Chinese investments in Africa's resource-rich economies have fuelled economic growth in the continent (Shelton & Kabemba, 2012) and these investments have changed the nature of bilateral relations between China and African countries. For instance, Chinese state-owned mining companies not only come with the required capital for investment but also support communities through infrastructural activities and aid programmes. However, Chinese state-owned enterprises can be the saving of autocratic governments because Beijing does not demand good governance, the rule of law, respect for human rights, or strict environmental rules from them (Tang & Pigato, 2015; Shelton & Kabemba, 2012; Cheru & Obi, 2010; Christensen, 2010; Brautigam, 2009).

MEASURING THE INSIGNIFICANT AND SIGNIFICANT PRESENCE OF CHINA

In this section, I describe how I measured the relative economic and political absence or presence of China. Indeed, the Chinese economic presence in South Africa and Zimbabwe is a result of nonliberal economic policies being implemented in both countries from the early 2000s. Also, China's political presence in both countries is related to this shift in economic nonliberal policy choices. Hence in Zimbabwe, implementing the Fast-Track Land Reform in 2000 and adopting the 'Look East' policy in 2002 for attracting Asian investors, particularly the emerging semiperipheral China, was a diplomatic shift which caused a breakaway from Western core countries and IFIs. The Chinese presence in Zimbabwe reduced the negative effects of Western sanctions and compensated for Western capital with beneficial trade relations and FDIs (Mason, 2017; Nyabereka, 2017; Burgess & Beilstein, 2013; Mukwereza, 2013).

Beijing and Pretoria established bilateral diplomatic relations in 1998 after South Africa recognised China over Taiwan during the early years of the BEE policy. South Africa never fractured relations with Western countries as Zimbabwe did in the early 2000s as the policy choices of the ANC were not extreme. However, implementing the First Mining Charter in 2004 was a nonliberal policy choice by Pretoria and was not welcomed by the existing white investors in the mining industry (Tangri & Southall, 2008; Ponte *et al.*, 2007; Chabane *et al.*, 2010; Southall, 2004). This consequently caused a shift in foreign policy in Pretoria during the 2010s under the Zuma presidency, and South Africa moved away from Western core countries to semiperipheral countries such as Brazil, Russia, India, and China (BRIC). Also, during the 2000s and onwards, South Africa-China economic relations developed gradually. One of the important consequences of this close relationship was South Africa joining the BRIC grouping in 2011 (Bond, 2018; 2013; Garcia, 2017a; Alden & Schoeman, 2015; 2013; Garcia & Bond, 2015; Taylor, 2014; Carmody, 2013; Vickers, 2012). This cooperation made South Africa a very obvious partner of China within the continent (Alden & Wu, 2016). Despite the good relations between South Africa and China, some argue that the Chinese presence is not beneficial for South Africa as it has created competition between two semiperipheral countries (Alden & Wu, 2016; Carmody & Taylor, 2010; Schoeman, 2007).

One of the most visible effects of China's influence on South Africa and Zimbabwe has been the dramatically increasing trade volumes during the last two decades. Examining the nature and degree of trade relations (exports and imports) between China and each case with the help of data from the National Bureau of Statistics of China (2017) is therefore crucial for seeing the alteration in the economic partners of South Africa and Zimbabwe. According to the National Bureau of Statistics of China (2017), bilateral trade relations between Zimbabwe and China gained momentum following the economic sanctions imposed by Western countries against the Mugabe administration in the early 2000s. From 1998 (US$132 million) to 2015 (US$1.3 billion), total trade between Zimbabwe and China multiplied nearly tenfold.

According to the same National Bureau of Statistics of China (2017) statistics, trade relations between China and South Africa have also increased during the twenty-first century. Total trade volume rose considerably, by more than forty times, from 1998 (US$1.5 billion) to 2013 (US$65 billion), showing the lowest and the highest amounts over the last twenty-year period. However, total trade volume decreased significantly, by almost 55 per cent, between 2013 and 2016 (US$35 billion) because of the sharply diminishing commodity prices, particularly minerals, from the early 2010s following the end of the commodity boom with the financial crisis of 2007–2008 (Bond, 2018).

Chinese FDIs in Africa is one of the significant demonstrators of China's economic presence in South Africa and Zimbabwe during the 2000s and 2010s. According to a SAIS China-Africa Research Initiative report on

Chinese foreign trade statistics, South Africa was the top recipient of Chinese FDIs, and Zimbabwe was the eighth-biggest Chinese FDI host country among all African countries in 2017. Chinese FDIs were worth US$7472.77 million and US$1748.34 million in South Africa and Zimbabwe respectively in 2017. As a result, these figures and statistics show that both South Africa (with a huge distinction in terms of total amount) and Zimbabwe have importance for Chinese economic activities in Africa.

CHINA-SOUTH AFRICA RELATIONS

China and South Africa created bilateral economic and political relations after President Mandela decided to recognise the People's Republic of China and not Taiwan in 1998. In addition to the diplomatic relations between the two countries, there had been a Sino-South African relationship following the discovery of diamonds and gold in South Africa in 1867 and 1884 respectively. Hence, Chinese miners came to South Africa around 120 years previously and worked as migrant labour workers who had previous experience of deep mining in China (Interviewee 5, 2017).

Following the establishment of Sino-South African relations in 1998, China's FDIs in South Africa soared more than six times from US$1.3 million to US$8.6 million within a year (*see* figure 3.2). In the same year, the Sino-South African trade volume was more than US$1.5 billion in total,

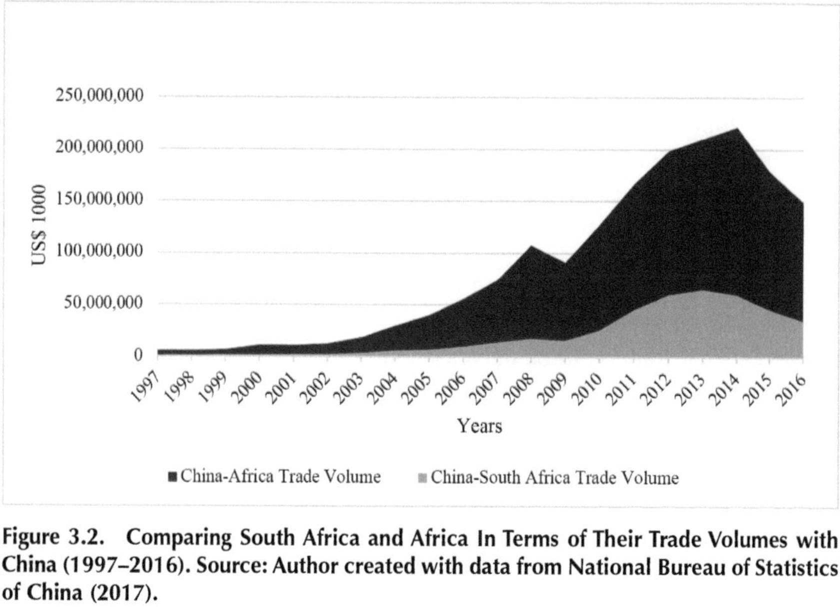

Figure 3.2. Comparing South Africa and Africa In Terms of Their Trade Volumes with China (1997–2016). Source: Author created with data from National Bureau of Statistics of China (2017).

which was 35 per cent of the total African trade with China, thanks to South Africa's sophisticated economic structure (National Bureau of Statistics of China, 2017). The Sino-South African trade volume peaked at US$65 billion in 2013 and three years later had almost halved to US$35 billion (National Bureau of Statistics of China, 2017).

South Africa developed a bilateral relationship with some rising semiperipheral countries such as Brazil, China, and India (*see* on BRICS, IBSA, and on South-South cooperation *see* Carmody, 2017; Garcia & Bond, 2015; Shaw, 2015; Alden & Schoeman, 2013; Carmody, 2013; Stephen, 2012; Vieira & Alden, 2011; Taylor, 2009; Shaw *et al.*, 2007; Alden & Vieira, 2005). South Africa's and China's economic relations boomed from the 2005 FOCAC summit to 2011, when South Africa joined the BRIC group (Grimm *et al.*, 2014, p. 16), adding the final S to the acronym, to make it the BRICS group. Grimm *et al.* (2014) believed that China needed good bilateral relations with South Africa because diplomatic and political support from Pretoria was, and still is, very important for China's strong position in the international community (pp. 15–16).

Burgess and Beilstein (2013) warned that South Africa could become a focus of conflict between China and the United States in Africa. However, during the last two decades, other African countries have challenged South Africa's pivotal position in the continent and the importance of South Africa for external actors has decreased slightly. In other words, countries such as Nigeria and Egypt have challenged South Africa's influential position in the continent in terms of economic growth during the last two decades. Inevitably, the increasing competition within and outside the country has affected negatively the pivotal position of South African mining companies in Africa, as well as domestic SBRs (Carmody & Taylor, 2010; Schoeman, 2007).

Despite South Africa having a diversified economy, China has primarily been interested in importing raw materials including mining products and precious minerals, as has been the case with imports to China from other mineral-rich countries of Africa (Grimm *et al.*, 2014, p. 18). Indeed, according to the sectoral allocation of GDP in South Africa, agricultural products (2.5 per cent) and mining and quarrying goods (8.4 per cent) formed 11 per cent of the total GDP (OECD, 2017). Beijing's primary interest in South Africa is in the country's raw materials, as is the case in the rest of the continent. South Africa's economy also depends on China like other African countries but with greater freedom than them, particularly Zimbabwe (Mason, 2017). According to International Trade Centre (2018) figures, South Africa exports not only extracted minerals, precious stones, and other kinds of metals but also agricultural products to China. Thus, China imports industrial metals, particularly coal, ferrochrome, iron ore, and manganese from South African mining companies and Interviewee 1 (2017) believed that Pretoria supports this type of trade relation. In fact, many South African mining companies benefit from a stable relationship by selling their products to the Chinese market.

On the other hand, the relatively sophisticated manufacturing industry in South Africa seems weaker against cheaper Chinese products as China exports similar products to South Africa and other African countries. According to figures from the International Trade Centre (2018), South Africa imports electrical machinery, machinery, furniture, clothes, and footwear from China. Indeed, South Africa and China compete in terms of labour-insensitive manufacturing goods and in selling them to other African countries (Arrighi *et al.*, 2010, p. 414). Arrighi *et al.* (2010, p. 414) sought an explanation for the lower Chinese wages than the South African wages for labour of about the same productivity and gave an example from Anita Chan's (2003, p. 44–45) study which compared the *hukou* (localised work permit) system in China and the apartheid administration in South Africa. Chan (2003) argued that it was the restricted human mobility which helped to generate a cheap labour force in China.

As a result, China can compete against South Africa's economic presence in Africa in two economic activities (Schoeman, 2007). First, Chinese manufactured goods are cheaper than the South African ones, and second, China can take over South African mining corporates' extractive activities in the rest of Africa. Martin criticised the fact that the Asian (Chinese and Indian) invasion in Africa had some negative effects on South African capital because the Asian corporations or investments brought similar technology to that of South Africa but more cheaply (2013a, p. 183). In contrast, Burgess and Beilstein (2013, p. 130) argued that South Africa's mining-extraction activities were more sophisticated than those of their Chinese counterparts.

Chinese large mining companies have not yet been very active in the South African mining industry because most of the South African mining corporates were traditionally white and English-speaking with few exceptions. According to Interviewee 5 (2017), although Gencor was an Anglo American gift to Afrikaner businesspeople during the apartheid regime, the tradition was for white English, Scots, and Welsh to undertake the mining sector in South Africa. In addition, Interviewee 1 (2017) stated that Chinese shareholders had started to take an active role in the South African mining industry even though their influence was slow. Interviewee 2 (2017) believed that the Chinese economic presence in South Africa had been surprisingly slow because of the sophistication of the mining sector in South Africa:

> Chinese investment in South Africa I think has been surprisingly slow compared to many other parts of the world and in many other parts of Africa. I am not sure . . . Maybe it is because the South African mining sector is far more

> developed than many other parts of Africa because it has been going [for a long time], it has had commercial rights in South Africa now since the 1860s and in gold since the 1880s. So, for that reason, I am not sure, what is the cause of the slow take of Chinese investment in South Africa in mining.

Moreover, Interviewee 6 (2018) also suggested that China is not a big player for the South African mining industries:

> Right now, Chinese investments cannot compete with the domestic mining industries of South Africa. They have so little investment than the West's. They are mostly junior companies who work with the South African mining industries. However, the Chinese are the main shareholders of Palabora Mining Company. They bought those shares from Rio Tinto in 2013. Chinese invest in the rest of Africa, for example in the DRC heavily. As a result, they are more effective in these countries. They are very important for those countries like the DRC or Angola.

Three Chinese state-owned companies and the South African state-owned IDC consortium announced that they would buy a 74.5 per cent stake in Palabora Mining Company from Rio Tinto and Anglo American in December 2012 (Jamasmie, 2012a). Rio Tinto had been looking to sell Palabora since 2007 because of a mineral rights dispute with the DMR (Harvey, 2014, p. 2). The Chinese Ministry of Commerce (MOFCOM, 2018) reported that the collaboration between the IDC and the Chinese consortium had been a success story for BRICS. MOFCOM (2018) stated that this kind of investment partnership among BRICS countries "can create [a] favourable environment for growth, technology exchanges and assist in building international cooperation platforms that embody the spirit and ethos of BRICS." Another partnership between the IDC and Chinese state-owned firms had been rumoured to be a R45 billion steel-mill project which would be the largest Chinese mining investment in South Africa from 2015, but Chinese investors have not yet materialised that intention because of decreasing steel prices in the market (Meng, 2017). The IDC and Chinese mining companies' collaboration is an example of how Chinese state-owned mining companies can bypass BEE demands and uncertainty in the mining policies of South Africa. Nevertheless, this collaboration might undermine the competitiveness of the mining industry in the long run (Harvey, 2014).

There have been other active Chinese-owned investment groups in the South African mining industry which have invested particularly in member companies of the Minerals Council of South Africa, such as Sibanye-Stillwater and Wesizwe Platinum, from the early 2010s. Grimm *et al.* (2014, pp. 20–21) stated that Chinese state-owned firms have effectively engaged in the South African mineral extraction sector. For example, in 2011 the Jinchuan

Group purchased a 45 per cent stake in Wesizwe Platinum and consequently became the biggest investor in the corporation alongside BEE partners, Anglo American, and other shareholders (Matomela, 2011). In 2011, the Chinese Investment Corporation (CIC) bought a 25 per cent stake in the Shanduka Group, which had been founded by Ramaphosa in the early 2000s and was 51 per cent owned by BEE investors (England, 2011). Moreover, Gold One South Africa, a Chinese-owned consortium, became the largest shareholder of Sibanye-Stillwater with a 19.35 per cent stake in 2017 (Prinsloo & Njini, 2018). So, after South Africa had joined the BRICS group, Chinese investors were active in the South African mining industry to fuel particularly newly founded, black-owned corporates.

Although Chinese organisations have purchased some significant stakes in South African diamond and gold companies, their overall intention is to invest in industrial metals in Africa (Interviewee 1, 2017). Towards this goal, China's President Xi Jinping announced a US$60 billion investment in Africa at the opening ceremony of the 2018 Beijing Summit of the FOCAC (France24, 2018). As part of this investment, Beijing also agreed with Pretoria to invest US$1.1 billion in South Africa, particularly in the industrial minerals sector (Stone, 2018).

The increasing Chinese presence in the South African mining industry inevitably affects the SBRs and makes it more complex. During the apartheid era, the mining industry was dominated by English-speaking, white businessmen and was less complicated than it is today because not only were the actors not diversified but also there was less political pressure on the mining industry. After the end of the apartheid regime, however, the structure of the mining industry changed to some extent through the BEE and indigenisation policies of the ANC government from the early 2000s. So, following the end of apartheid, the number of black-owned mining companies rose dramatically and the nature of the SBRs in South Africa changed.

Although Chinese investors have been active in some part of the South African mining industry, they still have only a restricted effect on the nature of the SBRs. Interviewee 4 (2017) claimed that Chinese economic involvement in the South African mining industry has not had any impact on the SBRs in South Africa. Similarly, Interviewee 2 (2017) thought that there was no effect on the South African mining industry from the involvement of the Chinese mining companies to SBRs. Nonetheless, Interviewee 3 (2017) argued that Chinese companies have a different relationship with the ANC government from other foreign investments because of the Chinese willingness to put more money on the table. Consequently, the stable Sino-South African relations might not have enough power to threaten the domination of English-speaking white businessmen along with the BEE policies of the ANC government. However, the partnership between IDC and Chinese state-owned mining firms was welcomed by the Zuma government. This partnership fuelled the deteriorating relationship between the domestic mining industry and the Zuma government.

Interviewee 1 (2017) thought that the BEE regulations, particularly those on the ownership rule, created obvious barriers to foreign investors, including China. Nevertheless, these regulations sometimes created opportunities for Chinese investors since some of the BEE investors could not provide the necessary money to buy a stake in a mining company. So many BEE investors want to bring Chinese partners to South Africa to become funding partners (Interviewee 1, 2017). Interviewee 4 (2017) claimed that the BEE policies regarding the mining industry, namely the Mining Charter, created neither barriers nor opportunities for Chinese mining companies:

> Chinese, Indian, and other countries, as long as they are bringing a BEE partner. All they need to do is bring a BEE partner. They can start new projects. They can even partner with bigger existing companies, but they just have to bring the required BEE partnership. So, they know that it is not going to be 100% theirs. They have to have local and indigenised representation in their structure. They do not have a problem with that.

Interviewee 6 (2018), however, suggested that foreign investors cannot survive in the medium and long term as the game changes frequently:

> Policy changes in the Mining Charter create barriers for foreign investors. These changes are not good for the lifecycle of foreign investment. Foreign investors experience more difficulty complying with these changes. This is also negative for Chinese investors. I have the same feeling for Chinese investors, they are affected badly by these everlasting discussions on the Mining Charter. They came here suddenly, and they are very pragmatic. They want a good return from their investments in the South African mining industries.

Interviewee 4 (2017) thought that the South African mining industry could learn something from the Chinese mining companies despite some concerns about China's ignorance of the rules and regulations regarding environmental and labour issues. However, as a member of the South African mining industry Interviewee 1 (2017) did not have positive feelings about the Chinese presence in South Africa, although he accepted that the lack of investment has opened a door for Chinese investors:

> A lot of western-based investors from Europe and the US, Canada, Australia are not investing here because of the policy and the uncertainty, because of the empowerment rules and so on and so on . . . because of the corruption in the government. People are not stupid. They do not want to invest in a country that

> is perceived as just corrupt. Therefore, someone has to fill the gap and maybe Chinese investors have fewer morals. They might be more likely; they have a more pragmatic approach to investment. They could feasibly take up the space left by some investors who are leaving this country.

In this section, I have shown that China's relationship with semiperipheral South Africa is more complicated and many-sided than its relations with peripheral African countries. Above all, South Africa is in a balanced position to China within the BRICS alliance because of its pivotal role in southern Africa. Second, the sophisticated mining industries and relatively rich mining corporates of South Africa reduce the country's dependence on Chinese investment and technology. Third, the detailed Mining Charter and BEE regulations have sometimes created uncertainty in South Africa but have also created opportunities for Chinese investors, such as becoming finance and investment partners with BEE shareholders, which has been beneficial for both sides. Consequently, as an external actor within the South African mining industry, China has affected SBRs from the early 2010s although its activities are more restricted than the domestic white and black mining companies.

CHINA-ZIMBABWE RELATIONS

China-Zimbabwe bilateral relations date back to the guerrilla warfare against the UDI in Rhodesia during the 1960s. Beijing supported black Zimbabweans against the white minority regime during the Cold War. Indeed, while the Soviet Union supported ZAPU, China supported ZANU under the leadership of Robert Mugabe during the Rhodesian Bush War. Beijing supported ZANU, or more directly Mugabe, during the Zimbabwean liberation war in four separate forms, all with long-standing consequences for both Zimbabwe and Sino-Zimbabwean relations (Alao, 2014, p. 6):

> The first was the provision of military assistance, which saw China sending military hardware to guerrillas in the Zimbabwe African National Liberation Army (ZANLA, the military wing of ZANU). The second form of support was the extensive military training that was given to ZANLA guerrillas. A significant number of ZANLA soldiers received military training in China that would advance the ZANLA insurgency. The third was the financial assistance given to the cause of Zimbabwean liberation through ZANU, while the final was the nature and extent of the ideological solidarity that resulted from the above.

Despite these historical ties, bilateral economic relations between China and Zimbabwe gained momentum after the imposition of Western economic sanctions in 2002 because of the human rights violations and the election rigging of the then-President Mugabe. The economic crisis in the late 1990s and the Fast-Track Land Invasion Programme of the ZANU-PF caused an economic meltdown with the collapse of GDP and economic growth and increasing hyperinflation. This economic meltdown posed a significant threat to the ZANU-PF government's hold on power. Consequently, Mugabe changed the government policy and moved away from established ties with Western core countries and IFIs such as the IMF and the World Bank. As the Western ties weakened, the Chinese economic and political influence in Zimbabwe started to increase (Carmody & Owusu, 2007). Mugabe's Zimbabwe withdrew from Commonwealth membership in 2003 because of the economic sanctions against the Harare government in the early 2000s (Farley, 2008, p. 82).

Mugabe announced the Look East policy in 2003 to reduce the effects of the Western economic sanctions and set up a close relationship with some developing Asian semiperipheral countries, including China, Indonesia, Iran, Malaysia, and North Korea instead of developed Western core countries (Youde, 2007, p. 10). Alao (2014, p. 5) argued that the "controversial relations" between Zimbabwe and China emerged from Zimbabwe's domestic politics (autocratic rule in Harare) and the reactions from the Western countries to them (economic sanctions). In addition to the economic sanctions and the Look East policy, China's economic expansion in Africa shaped close relations between the two countries during the 2000s and 2010s (Alao, 2014, p. 8).

After the first FOCAC summit in 2000, China expanded its bilateral economic relations with several African countries, including Zimbabwe (Chun, 2014, p. 8). Carmody and Owusu (2007, pp. 513–14) strongly argued that the start of Zimbabwe-China relations after the Western sanctions was one of the most important milestones in terms of the Chinese presence not only in Zimbabwe but also in Africa. Carmody and Owusu (2007) compared the geoeconomic strategies of Beijing and Washington towards Africa and argued that South Africa was one of the 'anchor' states for US influence and Zimbabwe was the 'anchor' state for China during the 2000s. Consequently, Beijing was able to easily apply its economic policy in Zimbabwe and to secure a new market (Chun, 2014, p. 15).

According to the trade figures published by the International Trade Centre (2018), China and Zimbabwe trade relations almost doubled from 2002 to 2007 before the international financial crisis of 2007–2008. Despite the financial crisis, China-Zimbabwe trade volumes soared during the 2010s and reached a peak in 2015 at US$1.3 billion (National Bureau of Statistics of China, 2017). The remarkable changes in the volume of trade during the 2000s and 2010s illustrate the growing importance of China in Zimbabwe. In fact, Mugabe's Look East policy saved the country (or his rule) until 2017 after the economic and political stagnation during the end of the 1990s and the early 2000s.

The trajectory of China-Zimbabwe trade relations was similar to that of the general China-Africa trade trajectories in terms of the range of products. China imported raw materials and unfinished products such as tobacco and minerals from Zimbabwe, and Zimbabwe imported mainly manufactured goods such as electrical machinery, machinery, and vehicles from China. Chinese interests were in nonprecious minerals during the early 2000s in Zimbabwe. Industrial minerals such as nickel and ferroalloys were the most imported products for China from Zimbabwe as they have fuelled China's economic development (Chun, 2014, p. 15). However, following the discovery of diamonds on a commercial scale in Marange during the late 2000s, Chinese companies invested in diamond companies along with the nonprecious metals (Alao, 2014, p. 9). In fact, this bilateral trade relationship had bigger importance for Zimbabwe than for China as the country had been facing economic sanctions from 2002 onwards.

In addition to China's imports of minerals from Zimbabwe, some Chinese firms were active in the Zimbabwean mining industry, particularly in diamonds, during the first two decades of the twenty-first century. Interviewee 5 (2017) summarised the link between the infrastructure investments and the extraction of resources in the continent:

> The Chinese have done [a lot] in East Africa, made big promises of infrastructure, built some of it—there is a brand-new [railway] line from Mombasa to Nairobi. It is unaffordable, just economically nonsense. So, they do all these things to set up the extractive systems, and in that case, they even have a passenger rail. But mostly it is to do standard neo-colonial extraction for which you need a port, they built up the ports, and you have a plantation, or you have mine and you need to get the minerals and the cash crops from here to there. You need to build or rebuild roads, bridges, ports . . . and that is the standard of neo-colonial or sub-imperial mining and extraction of resources that we can expect; the most extreme case in Zimbabwe is diamonds.

The Chinese state-owned and private mining companies were heavily involved in the distribution of the mining rights in the Marange diamond field during the late 2000s and early 2010s (Spiegel, 2014; Maguwu, 2013; Towriss, 2013; Bond & Sharife, 2012). For example, Chinese/Zimbabwean joint ventures, including Anjin Investments, Jinan Mining, and Kusena Diamonds, extracted diamonds from the Marange diamond field during the 2010s (Zimnisky, 2014; Bond & Sharife, 2012). The ZANU-PF government excluded Chinese activities from Zimbabwe's IEE, and China strengthened its position as a significant trade partner for Zimbabwe (Burgess & Beilstein,

2013, pp. 129, 135). Additionally, Shelton and Kabemba (2012, p. 99) argued that the Look East policy in 2003 supplied "the necessary framework" for the IEE and started a win-win relationship for Chinese and Zimbabwean elites.

Nevertheless, because of the IEE, some of the Chinese mining firms stopped their extraction activities in Zimbabwe because they did not want to indigenise their ownership structure at least to 51 per cent (for the 51 per cent black ownership rule, *see* Burgess & Beilstein, 2013, p. 135). Zimbabwe tried to compensate for the Western economic sanctions with the help of China but failed to do so after the IEE during the 2010s despite the better trade relations between the two countries (Mason, 2017). Interviewee 5 (2017) suggested that Chinese investment in Zimbabwe's mining industry has decreased in recent years:

> Zimbabwe's mining industries have always been under the thumb of South Africa; the platinum is controlled by Zimplats (owned by Impala Platinum) and there are some Russian platinum dealings. Russia is also interested in gold. The big question is what has happened with the Chinese?

For instance, in 2015, the ZANU-PF government cancelled the mining licence of Anjin Investments, which had been the largest producer of rough diamonds in 2011, as the company was operating illegally along with six other extraction companies (IOL News, 2016).

The increasing Chinese presence in the Zimbabwean mining industry during the twenty-first century has reconfigured the SBRs in Zimbabwe. Before the growing size of Chinese investments in Zimbabwe's mines, Western mining corporates were active. But along with the IEE, the structure of the Zimbabwean mining industry changed almost completely. Chinese mining firms and joint ventures participated in other non-Western semi-peripheral investments such as South Africa's mining corporates, Anglo Platinum, Impala Platinum, and Sibanye Stillwater, and boosted their effects in the SBRs. In addition to the foreign mining companies and investors, black-owned small mining firms, government-owned large mining firms, and artisanal miners were the other actors in Zimbabwe's mining industry. Therefore, the fracturing relations between the ZANU-PF government and foreign, mainly Western, mining companies during the late 1990s and the early 2000s were repaired by the Chinese and South African mining companies during the twenty-first century. However, the IEE did sometimes cause fractures in the relations between the government and Chinese mining firms.

China-Zimbabwe bilateral relations have been criticised on the grounds that the Chinese presence in Zimbabwe strengthened the autocratic Harare regime (Ojakorotu & Kamidza, 2018; Alao, 2014; Breslin & Taylor, 2008; Taylor, 2008). Human rights abuses by Chinese companies/employers against

Zimbabwean workers was a controversial issue in terms of China-Zimbabwe relations. Alao (2014, p. 9) thought that this was a result of China's "lack of environmental consideration" and the "contractual inequality" between the Beijing and Harare governments. In addition, Interviewee 5 (2017) criticised Beijing's support of authoritarian regimes such as the ZANU-PF government in Africa:

> The Chinese role in Zimbabwe shows they first nurtured Mugabe, who was their great friend. Mugabe looked east, so he had to run for election in 2002. They needed to overcome the opposition in March. In April, we found out that they were going to buy guns and ammunition imported into Zimbabwe through Durban. We had all protested. That was the kind of thing where the Chinese supported a dictator by three million bullets to kill his people (Mugabe). That is what I think is Chinese parastatalism on African dictators. Sure, the dictators are set up by the West, they have such a good record of it.

Before Mugabe was deposed by the Zimbabwean Army in November 2017, Interviewee 3 (2017) told me that China might maintain its economic presence in Zimbabwe with the help of elite-rent seeking:

> I know [there is] Chinese money in Zimbabwe. They probably paid Mugabe off. He said 'You do whatever you want to do.' He does not care because he gets his money in the bank. That is just the way Africa works. When you drive around Zimbabwe you see the roads being repaired; it is Chinese workers. Chinese people repairing the roads in Zimbabwe. Huge unemployment there but they are still Chinese people repairing the roads.

After Mugabe's resignation in November 2017, Beijing declared its support for Mnangagwa with an emphasis on the two countries' bilateral historical ties (Gao, 2017). The Chinese mining and retail corporation Sinosteel subsequently agreed with the Mnangagwa government that the company would invest US$1 billion in Zimbabwe (Kadzere, 2018). According to the agreement, Sinosteel, which has been active in South Africa and Zimbabwe from 1996, would invest in the energy and mining sectors in Zimbabwe. Washington was still concerned about human rights violations and the autocratic regime in Zimbabwe, according to the US Ambassador to Zimbabwe Brian Nichols (Mavhunga, 2018):

> President Mnangagwa's commitment to a transparent investigation of those events is very, very important for my government. The violence of August 1st, the death of six people in the streets here, intimidation of the opposition polling agents, violence in the areas around Harare, have all been issues of concern.

The new government in Harare relaxed the 51 per cent black ownership rule in the mining industry step by step. Initially, the ZANU-PF government cancelled the rule for all mining activity except for diamond and platinum extraction in order to attract new investors to Zimbabwe in March 2018 by the Finance Act, 2018 (No. 1 of 2018). Interviewee 6 (2018) told me that China had a remarkable impact on the Zimbabwean mining industry but that before the coup, Zimbabwe had not been in a good situation in terms of foreign investors:

> I believe that this worsened situation could change after the 30 July 2018 general and presidential elections in Zimbabwe. They could attract more foreign investors after the elections. This period could make them a more competitive investment area for foreigners. It would be a vigorous challenge for the ZANU-PF.

Furthermore, there were reports that the ZANU-PF government might relax the 51 per cent black ownership rule in diamond and platinum extraction as well during late 2018 (Karombo, 2018); this would create an opportunity to bring more investments to Zimbabwe and might therefore lead to the consolidation of SBRs. In this section, I have analysed the role of Chinese investments in Zimbabwe's mining industry during the last twenty years.

COMPARING CHINA'S PRESENCE IN SOUTH AFRICA AND ZIMBABWE

The significant presence of China in semiperipheral South Africa and peripheral Zimbabwe might change the trajectories and produce different outcomes in terms of fracturing and consolidation of the respective SBRs regarding the two mining industries. As I have already argued in this study, the significant Chinese presence in South Africa and Zimbabwe had different outcomes. Chinese mining investments in Zimbabwe compensated for the lost Western investments following the breakdown between Harare and the West during the early 2000s. Also, following the implementation of the IEE, Chinese state-owned extractive firms worked closely with Zimbabwean state-owned enterprises during the early 2010s. On the other hand, increasing Chinese investments in the mining industry of South Africa worsened the already deteriorating relationship between the domestic mining industry and the Zuma government from the early 2010s. I therefore suggest that Chinese investments had different outcomes for peripheral and for semiperipheral countries of the MWS in terms of their SBRs.

In contrast to the Western core countries, China does not intend to intervene in domestic indigenisation laws regarding mining because of the traditional Chinese foreign policy of the Five Principles of Peaceful Coexistence, which seek equality, noninterference, and mutual benefit (Ministry of Foreign Affairs of the PRC, 2016; Taylor, 2009; Ampiah & Naidu, 2008). Some commentators have argued that the indigenisation of the mining industries in South Africa and Zimbabwe was profitable for Chinese companies after the mid-2000s (for South Africa, *see* Grimm *et al.*, 2014, p. 19–21; for Zimbabwe, *see* Shelton & Kabemba, 2012, p. 99; Saunders, 2009, p. 74). Despite this noninterference policy, Chinese private and state-owned companies were not entirely cognisant of the local laws and indigenisation policies in South Africa or Zimbabwe, so the Chinese mining-extraction firms sometimes faced difficulties because of the BEE policy in South Africa and the IEE in Zimbabwe, despite the strong bilateral ties between Beijing and the respective governments in Pretoria and Harare (Burgess & Beilstein, 2013, p. 131).

Both Harare and Pretoria maintained their bilateral relations with Beijing after pursuing indigenisation and economic empowerment policies in their mining industries. Interviewee 2 (2017) stated that active Chinese mining companies in the South African mining industry are generally quite small companies and they are looking for more opportunities. In fact, he told me that Chinese mining companies are required to follow the same rules in South Africa as everybody else, so the balanced approach of the successive South African governments towards the Chinese mining firms had some differences from Zimbabwe's approach during the early 2010s. Because of the Look East policy and the lack of capital and technology in the Zimbabwean mining industry, the Harare government did not apply the full indigenisation rule to Chinese investors during the early 2010s (Shumba, 2018). In fact, a peripheral country such as Zimbabwe felt more pressure than South Africa to make exceptions for a new actor which was stronger, semiperipheral, and needed as a new external investor, in order to cover the absence of previous core actors (Western investors). As a result, Zimbabwe became more dependent on Chinese investment and technology than South Africa when applying the indigenisation policies regarding their mining industries.

I suggest that Chinese capital and technology might substitute for Western capital and technology in the mining industries of peripheral countries of Africa. In a semiperipheral country such as South Africa, however, Chinese technology might not replace the relatively sophisticated technology in the mining industry. Interviewee 4 (2017) believed that Chinese capital and extractive technologies could be a substitute for the Western ones in Zimbabwe. She also argued that Chinese manufactured goods had dominated both the South African and the Zimbabwean markets and that this domination provided them with an important basis for substituting the Western investments. Nevertheless, Interviewee 5 (2017) claimed that the Chinese sometimes bring the latest technology and sometimes not to the peripheral areas of Africa:

> The Chinese capitalists take the US, British and French model of looting Africa to a new level. [They have] the same tradition, even the extractivist mentality, but they have the capacity to do even worse. Sometimes their technology is better, sometimes worse (the Chinese goods break quickly). The critique is that their technology does not work very well here. The best example is just across the border in Botswana with coal. There is another example on the Zimbabwean side, which is sometimes alleged, that [damage] to the Kariba Dam followed very rapidly because the Chinese put in turbines on the Zambian side of the Kariba Dam which drained too quickly and lowered the volume of Lake Kariba too quickly a couple of years ago. I heard that, by the way, from the President of Zambia who had just lost the election. He was telling me that he was on the border crossing where the Kariba Dam is and he thought he could even tell us the train engineer was an economist, and that they made a huge mistake and then the water level decreased because that was really a drought period.

In addition, Interviewee 3 (2017) claimed that Chinese capital had already replaced Western capital in a few mining shafts of the South African mining industry:

> You look at Sibanye . . . They are like five years old, six years old. Basically, they came into existence and they bought three of the Gold Fields operations, about twenty old shafts. They just bought Anglo Platinum's Rustenburg operations with five or ten shafts. That is just Chinese money. There is a Chinese-owned company. They are managed by local South African people but they report to China. It is Chinese money and Chinese owned. For a lot of these companies which they listed, [there is] nothing stop to Chinese money coming and buying.

Moreover, Interviewee 6 (2018) told me that Chinese investments have already replaced Western capital and technology in Zimbabwe to some extent but "that will not happen in South Africa as happened in some part of the rest of the continent. For example, they are more involved in the Zimbabwean mining industries than the South African mining industries." Also, Shelton and Kabemba (2012, p. 136) have given an example on Chinese activities in the mining industry of South Africa in terms of technology transfer:

> Joint ventures between local and Chinese companies do not generate any significant compensating job creation or business opportunities. Executives of the partly Chinese-owned Aquarius, which mines platinum group metals, have confirmed that Zijin, the Chinese investor, did not bring any new technology to South Africa as part of the deal, nor were any new jobs created.

As an upwardly mobile semiperipheral country, China's money has been dominating the mining sector in African countries, but in South Africa, China has more sophisticated relations with domestic political and business actors.

Some have argued that South Africa's subimperial role and China's increasing influence have deindustrialised the economies and created a new dependency after the involvement of Western core countries and financial institutions in southern Africa (Interviewee 5, 2017; Carmody, 2017, p. 10; Garcia & Bond, 2015; Taylor, 2014, p. 142). China's and South Africa's cooperation within the continent, or more narrowly in the southern African market, have increased deindustrialisation and dependence on BRICS by South African retail companies such as Shoprite (Jenkins & Edwards 2015 cited in Carmody, 2017). By this means, Chinese companies have sold their manufactured goods, such as mining equipment, through Shoprite to southern African markets and little-known Chinese goods are therefore promoted by a more reliable South African firm (Carmody, 2017). Despite these negative interpretations of the Chinese presence in Africa, some businesspeople have claimed otherwise. For instance, Interviewee 4 (2017) argued that China or other new investors in southern Africa cannot act like colonisers as their policies do not allow it:

> It is a good thing they are coming to Africa and southern Africa at a time when all the countries are liberated. These kinds of policies are in place [so that] we make sure that they are not coming as the previous colonizers did. So, they are coming and knowing what is expected of them and what they can do. So, in the beginning, people who are concerned that they are the new colonisers [should know that] they did not get that opportunity because our policies would not have allowed it.

Moreover, Interviewee 6 (2018) suggested that Chinese mining firms are becoming more sensitive to environmental issues and pollution than they were in the past:

> Chinese companies intend to bring their own Chinese labourers to work in the mines. I think they are more sensitive to some issues if we compare it with ten years ago. For example, they ignored environmental issues and pollution, but now they care about these issues. They are well-managed nowadays and follow certain international principles.

In this section, I have analysed the overall impact of China's economic involvement on the mining industries of South Africa and Zimbabwe, which had different outcomes for both countries' SBRs. In Zimbabwe, Chinese state-owned and private mining companies worked with the ZANU-PF government through joint ventures despite the extreme demands of the IEE.

As a result of this close relationship, the ZANU-PF government found a chance to consolidate not only its power in Harare but also its SBRs during the first decade of the twenty-first century. However, after Mugabe declared that Chinese mining companies operating in Zimbabwe had to obey the 51 per cent ownership rule, the relationship completely fractured during the mid-2010s.

On the other hand, the sophisticated mining industry of South Africa has not left too much space for Chinese mining companies although Chinese investors have supported HDSAs not only for buying stakes in the existing mining companies but also to establish new mining firms. Consequently, the Chinese presence in South Africa's mining industry has sometimes distanced the relations between the ANC government and the white-owned, English-speaking mining houses. However, SBRs in South Africa have not fractured completely and they are coexisting with each other, except for the proposal of the nonnegotiated and the suspended third Mining Charter under the Zuma regime. During that period, SBRs were completely fractured because of the lack of communication and cooperation between the Zuma government and the domestic mining industry, as well as the increasing Chinese economic and political presence. Indeed, Chinese investments in the mining industry of South Africa have increased from the early 2010s along with the fractured SBRs.

CONCLUSION

In this chapter, I analysed China's role in this research in the respective SBRs regarding the mining industries of the two countries. I examined the influence of the Chinese presence on the fracturing and consolidation of SBRs regarding the mining industries of South Africa and Zimbabwe. I suggested that the Chinese economic presence or absence has had some effects on the SBRs of the peripheral and semiperipheral countries in the MWS which pursue indigenisation and economic empowerment policies in their mining industries. I also discussed how Chinese state-owned companies have reconfigured the SBRs in mining industries in the continent. Chinese investments in the mining industry in South Africa and Zimbabwe either caused breakdowns between the existing business and the government or repaired fractured relations respectively. I argued that Chinese capital and technology have been beneficial in repairing the fractured relations between the mining industry and government more in the periphery than in the semiperiphery. In fact, China can influence unsophisticated and nondiversified economies such as Zimbabwe within the MWS in terms of SBRs.

NOTE

1. For instance, the Governor of the Central Bank of Nigeria criticised China's presence in Africa in March 2013 (Taylor, 2014, pp. 13–14). Another example is a Zimbabwean analyst's criticism of China's noninterference policy in Africa (Taylor, 2014, p. 115).

Chapter 4

The Consolidation and Fracturing of State-Business Relations in South Africa and Zimbabwe

INTRODUCTION

Following the empirical examination of the relevant forces, shaping SBRs in South Africa and Zimbabwe, I shall now analyse how SBRs actually developed in the two countries and across the relevant time periods of liberalisation and indigenisation. The SBRs of South Africa and Zimbabwe have been analysed during the countries' respective periods of economic transformation (Bowman, 2019; Southall, 2012; Van Wyk, 2009; Andreasson, 2007; Taylor, 2007). The racially differentiated structure of the business sector and the general structure of the South African economy from the SBR perspective have been also examined in recent years (Seekings & Nattrass, 2011; Nattrass & Seekings, 2010; Handley, 2008). However, the significant Chinese presence and the effect of a country's position in the MWS on domestic SBRs are topics which remain undebated. I shall compare the SBRs, which is the key focus of the current study, of South Africa and Zimbabwe in regard to the outcomes of the previous chapters of this study. In order to redress the legacies of white minority rules in both countries, attracting more investments with the help of the consolidation of SBRs is crucial. This introductory section will therefore remind us how the position of a country in the MWS and the policy choices which it makes in regard to its mining industry, and the Chinese presence in the country, affect the possible outcomes of either the consolidation or the fracturing of SBRs.

The consolidation of SBRs in a country illustrates effective relations between the government and the business community. This effective relationship between these two actors is based primarily on not only accurate political choices which create a collaboration between the state and business, but also the frequency and volume of existing foreign capital activities in a country (*see* Cali & Sen, 2011; Maxfield & Schneider, 1997; Evans, 1995; Amsden, 1992). Qureshi and Te Velde (2013, pp. 912–13) defined the importance of stable and unstable SBRs for economic successes or failures: "Effective state-business relations—specifically, well-organised, responsive and public interactions between the state and business sectors—are considered to be important because both markets and states are subject to failures." Collaboration between the state and business might end up producing effective SBRs in developing countries in terms of providing public benefits and prodevelopmental outcomes (Taylor, 2012; Maxfield & Schneider, 1997). On the other hand, the fracturing of SBRs in a country might be a consequence of confrontation between the government and either foreign capital or private domestic investors. Moreover, foreign capital flight or diminishing private domestic investments might cause fracturing of SBRs in a country. In this chapter, I illustrate why a specific outcome occurred in the cases of South Africa and Zimbabwe under different circumstances.

The mining sector has been the key industry for SBRs in South Africa and Zimbabwe following the end of minority rules. On the one hand, in South Africa, the negotiations between the mining sector, officially the Minerals Council, and prominent government officers have been decisive for determining BEE rules, particularly the MPRDA and the Mining Charter during the last two decades (Bowman, 2019; DTI, 2003). Mining has been the most attractive industry following the implementation of BEE policies from the early 2000s (Bowman, 2019, p. 2). According to an Intellidex (2015, p. 15) report on the value of BEE deals, the mining sector has had "the largest generator of value," which was R101 billion, equivalent to 11.8 per cent of total BEE deals between 2000 and 2015 through equity sales of mining firms to HDSA. On the other hand, the mining sector has been the main target of racial economic transformation in Zimbabwe along with land redistribution policies. For example, when Mugabe implemented the 51 per cent indigenous ownership rule of IEE Act of 2007 towards the mining industry during the early 2010s, foreign investors—specifically Chinese state-owned mining firms—had to stop their extraction activities (Saunders & Caramento, 2017, p. 11). This policy shift has caused the breakdown of existing consensus between the foreign investors and the Harare government; in other words, SBRs in Zimbabwe (Saunders & Caramento, 2017, p. 14). Moreover, following the end of thirty-seven-year Mugabe era in Harare, Mnangagwa relaxed 51 per cent indigenous ownership rule, except diamond and platinum industries (Dzirutwe, 2018a). These kinds of policy shifts and their effects on the business environment demonstrate the importance of the mining industry to SBRs in both countries.

Policy choices regarding the mining industry might have different outcomes in semiperipheral and peripheral countries. However, the presence of China might cause these outcomes to differ. Apart from other effects, liberalisation policies provide consolidation of SBRs in semiperipheral and peripheral countries of the MWS for a limited time. I therefore suggest that if a country such as South Africa or Zimbabwe chooses to use indigenisation in order to complete economic transformation as a policy tool regarding its mining industry not only to bring about socioeconomic and black transformation policies but also to tackle the legacies of white-minority rule, SBRs might consolidate or fracture over time. When I consider the significant Chinese presence in semiperipheral and peripheral countries of the MWS, I assume two different outcomes for them respectively.

I claim that if a peripheral country applies an indigenisation and economic empowerment policy regarding its mining industry and moves away from core countries, it is expected that its SBRs will fracture. For instance, the implementation of the IEE Act of 2007, which had extreme demands, such as 51 per cent of indigenised ownership rule for nondomestic investments, in Zimbabwe has not yet achieved an economic transformation in the mining industry, which is highly dependent on foreign investors. So if a peripheral country applies an indigenisation policy to its mining industry and moves away from core powers but then approaches a semiperipheral country or countries such as China, India, and South Africa, its SBRs might consolidate over time because of the required capital and technology from the external actor(s). For instance, following the fracture in relations between Zimbabwe and Western core countries' financial institutions at the start of the new millennium, the ZANU-PF government introduced the Look East policy and developed more intense relations with noncore countries of the MWS. Therefore, mining investments from South Africa and China were helpful for repairing the fractured SBRs for some short periods during the last two decades.

On the other hand, if a semiperipheral country applies indigenisation and economic empowerment policies to its mining industry and moves away from core powers, it is expected that its SBRs might be consolidated as they might have more options than peripheral countries and the manoeuvrability to maintain the existing condition. For example, although the implementation of the Mining Charter and the MPRDA in South Africa caused some tensions between the different ANC governments and the mining industry during the 2000s, the SBRs did not fracture until the country's inclusion in the BRIC group in 2011. As I have already argued, if a semiperipheral country moves away from Western core countries to semiperipherals such as Brazil, China, and India, its SBRs might be fractured over time because of the increasing competition between the new foreign and the old domestic actors in the country. Bilateral relations between China and South Africa have increased the Chinese presence in South Africa's domestic sectors, but only to some extent in the mining industry. In order to develop these assumptions, I shall examine the fluctuation of SBRs under majority rule in South Africa and then in Zimbabwe.

MEASURING THE NATURE OF SBRS: CONSOLIDATION AND FRACTURING

In this section, I explain how I measured SBRs in South Africa and Zimbabwe, which constitutes the final outcome of this comparative study. I define the nature of SBRs as being characterised as either consolidating or fracturing, by means of referencing the qualitative literature on SBRs generally and by providing a summary of SBRs in these two countries. The following the pursuit of privatisation policies in the Third World during the 1970s, 1980s, and 1990s, SBRs have become a vital issue not only for international political economy scholars but also for development studies. The successful economic transformation in East Asia, notably in South Korea, gave inspiration to other developing countries in Latin America and Asia. Market-driven or developmental policies were discussed in political science and economics literature. For instance, Evans (1997; 1992) and Haggard and Kaufman (1997; 1992) analysed the state's economic role, reflecting on economic crises and performance during democratic transitions. Sen (2013, p. 7) also discussed the opportunities in Africa from an economics perspective for the SBRs analysis "whether the emergence of effective SBRs has had growth-enhancing effects." In fact, the respective political transitions in South Africa, which was democratic, and Zimbabwe, which was less democratic, have left the ANC and ZANU-PF governments with unresolved deep divisions in each country relating to economic transformation.

The literature on SBRs in developing countries has focused on collaboration between the government and business for enhancing economic growth (Cali & Sen, 2011; Maxfield & Schneider, 1997; Evans, 1995; Amsden, 1992), a collaboration between the government and the business sector which ends up producing good SBRs, in terms of providing public benefits and prodevelopmental outcomes, in developing countries (Taylor, 2012; Maxfield & Schneider, 1997). Collaboration between the government and business, therefore, represents the involvement of the state in the market alongside the business sector rather than the nonintervention of the state through respecting private property rights (Cali & Sen, 2011, p. 1542). For instance, as happened in East Asia, strong collaborative relations between the state and business actors might produce economic growth (Cali & Sen, 2011, p. 1542). In South Africa and Zimbabwe, collaboration is a good way of enhancing economic growth as the indigenisation policies need the engagement of both state and business actors.

Te Velde (2006, p. 7) identified four main elements responsible for good SBRs in developing countries:

i. The way in which the private sector is organised vis-à-vis the public sector,
ii. The way in which the public sector is organised vis-à-vis the private sector,
iii. The practice and institutionalisation of state-business relations,
iv. The avoidance of harmful collusive behaviour.

He, therefore, considered that the participation of the private sector was vital for sustaining good SBRs. He also suggested that business associations, such as the Chamber of Mines of Zimbabwe and the Minerals Council in South Africa, had more impact on government "because they can provide a more coherent and consistent case" (Te Velde, 2006, p. 7). Moreover, the business associations might have an important role in "facilitating the formulation, implementation, and monitoring of economic policies and provision of feedback to the government" (Hisahiro, 2005 cited in Te Velde, 2006, p. 7). On the other hand, the government's approach to the interaction with the business might be provided with the help of an investment promotion agency and government institutions for interacting with the business sector, which can be formal or informal (Te Velde, 2006, p. 8). He, therefore, suggested that if formal interaction between the state and the business sector is present, then cooperation can be achievable. Also, if the competition is regulated and business practices are protected by laws, the parties can avoid "harmful collusive behaviour" (Te Velde, 2006, p. 8).

Te Velde (2013) explained the methods of measuring SBRs in Africa and argues that there was a lack of discussion on the measurement of SBRs in Africa. In the same study, he answered how is the private sector organized or how are the SBRs organized in sub-Saharan Africa. He uncovered that Botswana, Mauritius, and South Africa are above average in terms of private sector organisations among twenty sub-Saharan African countries (te Velde, 2013, p. 23). Evans (1997, p. 73) considered that the state and business reshape each other during transformation periods, which South Africa and Zimbabwe have already experienced during the postapartheid and postcolonial periods, respectively. He also claimed that the government needs to be linked to business to create a coherent state structure (Evans, 1997). In the same manner, it is my contention here that the nexus between the government and the mining industry should be carefully consolidated by each party to reduce problems about the business environment and disagreements between each other in posttransition communities such as South Africa and Zimbabwe.

Jilberto and Hogenboom (2007) approached SBRs from the perspective of relationships between conglomerates and governments in developing countries and transition economies, which included South Africa and Zimbabwe. They analysed the causes of privatisation, economic, and financial liberalisation and neoliberal globalisation and the economic, social, and political effects of the rise of 'big business' in Africa, Asia, Eastern Europe, and Latin America. Sen and te Velde (2013) investigated the correlation between the SBRs and economic growth in sub-Saharan Africa. They found that Kenya, Senegal, Tanzania, and Uganda were the star performers and Mali, Nigeria, and Zambia were the worst performers in terms of eliminating poverty and inequality through effective SBRs (Sen & Te Velde, 2013, p. 64–65). They suggested that effective SBRs contribute significantly to economic growth in sub-Saharan Africa according to the results of their study.

In addition to the literature on the measurement of SBRs in developing countries, this research considers the frequency and volume of existing foreign capital activities (for example, FDIs) and domestic private investments to measure the SBRs of South Africa and Zimbabwe. Cali and Sen (2011, p. 1544) hypothesised that "effective SBRs can have a positive impact on economic growth by increasing both the rate of investment and the productivity of investment," and I, therefore, argue that increased FDIs and an improving investment climate are important indicators of effective SBRs in developing countries. Also, effective SBRs can be useful for reducing the uncertainties of future policies and raising investment (Ibarra, 1995; Rodrik, 1991 cited in Cali & Sen, 2011, p. 1544).

In this study, consolidation of SBRs means domestic and foreign capital are not only in cooperation with domestic government but also coexist together within a country. In addition to this, fracturing of SBRs means conflict between domestic and foreign capital and government policies exists in a country. So on the one hand, if a country provides a healthy environment for both domestic and foreign companies, it might consolidate SBRs. Additionally, consolidation of SBRs entails the durable existence of domestic and foreign capital. Cooperation (and harmonious relations more generally) between foreign/domestic businesses and states constitutes the primary evidence of the consolidation of SBRs.

On the other hand, a conflict between foreign/domestic business and government policies results in a fracturing of SBRs whereas maintaining collaboration or cooperation results in the consolidation of SBRs. The fracturing of SBRs involves not only international capital flight but also deteriorating relations with domestic business. Moreover, confrontation with, or outright rejection of, IFIs and foreign firms by governments also constitutes a type of fracturing of SBRs in developing countries.

This study targets to analyse the relations between the domestic state and domestic and foreign capital, narrowly in the respective mining industries of South Africa and Zimbabwe. Thus, the complex relationship among these three actors differs from a country's position in the MWS. For instance, the domestic mining industry has been more important in semiperipheral South Africa than in peripheral Zimbabwe, which has depended on foreign investors. Hopkins (1982, pp. 86–87) stated that the modern capitalist world-economy is not built upon "nationally organized political economies." Indeed, "the firms have become the typical production units" of the modern capitalist world-economy "by overcoming the historically limited markets" (Hopkins, 1982, p. 87). The MWS has two respective economic and political organisations as I have discussed above: the international division of labour and the inter-state system. The international division of labour includes local or international markets, which have been the major components of the capitalist world-economy. Therefore the relations between domestic and foreign companies and domestic governments are central to not only for South African and Zimbabwean domestic markets but also for the entire world market. In fact, the fracturing or consolidation of SBRs in these countries has not been independent of the rest of the capitalist world-economy.

In this study, I analysed SBRs in South Africa and Zimbabwe from a comparative perspective. These former settler-colonies both experienced alternating periods of conflict and cooperation in terms of their SBRs before and after the onset of majority rule. Thus foreign and local (white) companies dominated the domestic markets in these countries during the periods of minority rule. Following the end of minority rule, the governments of South Africa and Zimbabwe both attempted to empower local black capitalist classes with the aid of indigenisation policies (Bowman, 2019; Shumba, 2018; Zvoushe *et al.*, 2017; Leon, 2012; Magure, 2012; Cargill, 2010; Saunders, 2009; Tangri & Southall, 2008; Andreasson, 2007; 2006; Bond, 2000). These economic transformation attempts (BEE and indigenisation law) caused foreign capital flight (primarily Western capital as it was dominant in the region) from South Africa and Zimbabwe. That said, in the last two decades, state-led, non-Western foreign capital had substituted Western capital mainly in Zimbabwe and, to some extent, in South Africa largely because of (race-based) economic transformation processes.

SBRS IN POSTAPARTHEID SOUTH AFRICA

Before developing a discussion on SBRs under majority rule I shall briefly illustrate the mixed SBRs during the isolation period under minority rule to show the importance of the economic transformation for the business sector. English-speaking white business was against the segregationist policies of the NP during the height of apartheid because they caused isolation from the world economy (Handley, 2008; Lipton, 1986). During the height of apartheid, the relationship between the NP government and the mining business was strained. One of the main reasons behind the 1980s turmoil was the worries of the corporate sector. According to Louw (2004, p. 134), the English-speaking corporate sector circulated propaganda against the apartheid regime through its international news agencies:

> South Africa's corporate sector [which] saw apartheid as 'bad for business' (corporate hostility became internationally significant because they owned South Africa's Anglo press, which distributed antiapartheid stories to the international media via Reuters news agency).

However, there was also progovernment business under the apartheid regime, mainly from the Afrikaner community which supported the regime through the progovernment press (Berger, 1999). SBRs in South Africa throughout the twentieth century were framed by the consolidation of a strong state and powerful corporate capital (especially Afrikaner) (Seekings & Nattrass, 2011, pp. 343–44). The first convergence between the NP, the ANC, and the white English-speaking business community happened in 1985 after the then-president P.W. Botha declared that the NP government "was ready to release imprisoned ANC leader Nelson Mandela" (Van Wyk, 2009, p. 7).

Despite these restricted business activities under the apartheid regime, white business was cautious about black majority rule not only because of the nationalisation policies in the *Freedom Charter* (1955) of the ANC and the SACP, but also because of the polarised world system during the Cold War, which caused a fear of a socialist state in South Africa. In fact, the white businesses, particularly the mining industry, feared that under black majority rule the new government might seize their assets and operations under the South African soil (Van Wyk, 2009, p. 7). Thus, despite some concerns, the white-owned businesses in South Africa largely supported the democratic transition from the late 1980s (Seekings & Nattrass, 2011, p. 345). For example, in 1991 before he was elected leader of the ANC, Mandela signalled a policy shift on the nationalisation policies. The ANC reflected this shift with a working paper and declared that "we need to look more carefully at the economic reality and begin to find a more overall economic policy that will begin to solve our problems" (Wren, 1991). This was a sign of a more reasonable economic policy than the full nationalisation of the mines, banks, and other powerful sectors under the economic policy of the *Freedom Charter*. The transnational mining companies in South Africa as the corporate fraction and the prospective ruling party as the state fraction of the TCC in South Africa found a way to develop a consensus between each other during the political transition period (*see* Sklair, 2002, 2001, 2000, 1997).

Mandela had close relations with the pioneers of the mining industry before and after the end of apartheid. The Deputy Chairman of AngloVaal, Clive Menell, and the Chairman of Anglo American, Harry Oppenheimer, had close relations with Mandela. Menell and Oppenheimer were founders of the Urban Foundation in 1977 to support black South Africans after the Soweto Uprising in 1976 (Hansell, 1996). Menell stated that the reason behind the establishment of the Urban Foundation was a concern both for the country and for their corporate assets (Hansell, 1996). Also, Mandela attended regular meetings with fifteen leading businessmen whom Oppenheimer called the 'Brenthurst Group' (Seeking & Nattrass, 2011, pp. 347–48). The leader of the NP was F.W. de Klerk, Botha's successor, and he announced that the government would lift the ban on trade unions, the ANC, and other liberation movements; release political prisoners; and give permission for the return of exiled politicians and members of liberation movements as the final steps towards black majority rule in 1990 (Van Wyk, 2009, p. 8). During this period of political transition in South Africa, SBRs were multifaceted and more sophisticated than those in other sub-Saharan African countries. This demonstrates that the developed structure of the business sector was an outcome of the country's semiperipheral position.

Although the black majority government applied the sociodemocratic RDP in 1994, it moved swiftly away from this policy and pursued liberalisation policies through the implementation of a homegrown neoliberal policy of GEAR in 1996. The newly elected ANC government therefore discarded its nationalisation policies and took up liberalisation policies, which provided a basis for the consolidation of SBRs during the transition period. In addition to GEAR, the first elected majority government in South Africa abolished the dual exchange rate and launched the liberalisation of the foreign exchange market in 1995. GEAR was written by progressive corporate (pro-ANC) economists (Seekings & Nattrass, 2011, p. 347) and the ANC therefore discarded its nationalist and proredistribution of wealth policies to undo the socioeconomic legacies of apartheid.

There were two major targets in undoing the legacies of apartheid (more broadly white minority rule) in the new South Africa under black majority rule: political transition and economic transformation. So although several thousand South African citizens died in the political turmoil during the early

1990s, the political transition from white minority rule to black majority rule in South Africa was completed during the mid-1990s less violently than Zimbabwe, where a civil war was experienced during the 1970s before the end of white minority rule. However, the economic transformation from white business to black business had not yet been achieved during the early postapartheid period. For example, as a member of the mining industry, Interviewee 2 (2017) believed that the racial economic transformation was inevitable during the early 1990s in the industry:

> I think in terms of equality of opportunity if you are talking about equality of opportunity between people of different races, and for that matter different genders because historically women were excluded from the industry as well. The approach has done a great deal to improve equality of opportunity for people. Of course, to change what was in the industry until the early 1990s, it was in the industry, as I said, whites had all of the best jobs. There weren't many black people with the ability to own shares in the economy because the entire apartheid system was designed to prevent those people from acquiring wealth. It has made a significant difference.

The ANC pursued probusiness/market policy choices not only to transform the economy but also to stabilise it and attract more FDIs (Van Wyk, 2009, p. 8). Seekings and Nattrass (2011, p. 340) also argued that the new majority government applied liberal trade and economic policies, but without 'active cooperation' with South African white business. This means that the ANC government implemented promarket policies for transforming the South African economic structure in accordance with foreign business.

Even though the ANC pursued neoliberal policies without active cooperation with domestic business, white business and capital in South Africa benefitted from the neoliberal policies of the ANC government and lost their fears about black majority rule in South Africa. For example, the postapartheid regime permitted international stock market relistings by some of the largest JSE corporations, including Anglo American Corporation (mining), De Beers (mining), Old Mutual insurance (finance), South African Breweries (brewery), Didata (IT), Investec Bank (finance), and Mondi Paper (manufacturing) in 1999 (Bond, 2018). Domestic white-owned mining houses also moved their headquarters from Johannesburg to other countries from the late 1990s as a result of the neoliberal policies of the Mandela government. Julian Ogilvie Thompson, who was the executive chairman of Anglo American, for instance, welcomed "the end of the financial structures that were imposed on us by apartheid" in 1999 (Gapper, 2016). The stable relations during South Africa's turn to neoliberalism under the Mandela presidency had actually started with his close relations with the pioneers of the business sector during the early 1990s. Also, during the 1990s the second phase of economic transformation, namely the BEE, was immature as the government did not have a particular strategy on it. As a result, SBRs were consolidated by pursuing a liberalisation policy in South Africa during Mandela's presidency (Nattrass & Seekings, 2010, p. 6).

In addition to the liberalisation policies, the ANC government implemented the BEE policies during the early postapartheid era in order to complete the economic transformation. The ANC government pursued state-led policies such as affirmative action and employment equity for redressing the legacies of the apartheid regime, but these policies were not like the sophisticated B-BBEE policies since the 2000s. As a result, the first ANC government under Mandela established the BEE Commission in 1998 for classifying empowerment progress and it was chaired by Ramaphosa, who was the founder of NUM and Secretary of the ANC between 1991 and 1997 (Andreasson, 2007, p. 284). This initial BEE policy did not affect the stable relations between the ANC government and the mining corporations of South Africa.

Some of the large corporations of South Africa "had initiated and embarked on a series of voluntary 'unbundling' exercises" before black majority rule for preventing the "more state-driven transformation initiatives" (Van Wyk, 2009, p. 35; Handley, 2008, p. 70). In addition, the white-owned conglomerates sold off their noncore assets to the initial BEE companies along with foreign transnationals (Van Wyk, 2009, p. 35; Carmody, 2002, p. 264). According to Carmody (2002, pp. 264–265), these unbundling efforts had two main reasons:

> They were keen to unbundle because of falling rates of profit and the desire to pre-empt domestic competition actions; gaining political capital in the process. From 1995 to 1998, the proportion of shares on the JSE owned by black economic empowerment companies, and purchased using debt, rose, by some estimates, from 0.5 per cent to almost 20 per cent.

To do this, some of the ANC-linked prominent black South Africans such as Ramaphosa and Tokyo Sexwale, who was premier of Gauteng province between 1994 and 1999, emerged as black entrepreneurs as a consequence of the unbundling efforts of the white-owned conglomerates. Moreover, Ramaphosa became a shareholder of the first BEE company listed on the JSE, New Africa Investment Limited (NAIL), and Sexwale took a share in the Johannesburg Consolidated Investment (JCI) Group which had been an active mining company for more than a century in South Africa from the late nineteenth century to the early twenty-first century; even so, it was suspended due to bad management and fraudulent activities in the mid-2000s and delisted from the JSE in 2013 (JCI Limited, 2019; Mandla, 2005, p. 43; Koelble, 1998, p. 161 cited in Van Wyk, 2009, pp. 35–36).

The first phase of BEE attempts gave way to more sophisticated and broad-based empowerment policies during the 2000s under the presidency of Thabo Mbeki. The second president of the black majority rule of South Africa became 'business-friendly' Mbeki in 1999. Indeed, Andreasson stated that "President Mbeki has a long-standing practice of hosting indabas (gatherings) with the business 'working groups,' representing key domestic and foreign corporate interests as part of a larger lobbying network" (Andreasson, 2007, p. 279). These working groups were functional tools for Mbeki to maintain contact with the business sector (Seekings & Nattrass, 2011, p. 348). Moreover, Van Wyk (2009, pp. 40–41) stated that "Mbeki was associated with several informal economic/business coalitions" and to do this he had developed close relations with some businesspeople and political elites including trade union leaders, presidents, and chairmen of government-sponsored enterprises (such as the Development Bank of South Africa and the National Olympic Council of South Africa), corporation managers, and BEE beneficiaries during his presidency from 1999 to 2008. Nevertheless, after Mbeki came into power, the relationship with white business soured (Handley, 2008).

Despite Mbeki having close relations with the white business community before his presidency, he implemented indigenisation policies to redress the legacies of the apartheid and complete the economic transformation of the country. Mbeki introduced an initial document on empowerment in the mining industry in 1999, namely the Mineral and Petroleum Resources Development Bill, which was an immature version of the MPRDA of 2002. To reduce the negative reactions of the industry, Mbeki stated that "there is no vision to nationalise the industry, this is not part of the mining charter" (*IOL News*, 1999). Mbeki also pointed out the importance of the mining industry for the economic transformation: "the mining industry has played a critical role in our economy in the past and has the potential to be a cutting-edge and important player in the promotion of transformation" (*IOL News*, 1999). As a result, during the early years of the twenty-first century, liberalisation policies gave way to indigenisation and economic empowerment policies as the ANC government announced the MPRDA in 2002 and the Mining Charter in 2004. The world's largest mining companies welcomed the first Mining Charter draft, which demanded deracialisation by 15 per cent in a five-year period and 26 per cent in a ten-year period of the ownership structures of the mining companies. AngloGold, BHP Billiton, and Harmony Gold declared their approval of the Mining Charter draft and found that its target would be achievable because it was far less than the rumoured 51 per cent (*BBC News*, 2002a).

The B-BBEE legislation had some positive results for the ANC government, such as the creation of new elites, elite circulation, and the establishment of growth coalitions on behalf of the black entrepreneurs of South Africa. However, these were not the broad-based achievements which the ANC government had suggested in the name of the legislation (Van Wyk, 2009, p. 38). The ANC government had supported emerging black businesspeople during the 2000s instead of white-owned foreign business and capital (Seekings & Nattrass, 2011, pp. 349–50). Thus, the B-BBEE legislation provided an opportunity for the promotion of a black capital class in South Africa by offering discounted shares for black South Africans only (Van Wyk, 2009, p. 43).

Politically connected elites, such as Mandela, Oliver Tambo, Govan Mbeki, and Walter Sisulu, and their family members, benefitted from the 'elite transition' in the South African economy, particularly during the 1990s (Seekings & Nattrass, 2011, p. 351; Van Wyk, 2009, p. 38). Bond (2000) argued that the stipulated economic transformation regarding the South African economy was replaced by an elite transition through the neoliberal and uneven BEE policies. For example, Patrice Motsepe was one of the most notable winners of the promotion of BEE in the South African mining industry. Motsepe, who was the brother-in-law of Ramaphosa and former Minister Jeff Radebe, bought the insignificant mineshaft of an old mining company AngloGold (now AngloGold Ashanti) in the late 1990s when gold prices low in the world market (Wild & Cohen, 2013). Motsepe subsequently founded African Rainbow Minerals and became one of the richest people in South Africa.

Unsurprisingly, South African white business corporations, more narrowly the mining houses, were not satisfied with the policy shift by the ANC in the mid-2000s because of the increasing demands made on them, which included changes in the ownership and management structures of the private companies on behalf of the HDSAs through the MPRDA and the Mining Charter. Interviewee 4 (2017) argued strongly that even though there were some differences in the discourses of the mining industry and the government, the mining industry was committed to transformation and to making the country work. Interviewee 5 (2017) stated that the mining houses did not like the BEE and the charters, which required them "to give chunks of their company partly because the black entrepreneurs who are given the chunks of companies can somehow sell them and you have to start all over again." Although the mining industry did not like the BEE policies, the Mining Charter or the MPRDA, they took a supportive attitude towards adjustments of this type as they needed the South African community to invest more and make more profits.

Interviewee 4 (2017) told me that the economic transformation process, which had to happen in order to achieve economic emancipation and stabilise the economy, resulted positively in terms of increasing the numbers of black managers:

> I told you just now and gave you an example of what happened in my company where 64% of the managers are black people. This shows that they embraced the changes which were supposed to happen and the transformative changes that had to be made. We did not just comply; we realized it was the right thing to do. Therefore, for South Africa to be stable to achieve like the economic emancipation, if you do not bring the blacks into the economy, it is not going to happen . . . and it is never going to be a stable country for anyone who wants to do business here. Consequently, we realized that change had to happen.

Interviewee 2 (2017) said that the mining industry needed more transformation in terms of the number of black managers as he believed that the proportion of black managers did not reflect the demography of South Africa:

> If you look at the mining industry today, 25 years later, compared with what it was, it is very different. For example, in skilled positions, any management positions, about more than 50% today are black people whereas in the early 1990s it was more or less 0% maybe 1%. Of course, that means if you compare the 50% with the demography of the country that means it is still not equal because 90% of the population is black. But it does indicate that this is a law that started to come in to effect really in 2004. That means that in the last thirteen years there was movement, there wasn't any regulation enforcement by 2004, maybe 20% of senior positions [were held by] black people, and today it's 50%.

A row between Mbeki and Anglo American tensed the relations between the ANC government and the mining industry. The reason for this tension was that Mbeki accused Anglo American of not being committed to the economic transformation and withheld its overseas assets under majority rule (*BBC News*, 2004). On the other hand, Anglo American declared that "it has full confidence in the country and denies that it is sitting on unvested cash reserves" (*BBC News*, 2004). Thus, SBRs in the South African mining industry were sometimes nervous during Mbeki's presidency because of the indigenisation policies (Andreasson, 2007, p. 282). In addition to the B-BBEE Act, in foreign policy, South Africa started to move away from core countries, capital institutions and businesses and approached instead upwardly mobile, semiperipheral countries such as China and India from the late 2000s onwards.

South Africa underwent radical changes in its political and economic areas during the late 2000s. Jacob Zuma, former deputy president of South Africa, was elected party leader at the ANC Congress on 18 December 2007 and Mbeki had to step down on 21 September 2008. The ANC leader Zuma was elected president of South Africa on 22 April 2009 and a new period was launched. In 2010, Zuma and his cabinet prepared an amendment to the first Mining Charter of 2004 which increased the BEE ownership rule in the mining industry from 15 per cent to 26 per cent. The second Mining Charter of 2010 not only sought to increase the numbers of promoted black entrepreneurs but also expanded the calibre of the inclusivity of HDSAs through changes in employment equity, procurement, and mine community development. Nolke and Claar (2013, p. 45) claimed that "the co-option of black elites into national capital has contributed to preventing major economic ruptures after the end of apartheid." Nevertheless, there was a risk to the white-owned domestic and foreign mining houses and investors from the amendments to the Mining Charter.

The first years of the Zuma presidency was a transition period from the Mbeki era. The relationship with the mining sector was complex but did not completely deteriorate during this period. For example, Interviewee 1 was a member of the negotiation team for the second Mining Charter of 2010 on behalf of the mining industry over a six-month period and told me that they met with the government every two weeks during this period. Although there were some disagreements between the two parties, they negotiated the proposal and could work on this basis. This shows the importance of the negotiation process as a satisfactory tool for the mining industry for keeping the SBRs stable.

In addition to these domestic developments, the financial crisis of 2007–2008 had devastating effects on the commodity boom and the prices of precious minerals and industrial metals. The prices of precious minerals and industrial metals decreased in the early 2010s and the mining industry became less profitable for investors (Allen, 2015; Pratley, 2015). According to PWC (2016) data, the market capitalisation of the Top 40 mining companies against and the adjusted price index for some commodities such as copper, coal, nickel, zinc, gold, silver, and iron ore decreased by 145 per cent from 2010 to 2015. Moreover, Chinese state-owned and private companies invested in the mining industries of sub-Saharan Africa from the mid-2000s and this raised the competition within the continent with other investors, including South Africa. As an important part of a semiperipheral country, the business community in South Africa also considered its investments beyond the domestic level and the significant Chinese presence was harmful to its interests.

Relations between the ANC government and the mining industry were relatively fractured during Zuma's presidency in the mid-2010s. There were tensions related to the state-capture and the nonnegotiated third Mining Charter draft in 2017. For example, according to Interviewee 4 (2017), there was 'no trust' between the Zuma administration and the mining industry due to the nonnegotiated third Mining Charter draft. She claimed that the government thought that there was still a 'white monopoly capital' phenomenon within the mining industry and that it intended to perpetuate this phenomenon with its policies. In fact, the government believed that white-owned mining corporates were taking money out of South Africa and moving it overseas to place it off-shore. The government also believed that white-owned mining corporates such as Anglo American did not pay enough taxes to South Africa (Interviewee 4, 2017). Overall, she stated that the ANC government under Zuma did not trust the white-owned mining corporates.

The former Minister of DMR Joseph Zwane argued that the suggested increase in BEE ownership from 26 per cent to 30 per cent in the new Mining Charter was not enough for completing the economic transformation of South Africa's mineral resources according to the ANC members, and he told ANC delegates that he would target the BEE ownership rule at more than 50 per cent (Macupe, 2017). Consequently, relations between the white-owned mining industry, particularly the Chamber of Mines, and the ANC government was tense during Zuma's presidency. Van Wyk (2009, pp. 45–47) argued that Zuma had pursued more intense BEE and indigenisation policies during his presidency after the policies of political transition and economic transformation which were pursued in South Africa from 1994 to 2008.

There were three major reasons for the deterioration of the nexus between the Zuma government and the mining industry from the early 2010s to mid-2010s. First, the government was influenced by ANC-linked black entrepreneurs when it was formulating the laws. Second, the relatively higher cost of labour in the South African mining industry than in the rest of the continent and the traditionally high influence of trade unions were obstacles. Third, incompetent politicians and the deteriorating relations between the mining industry and the former Minister of Mineral Resources Zwane were the other major obstacles to the effective SBRs regarding the South African mining industry (Interviewee 1, 2017):

> Firstly, we believed they [the Zuma government] were unduly influenced by many black entrepreneurs who believed they were not getting enough from the government. Therefore, we believed but they [the Zuma government] could not believe that there is the vested interest of black capital who wanted more without putting the money in. Secondly, I think the trade unions were very unreasonable. South African labour costs for mining were among the highest in the world. We had one of the least productive labour forces in the continent. Thus, it's an issue we have with the trade unions to set the ways to demand, ways which cost 56% of our cost and they are going up by 11% without any parallel increases in productivity. Therefore, we found our labour forces very unreasonable. Thirdly, we did not have enough capable black managers. They had no experience in mining, they were not capable managers. They were useless managers, to be

> very blunt. We believed the current Minister [of Mineral Resources Zwane] was also corrupt. The laws which were put on the table were influenced by the party [the ANC] which had its own interests at heart. They [the Zuma Government] were not looking at long-term sustainability in the industry. There is a complete breakdown between the mining industry and the government at the moment.

The mining industry in semiperipheral South Africa would expect fewer expenses for the workers as they are not in a core country. The irony is semi-peripheral states have not only core-like industries but also core-like working classes as the wages are more important than the prices of minerals (Hopkins, Wallerstein *et al.*, 1982, p. 48). Therefore, South African originated mining corporates do not make profits as when they did under the apartheid regime. The mining industry expected to cooperate with the Zuma government for oppressing the demands of the mineworkers, particularly the trade unions (for the embedded cooperation between semiperipheral states and large corporations for exploiting the raw materials in noncore areas *see* Garcia, 2017b, p. 501).

Interviewee 3 (2017), who had worked in the mining industries of both South Africa and Zimbabwe as a mining consultant and engineer, thought that SBRs during the early and mid-2010s were affected by the policy choices of the government "very badly." He believed that the government did not consult the industry at all and just said: "here is the new Mining Charter." Moreover, he blamed the government for not talking with the mining industry and for saying to the industry "it is our country, we can do it and you just have to obey the law." Interviewee 3 (2017) also claimed that the mining industry wanted to talk and negotiate with the government about the draft of the third Mining Charter. Despite these efforts of the mining industry, "the Zuma government have gone on their own" (Interviewee 3, 2017). Zwane argued that the business community should focus on business instead of trying to govern the country (Macupe, 2017):

> I think we must also take the blame as the government, partly, that we have not been clear enough to say at a particular point when we are governing, 'we will have legislation that takes this country forward.' And business should do business, they can't do business and govern at the same time. It won't work because we will not achieve [anything].

According to Interviewee 4 (2017), the mining industry thought that the ANC government under Zuma did not understand what the mining corporates wanted. She stated that the mining industry wanted certainty from the government's policies such as the Mining Charter and the MPRDA. Additionally, she believed that the ANC government was asking too much and moving goalposts frequently under Zuma's presidency.

Nevertheless, the main problem between the government and the mining industry was not only uncertainty over the policy choices and nonnegotiated laws regarding mineral rights but also the favoured BEE entrepreneurs. For example, Interviewee 2 (2017) argued that there were other reasons in South Africa which affected the deterioration of the relationship between the ANC government and mining industry:

> In those days, the relationships between the industry and government had deteriorated over the last few years. But that is actually because of other factors. Some elements in the government have been favouring some families and groups, which had discouraged a lot of investment in the industry [When I was doing this interview with Interviewee 2 the 'State Capture' inquiry and corruption allegations against then-President Zuma and his rich close allies, namely the Gupta family, had been dominating the headlines in South Africa during November 2017].

Also, the demands of the labour unions and HDSAs were other obstacles to an effective SBRs in South Africa's mining industry. Interviewee 5 (2017) pointed out another aspect of the deteriorated SBRs in the industry by stating that the labour force had remained very militant against the mining companies of South Africa. Moreover, Interviewee 2 (2017) told me that in addition to the BEE policies there were other changes in the mining industry during the postapartheid period:

> In fact, employment in the mining industry fell for a couple of reasons. First of all, because particularly the mining industry in diamond was very old, starting in the 1800s. They had paid basic wages very substantially lower than was meant and the vast bulk of the workforce were non-skilled and doing very low-skilled kinds of work. Workers are now more skilled. They have trained to have better skills and that has also meant that the number of people has declined and the number of workers in the industry has declined. I think that's related to the incidents of unionisation in collectives rather than due to the BEE policies which you are talking about.

In addition to Interviewee 2 (2017), Jean-Sébastien Jacques, from 2016 the chief executive of Rio Tinto which had extracted several minerals such as iron ore and bauxite in South Africa, warned the mining industry and told that the rising costs of extraction and political uncertainty were affecting the extraction activities (Hume, 2018). He believed that the rising oil prices and resource nationalisation policies of the governments in mineral-rich countries (Saunders & Caramento, 2017; Zvoushe *et al.*, 2017; Saunders & Nyamunda, 2016; Andreasson, 2015; Jackson *et al.*, 2013; Burgess & Beilstein, 2013), including South Africa, the DRC, and Indonesia, were the major reasons for the volatility in markets (Hume, 2018). Also, Gold Fields CEO Nick Holland said that "higher wages and power prices, combined with the geological challenges of the world's deepest mines, will mean more job losses and less production in the country over the next five years" (Njini, 2018b).

In addition to this, Interviewee 2 (2017) told me that there had been a significant change in the nature of the mining industry:

> Obviously, we can debate whether it has moved fast enough, and many people argue it hasn't. Nonetheless, there has been a significant change in the nature of the industry. Some of the new . . . there are many mining companies today that are owned by black people who have held shares in mining companies. Therefore, there have been many significant changes in employment and ownership structures. As we are saying, there is more that still needs to be done.

A well-known political economist Moeletsi Mbeki, the brother of former president Thabo Mbeki, talked about the changing nature of the industry in 2013 when the industry was in crisis because of increasing demands by the mineworkers and the reducing profitability of the sector (Smith, 2013):

> People forget that the mining industry is 140 to 150 years old and its foundation was migrant labour and cheap labour. This model has not changed. The mining companies want to preserve the cheap labour system but in any country you can't expect the workers to accept the conditions of 100 years ago. You can't sustain the use of force that has been the character of the mining industry. The workers themselves are now voters and much more politically savvy.

The reducing investments in the mining industry in South Africa was a result not only of the policies of the ANC government but also of global issues beyond the control of the government in Pretoria. In addition, according to Interviewee 5 (2017), another problem causing this deterioration was the fact that the commodity super-cycle from 2002 to 2011 did not contribute to the South African economy as expected in terms of GDP, savings, and investments because the mining houses were just operating for the short term in South Africa.

Attracting more FDIs and an improving investment climate are important indicators of effective SBRs, as well as tools of measuring the variations of SBRs in developing countries. Nolke and Claar (2013, pp. 46–47) believed that South Africa attracted fewer FDIs than other semi-peripheral countries during the 1990s and 2000s because of "the small size of the South African domestic market, due to a much smaller population than in other major emerging economies, but also to a continuation of extreme inequality." According to UNCTAD (2018) figures, the FDI flow towards South Africa declined after 2014 despite the same data demonstrating that FDI stock had increased slightly from 2014 to 2017 (*see* table 4.1). According to the then Chamber of Mines of South Africa, the mining industry had lost thirty thousand workers from 2014 to 2018 and the net investment had declined 57 per cent during the last decade (Hume, 2018).

According to Interviewee 3 (2017), although the former DMR minister Zwane had told the mining industry that the new Mining Charter was set in law, the head of the Chamber of Mines (now the Minerals Council of South Africa) claimed that it was not law and they were in court as the implementations were being suspended by the court. As a consequence, there was no relationship between the government and the mining industry in South Africa during the last years of Zuma's presidency. To conclude, there was no trust between the mining industry and the ANC government, and Interviewee 4 (2017) therefore asked: "Are they just protecting their interest or is this a genuine relationship [on behalf of both sides]?"

Following the end of the Zuma era with high tension and nonnegotiation between the ANC and the mining businesses, the business-friendly presidential candidate Ramaphosa was expected to follow a negotiated Mining Charter and therefore provide more stable SBRs. The South African mining industry therefore supported Ramaphosa at the 54th National Conference of the ANC. The South African rand reacted well to the election of Ramaphosa as the new ANC leader and gained value against foreign currencies, which was termed "Ramaphoria" (Groenewald, 2018; Masinga, 2018; Monteiro & Gumede, 2018). After Ramaphosa became the leader of the ANC in January 2018, South African rand "broke the barrier and reached" 11.95 to the US dollar for the first time since 2015 (Chutel & Kopf, 2018). Nevertheless, some disagreements on the third Mining Charter of 2018, land invasion discussions, and Ramaphosa's populist approach affected the Ramaphoria negatively (Goko, 2019; Burke, 2018; Mattes, 2018). Despite these controversies

Table 4.1: FDIs in South Africa

Years	*2005-2007 (Precrisis annual average)*	*2014*	*2015*	*2016*	*2017*
FDI Inward Flow	4,499	5,771	1,729	2,235	1,325
FDI Inwards (in % of GFCF[1])	8.6	n/a	2.7	3.9	2.1
Years	1995	2014	2015	2016	2017
FDI Inward Stock (million US$)	15,014	138,906	126,755	135,454	149,962
FDI Inward Stock (in % of GDP)	9.7	n/a	40.3	46.1	47.2

Source: Author created with data from UNCTAD (2018)

about the Ramaphosa government, the Minerals Council South Africa welcomed the president, his cabinet and his 'ethical leadership' with respectful media statements (Minerals Council South Africa, 2018, 2019; Chamber of Mines of South Africa, 2018b, 2018c, 2017). The suspended third Mining Charter of 2017 was revised by the Ramaphosa government in agreement with the mining industry in 2018.

During the negotiations on the third Mining Charter of 2018 between the mining industry and the Ramaphosa government, Minister of DMR Gwede Mantashe reiterated the Ministry's intention to find solutions to the ongoing problems of the South African mining industry at the Minerals Council South Africa's Annual Meeting (Van Vuuren, 2018b). The Minister believed that the DMR would address four key points for resolving the impasse in the mining sector. Hence, (i) the uncertainty and the need for regulation were the main issues related to legislative frameworks such as the Mining Charter and the MPRDA; along with (ii) health and safety issues in the workplace, and (iii) confronting the complexities of the granting of mining rights and mining licences as other key points. Finally, Mantashe thought that (iv) the DMR and the mining industry should cooperate to fight the illegal mining activities in South Africa (Van Vuuren, 2018b).

The tensions between the mining industry and the government have not ended despite the implementation of negotiated third Mining Charter of 2018 and they might keep going during the next decade and further. The Minerals Council South Africa has some concerns about the new Mining Charter although it is happy about the negotiations between the mining industry and government. The concerns of the Minerals Council South Africa focus on the procurement rules, services and turnover threshold for junior miners (*Reuters*, 2018). The President of the Minerals Council South Africa Mxolisi Mgojo said that the mining industry had concerns about the three issues in the third Mining Charter after the South African parliament passed the law on September 2018 (Seccombe, 2018b).

First, Mgojo believed that the 'once-empowered always empowered' rule, which was a major concern for the mining industry as past empowerment deals before the third Mining Charter of 2018 had not achieved transformation (Njini & Burkhardt, 2018), should be considered by the government. Second, raising the percentage of the mining ownership rule from 26 per cent to 30 per cent was another concern for the industry. Indeed, changes in the ownership structures of the mining companies had started to increase after the financial crisis of 2007–2008 as the mining industry had not been the most lucrative industry (Interviewee 2, 2017). Hence, some of the black entrepreneurs had sold their BEE shares and created a re-empowerment problem for the mining industry. Interviewee 3 (2017) thought that the ANC government must solve this problem together with the mining industry as the capital owners or investors could not solve it on their own without the power of legislation:

> You go to the government and say that we are busy trying; all these people have done is create a gap. Using the fact that the blacks get a good deal and they are making money out of it, then we are losing the money, and then we are going to be black-empowered again. After buying their shares, they sell them back at a higher price. They cost the company money and he [President Zuma] says no. It is not like a sustainable thing.

Third, the procurement targets demanded in the third Mining Charter of 2018 were too high for the industry since there were not enough locally manufactured goods from black economic empowered companies for the industry in South Africa (Seccombe, 2018b). Although the Minerals Council South Africa still has some concerns about the third Mining Charter of 2018, the consensus between the Ramaphosa government and the mining industry has been a significant development for the consolidation of SBRs.

In addition to the concerns of the Minerals Council South Africa, the chairman of AngloGold Ashanti Sipho Pityana argued that the new mining rules in South Africa are "reckless" as the regulations in the third Mining Charter of 2018 are driving away foreign investors from South Africa and the consequent lack of investment is crippling the mining industry (Njini *et al.*, 2018). For a declining industry, the 30 per cent empowerment rule might be a disaster for the mining industry since foreign investors continue to flee from the country and avoid investing in South Africa. The fear of nationalisation and driving away foreign investors have always been on the table from the last years of apartheid and the postapartheid period.

Despite some breakdowns between the ANC government and the mining industry from 1994, South Africa has been a safe and profitable place for the mining houses. Some have argued that South Africa's effective SBRs were an example for other southern African countries such as Zambia and Zimbabwe during the postapartheid period (Seekings & Nattrass, 2011; Handley, 2008; Taylor, 2007). For example, Anglo American CEO Mark Cutifani said that the company would like to maintain its investments in South Africa as the profitability of mining investments in the country were still beyond their minimum expectations in 2013 (Armitage, 2013). He also said that he was more optimistic about the future of the business environment in South Africa as the ANC and the mining industry were working together on the new Mining Charter, which became a disaster for the relationship during the mid-2010s. The relationship between the mining industry and the ANC government has always had some tensions and fluctuations, but the government and the industry have worked together for their own interests, except for the fractured relations during the mid-2010s because of the suspended third Mining Charter of 2017. The ANC, the white-owned businesses and the black empowered businesses have searched for solutions and dialogue between them about these tensions.

Interviewee 5 (2017) shared a personal example, which was one of the worst examples for him, of coal mining in KwaZulu-Natal which had not only ruined the oldest game park in Africa, namely Imfolozi, but had also caused a climate struggle as South Africa had rights for digging and then exploiting eighteen billion tonnes of coal. Exceptionally disruptive and mega projects of this kind have benefitted not only the ANC-linked mining companies, such as Guptas, Shanduka Gold, and Lonmin, but also the white-owned mining houses such as BHP Billiton, Exxaro, and Glencore. In addition to these mining firms, Transnet and Sasol have been the other main beneficiaries of all this state investment. As a result, although opportunities like these have been harmful to both the climate and the history of South Africa and humanity in general, they have been functional for holding the government and black-owned and white-owned mining companies together as they have been profitable investments for all parties. This therefore represents an example of collusion between the ANC government and businesspeople because they were looking for only their own profit and ignored the public. In other words, collusive behaviour of the state and the business is unproductive for society and the economy (*see* Evans, 2012; Cali & Sen, 2011; Te Velde, 2006; Maxfield & Schneider, 1997; Evans, 1995).

Another example of collusive behaviour from South Africa is the so-called Marikana Massacre, in which thirty-four mineworkers were shot by the security forces while they were on strike against Lonmin Platinum in 2012. After the massacre, the South African press during the court hearing after the Marikana Commission uncovered the story behind the shootings and found that Ramaphosa, who was the chairman of the company's BEE partner, had requested security forces to the Marikana mining site to quell the 'criminal' acts of mineworkers with 'concomitant action' (Alexander, 2016; 2013; Bond, 2018; 2014; Bond & Mottiar, 2013; Gumede, 2012; Hlongwane, 2012). Interviewee 5 (2017) told me about this collusion between the state and Ramaphosa during our interview:

> So, there are a lot of techniques in this new phase and then there is, . . . you get people like Cyril Ramaphosa as a major shareholder in a foreign company Lonmin, who was called upon to do the worst thing you can imagine which was to email a request more or less for a massacre [Although Bond told me that Ramaphosa clearly asked the police to be forceful in dealing with what the mine operators said were aggressive and dangerous mineworkers]. But he said "I did

> not want a massacre. I wanted them to deal with these criminals in a peaceful way." He was very embarrassed, but he still would be the next president.

These examples demonstrate that the mining sector of South Africa has been the centre of SBRs, which might sometimes include collusive behaviour. However, in order to attract more FDIs to the mining industry of South Africa, SBRs should be consolidated. For providing public benefits and prodevelopmental outcomes the SBRs also should be based on collaborative behaviour, instead of collusion (Taylor, 2012; Maxfield & Schneider, 1997). Also, the collusive behaviour between the government and business prevents competition between private investors in the mining industry and pushes out foreign investors (Te Velde, 2006). This therefore reduces the attractiveness of the mining industry of a country that results in fracturing of the SBRs over time.

To conclude, even in the early 2020s, the economic transformation has not yet been successfully achieved in South Africa. This ongoing process is a sign of future policy changes in regard to mining rights. Changes of this kind create uncertainties for the domestic industry as well as for foreign investors. The economic transformation in South Africa has been relatively achieved in terms of ownership structures, managerial positions, employment equity, and community development, but even so, the ANC government should do more to tackle collusive behaviour and corruption for the consolidation of SBRs in the mining sector.

SBRS IN INDEPENDENT ZIMBABWE

Before independence in Zimbabwe, state and business relations were consolidated by the white ruling elite and white businesspeople who ignored the black majority population of Rhodesia. Indeed, the white minority government denied the economic and political rights of the black majority population by marginalising and oppressing them. In 1965, the white population of Rhodesia was about 5 per cent, which was around 224,000 out of a total population of four and a half million (Phimister, 2011; Brownell, 2010). Thus, there were no established black businesses or political institutions in Rhodesia until 1980. Following the UDI in 1965, the Rhodesian state protected the economic interests of white citizens over the blacks and the government "strengthened state capacity by expanding bureaucratic apparatuses and deepening state planning and collaboration with white capital targeted at midwifing the agriculture and manufacturing sectors" (Shumba, 2018, p. 97). Zimbabwe's domestic mining industry was traditionally white like the South African mining industry. However, the main differences between these countries were visible during the early years of majority rule. On the one hand, semiperipheral South Africa started to promote black-owned mining businesses from the early years of majority rule but on the other, peripheral Zimbabwe maintained the country's dependence on white-owned domestic or foreign investments throughout the majority rule.

Despite the Western economic sanctions, the Rhodesian state "provided a regime of incentives that included cheap credit, controlled labour and a protective tariff system" (Shumba, 2018, p. 97). As a result of these efforts, the Rhodesian economy experienced a relatively successful growth period from 1965 to 1973 and continued to attract foreign investment and trade (Shumba, 2018, pp. 97–98). Subsequently, the breakdown of relations between the ZANU-PF government and the business community during the late 1990s caused the violent land redistribution policies in the early 2000s through an increasingly authoritarian government in Harare. There were some similarities between post-2000 Zimbabwe and post-1965 Rhodesia in terms of their fractured relations with both domestic and foreign capital. Although the Rhodesian white ruling elite had resisted the economic sanctions after UDI in 1965, some domestic and foreign developments, such as the Rhodesian Civil War, the global recession after the petrol crisis in the early 1970s, and rising numbers of independent African (particularly southern African) countries broke down that resistance (Shumba, 2018, p. 36).

After gaining independence from the white-settler rule, Zimbabwe established strong bilateral relations with Western countries and IFIs during the late 1980s and 1990s. These close ties between core countries and actors of the MWS and the Zimbabwean government helped to consolidate the SBRs in Zimbabwe. Diminishing interest in mineral production during the 1980s on the world market complicated the relations between the new black political elite and white-owned businesses in Zimbabwe. There was mutual mistrust between them and both parties had concerns over controlling the mining resources in Zimbabwe. On the one hand, the government blamed the foreign mining capital for cheating Zimbabwe in terms of the earnings from the mineral resources. On the other hand, the foreign mining capital feared the initial steps towards the nationalisation of the mining sector through the establishment of the Minerals Marketing Corporation of Zimbabwe, which gave the right to the government "to handle all external selling and marketing of minerals" (Shumba, 2018, p. 99). In spite of the tensions between the government and foreign mining capital, the SBRs were consolidated during the postindependence era.

From the early period of postindependence in Zimbabwe, President Mugabe had close British friends, who invested heavily in the mining industry even during the Rhodesian era. Tiny Rowland was the owner of the London and Rhodesian mining company (Lonrho), lately Lonmin. He was born in

India as a German in 1917 and gained British citizenship (Davies, 1990). He grew up in Hamburg and joined the Hitler Youth Movement before the Second World War (Kay, 1995). His father sent him to Hampshire to protect him from the Nazis and, therefore, he changed his surname from Fuhrhop to Rowland (Davies, 1990). He was a private in the Royal Army Medical Corps until the army discharged him within four years (Davies, 1990). Although he was a supporter of Hitler from a young age, he was not a racist and had close relations with some newly independent African leaders, including Mugabe (Kay, 1995). In 1947, he went to South Rhodesia and started the business by buying two farms (*BBC News*, 1998). During the Rhodesian era, he was an upmarket car dealer in Salisbury, lately Harare (Kay, 1995). In 1962, he became the chief executive of Lonrho and expanded the company to become an international conglomerate (*BBC News*, 1998). However, in 1993, he lost control of Lonrho and was excluded from the honorary presidency. Despite that, Nelson Mandela honoured Rowland with the Order of Good Hope in the mid-1990s (*BBC News*, 1998).

Nicholas van Hoogstraten was another close friend of Mugabe from the United Kingdom. He owned a stake in Hwange Colliery, which is a pioneer mining company in Zimbabwe (*The Times*, 2006). He was born in 1948 as Nicholas Marcel Hoogstraten, but he added "van" to his name later. He was a famous criminal and some judges called him a "bully" and an "emissary of Beelzebub" (*BBC News*, 2002b). He was in prison for four years during the 1960s as the court convicted him for ordering a grenade attack on a Jewish clergyman (*BBC News*, 2002b). Although he received a ten-year prison sentence for manslaughter during the early 2000s, he escaped with only a monetary fine as a result of his appeal to the court after thirteen months of imprisonment (Barber, 2006; *The Times*, 2006). He was one of the richest people in the United Kingdom during the twentieth century as he had the most expensive house, which cost £40 million, in Britain (*BBC News*, 2002b). He was the biggest foreign investor in Zimbabwe during the mid-2000s and had special mining rights (Barber, 2006). Despite his close relations with Mugabe, he was arrested in Zimbabwe in 2008 as he collected rent in overseas currency, which was forbidden, for his almost two hundred properties (*BBC News*, 2008). A Zimbabwean court cleared him in 2009 and he told the judge that he is a close friend of Mugabe, as reported by witnesses (*BBC News*, 2009).

In the 1980s and 1990s, privatisation seemed the best method for economic development and for tackling foreign debts for sub-Saharan African countries (Hawthorn, 1993, pp. 330–31). "International governance" was the main theme of the liberalisation of the mining sector in Africa during the 1980s and 1990s (Campbell, 2003, p. 2). Sub-Saharan African countries attracted more FDIs because of the positive climate in SBRs during the 1990s, compared with the 1970s and 1980s (Maponga & Maxwell, 2001, p. 18). However, Ambe-Uva (2017, pp. 9–10) claimed that in spite of the rising number of foreign investments in the mining sector during the neoliberal transformation in sub-Saharan Africa, private mining companies did not promote sustainable development, especially for local people. Furthermore, rapid trade liberalisation of mining industries in developing countries, particularly in sub-Saharan African countries, had a negative effect on local industries (Brautigam *et al.*, 2002, p. 542). Brautigam *et al.* (2002, p. 542) suggested that contrary to expectations, African businesses were not winners in the rapid trade liberalisation. In fact, due to the failure of SAPs and economic liberalisation policies, they lost their significance for most sub-Saharan African countries at the end of the 1990s.

Zimbabwe did not go against this trend and it was not a distinct case in the continent, and Harare pursued a neoliberal policy with a homegrown name, ESAP, for applying privatisation and liberalisation policies to its mining industry. The Confederation of Zimbabwe Industries (CZI), which was an "umbrella organisation representing manufacturing interests (predominantly large, white-owned firms) in a number of sectors," was the main actor for applying neoliberal adjustment policies in the late 1980s (Brautigam *et al.*, 2002, p. 533). Moreover, the CZI supported its ally, the then minister of finance Bernard Chidzero, in adopting ESAP as an economic policy in the early 1990s (Brautigam *et al.*, 2002, p. 535). After the first years of the postindependence period in Zimbabwe, the ZANU-PF government pursued stable relations with foreign businesses because it could not afford to lose the support of "entrenched economic groups and their international compatriots" (Andreasson, 2007, p. 285).

During the economic liberalisation period, the ZANU-PF government supported the expansion of white foreign mining capital in Zimbabwe by providing state incentives (Shumba, 2018, p. 101). So following independence, Zimbabwe established better relations with white-owned big businesses than with the black-owned small businesses (Andreasson, 2007, p. 286; Bond, 1998). The newly independent black government elite did not want to promote a black business class as a rival to themselves (Shumba, 2018; Raftopoulos, 1996; Nicholas, 1994, p. 95 cited in Magure, 2012, p. 69), so the government did not support the domestic and indigenous mining activities since they feared the "development of an independent indigenous class that could pose a threat to its political ambitions" (Shumba, 2018, p. 100). According to Shumba (2018, p. 101), this undermining of small-scale miners and domestic black capital had two purposes; it "undermined the vital role of domestic capital in emulating the 'triple alliance of the state, domestic and international capital' as a vital source of transformative capital, but also exhibited predatory behaviour in repulsing potential threats to the power interests of the ruling elite." Large-scale mining capital providers were among the closest allies of the postindependence state and the government developed a stable relationship with the mining sector through investment incentives, direct participation, and increasing regulation and oversight (Shumba, 2018, pp. 89–90).

Sub-Saharan African countries governed their mining industries more conscientiously than simply "the disengagement of the state and the ascendancy of market-style operations" in the mineral industries during the 1980s and 1990s (Ambe-Uva, 2017, p. 13). During the SAP period, foreign private businesses enjoyed the liberalisation of economies in sub-Saharan Africa, and specifically in Zimbabwe. However, domestic businesses in sub-Saharan African countries, including Zimbabwe, were affected negatively by these economic liberalisation policies. The economic crisis in the late 1990s and early 2000s depressed the Zimbabwean mining industry. By 2000, some of the most active chromite, copper, gold, and nickel mines in Zimbabwe had closed down as a result of the economic crisis (Shumba, 2018, p. 105).

In addition to the failure of ESAP, corruption and mismanagement by the ZANU-PF reduced the trust of the government in the neoliberal policies as the country faced an economic crisis by the end of the twentieth century. Even though the government attempted to develop small-scale mining operations to avert an unemployment problem during the 1990s, the ruling elite failed to achieve it. As a result, the number of illegal artisanal mining activities were set up, which led to social and environmental disasters in Zimbabwe (Shumba, 2018, p. 102). Nevertheless, the ZANU-PF inevitably turned a blind eye to the illegal mining activities as it needed their support in the forthcoming elections in the late 1990s (Shumba, 2018, p. 103). The relationship between the white-owned businesses and the government deteriorated from the late 1990s.

The economic crisis in the last years of the twentieth century shaped the policy choices of the 2000s regarding the mining industry. Moreover, similar to South Africa's experience, in addition to the political transition in Harare, the ZANU-PF-connected individuals and elites expected legal support for promoting the black business capitalist class in Zimbabwe (Hammar, 2014). Before the IEE in Zimbabwe, the government had acted to indigenise the businesses (Pedersen & McCormick, 1999, p. 128):

> To increase the competitiveness of small and medium-sized indigenous enterprises, the government of Zimbabwe has established a policy of 'affirmative action' which prioritises indigenous businesses on public tenders below a certain size and requires large white-owned enterprises winning larger tenders to subcontract part of the contract sum to indigenous businesses. Similar policies have been discussed in South Africa.

So as a result of the policy choices, indigenisation demands, and economic failure, the Zimbabwean government moved away from core countries of the MWS and approached semiperipheral powers such as China and South Africa during the 2000s. The IMF, for instance, did not support the policies on property rights in Zimbabwe, such as the indigenisation policy (*Zimbabwe Independent*, 2006).

Brautigam *et al.* (2002, p. 537) stated that "many business groups were cast as enemies of the state" and SBRs in Zimbabwe therefore fractured in the late 1990s as a result of the major policy shift of the ZANU-PF government. Hence, during the 2000s new foreign players took place in the Zimbabwean mining industry:

> The collapse of domestic finance markets in the early 2000s, severe foreign exchange shortages and an effective boycott of development lending to Zimbabwe, placed foreign mining capital in a privileged position. In the 2000s, foreign players would dominate leading mining mergers, acquisitions and new projects; domestic capital involvement, with the exception of state involvement in the problematic diamond sector in Marange, remained negligible (Saunders & Caramento, 2017, p. 12).

An indigenous capitalist class emerged slowly until the land invasions in Zimbabwe. There was an "elite consensus" between the majority government and the old white business community (Andreasson, 2007, p. 277). However, following the fractured relations between the ZANU-PF government and the old white businesses during the early 2000s, the indigenous capitalist class has emerged as a "crony project" of the party (Moore, 2003; Sahikonye, 2003 cited in Andreasson, 2007, p. 277). The ZANU-PF government easily broke with the mining sector as no Zimbabwe-based investors or new investors from other countries were available. In South Africa, however, the ANC government needed to find a balance between the domestic pressures to implement indigenisation and the liberalisation policies. This shows that extreme policy shifts in semiperipheral countries are not easy decisions for governments as they affect a wide range of domestic actors.

Because of changing policies moving away from neoliberal ones, the nature of sub-Saharan Africa's external engagements changed with a corresponding shift in business actors, notably an increase in Chinese and other business actors from the Global South. Correspondingly, Ambe-Uva (2017, p. 14) stated that:

> The demand for resources from Africa has increased significantly due to the involvement of the BRICS, which are displacing Western countries in accessing African natural resources. Informed by South-South cooperation, these new players appear to be redefining the governance of the mining and extractive

> sector. China's policy of non-conditionality and non-political interference appears to have given it an edge over old players in the sector.

The Look East policy of Harare formally shifted the country's FDIs destination from the west to the east. Former CEO of Zimbabwe National Chamber of Commerce Innocent Makwiramiti championed the policy shift of Harare and stated that (*IRIN News*, 2005):

> Given that Zimbabwe's traditional trading partners in the European Union and the United States have drastically scaled down on business or stopped completely, it is natural for the government to look elsewhere in order to save the country from total collapse, and there is nothing bad about that. But there is no need to be over-enthusiastic about doing business with China, particularly because the Chinese are here, first and foremost, because of their own business interests—they have identified Zimbabwe as a viable market for their mass-produced goods.

The significant Chinese presence in Zimbabwe, particularly in the mining sector, was therefore expected to replace the traditional Western investments from the mid-2000s.

In addition to the Look East policy, the ZANU-PF government formulated an indigenisation law for foreign economic activities in Zimbabwe as well as promoting party-linked entrepreneurs. Indigenisation policies in Zimbabwe "created a 'state-dependent petty bourgeoisie' of well-connected black Zimbabweans" (Andreasson, 2007, p. 286). The Chamber of Mines of Zimbabwe was against the extreme indigenisation policy of the ZANU-PF government since it had argued that the policy was scaring away potential investors in the mineral sector (Magure, 2012, p. 79). Also, South African investors, including Anglo Platinum and Impala Platinum, did not welcome the government's decision on the indigenisation of the mining resources and foreign companies in Zimbabwe (*Zimbabwe Independent*, 2006). Despite this concern, the South African mining companies maintained their extraction activities in Zimbabwe (Shumba, 2018, p. 108). Anglo American, for instance, defended the company's investments on the grounds that they would benefit the economic future of Zimbabwe and declared that "the responsible development of the Unki mine will create a long-term viable business which will be important to the economic future of Zimbabwe for years to come" (Wearden, 2008).

ZANU-PF-linked entrepreneurs, politicians, and military elites benefitted from the indigenisation policies of the government in collaboration with Chinese investors during the late 2000s, particularly the inclusion of joint ventures, including Anjin Investments, Jinan Mining, and Kusena Diamonds extraction activities in the Marange diamond field (Zimnisky, 2014; Bond

& Sharife, 2012). Beijing, for example, granted 'special mining rights' to Zimbabwe's uranium and diamonds in exchange for providing military hardware and building a nuclear power plant for generating electricity (*Bulawayo24 News*, 2013; *Mining Technology*, 2013). Inevitably the mining sector was the most attractive sector until the early 2010s because of the commodities boom and rising mineral prices worldwide, and for Zimbabwe, the mining sector became the only rescuer of the economy after the meltdown which followed the land invasions (Shumba, 2018, p. 107–08). President Mugabe stated that "Zimbabwe has not collapsed under the heavy weight of sanctions" (Nelson, 2013). Consequently, the SBRs consolidated again and included an operating mining industry with restricted actors because of the economic sanctions, and foreign investments through Chinese state-owned and private mining companies, thanks to Sino-Zimbabwean and South African-Zimbabwean bilateral economic relations respectively during the late 2000s and early 2010s.

In 2012, Zimbabwe's Black Empowerment Minister Saviour Kasukuwere announced that foreign investors in Zimbabwe's mining industry would no longer be permitted to own the majority of the stakes (Jamasmie, 2012b); he stated that "all mining companies that have not complied . . . should note that 51% of their shareholding is now deemed to be owned by the state" (Jamasmie, 2012b). That meant that the 51 per cent indigenised ownership rule, which had first been introduced in 2010 for updating the IEE Act of 2007, was implemented for the mining industry by the ZANU-PF government and became a specific obstacle for foreign investors from 2013. The Ministry of Mines and Minerals defended this policy shift in mineral rights and declared that "the current free mining colonial mineral regime is inappropriate for using national mineral assets to underpin wider development and industrialisation" (Marawanyika, 2013). The country had already lost the business-friendly environment in the mining industry after the Western economic sanctions after 2000, but there were still some investors from mainly semiperipheral countries such as South Africa and China who sought to invest in Zimbabwe's mining sector. This 51 per cent indigenised ownership rule ended the hopes of the mining sector and FDIs to Zimbabwe diminished swiftly.

As I have mentioned in the previous section one of the measurement tools of the variations of SBRs in developing countries is the fluctuations in FDIs, as well as improving the investment climate. According to UNCTAD (2018) figures, the FDI flow towards Zimbabwe decreased year-by-year from 2014 to 2017 despite a slight increase in FDI stock in the same period (*see* table 4.2). Moreover, there had been a gradual improvement in Zimbabwe from the early years of the economic sanctions (the mid-2000s) to the mid-2010s in terms of FDI inward flow thanks to China's state-owned and private investments. Thus, the trade volume between China and Zimbabwe rose rapidly from US$134.6 million in 2000 to US$1.3 billion in 2015 (National Bureau Statistics of China, 2017). Another reason for the decreasing numbers of FDIs was the hyperinflation which had affected Zimbabwe from the late 1990s onwards.

The aggressive acts of President Mugabe for controlling the Marange diamond field and the looting of US$13 billion from the extraction activities on this field are signs of the fracturing relations between state and business during the early 2010s (Saunders & Caramento, 2017). The Marange diamond field was under the control of senior Zimbabwean military officers who were obviously connected with the Mugabe regime (Moyo, 2016; Spiegel, 2015; Mangongera, 2014; Kerr & England, 2013; Maguwu, 2013; Towriss, 2013; Bond & Sharife, 2012). Thus, the ZANU-PF government allegedly benefitted from the Marange diamond field and this closed the door to foreign investors from the discovery of the diamonds in 2006 to the mid-2010s (Global Witness, 2017). According to Interviewee 5 (2017), one of the main problems regarding Zimbabwe's mining industry is ensuring an electricity supply for digging platinum mines. But they did not need electricity for digging the diamonds on the Marange mine site since they only needed bulldozers for extracting them. Interviewee 5 (2017) pointed out that the miners in the Marange diamond field just stripped the diamonds and left. Mugabe accused the mining companies which extracted diamonds in Marange of robbing the country's wealth from the field, and he banned all mining activities in Marange, and the government took possession of all diamond operations there (*The Guardian*, 2016). Nevertheless, six mining companies, Anjin Investments, Diamond Mining, Jinan Mining, Kusena Diamonds, Marange Resources, and Mbada Diamonds, rejected the government's decision not

Table 4.2: FDIs in Zimbabwe

Years	*2005–2007 (Precrisis annual average)*	*2014*	*2015*	*2016*	*2017*
FDI Inward Flow	71	545	421	372	289
FDI Inwards (in % of GFCF)	n/a	n/a	21.6	15.3	12.3
Years	1995	2014	2015	2016	2017
FDI Inward Stock (million US$)	496	3,546	3,967	4,339	4,628
FDI Inward Stock (in % of GDP)	6.9	n/a	28.0	30.6	30.3

Source: Author created with data from UNCTAD (2018)

to renew the mining licences and to nationalise the Marange diamond field (Jamasmie, 2016).

In addition to these domestic developments, following the financial crisis of 2007–2008, mineral prices plummeted, and the commodity boom came to an end during the early 2010s. As a result, implementing the extreme indigenised ownership rule, the allegations of corruption in the Marange diamond field and beyond against the Mugabe regime, and the globally diminishing mineral prices caused a fracturing in SBRs in Zimbabwe during the early and mid-2010s.

Interviewee 4 (2017) stated that uncertainty over the policy choices of the ZANU-PF government was one of the most important problems facing the mining industry. She argued that foreign mining companies such as Anglo American would not invest comfortably under these circumstances as it would be wondering what is coming next in Zimbabwe. In addition to this uncertainty, during the last years of the Mugabe administration, everyone had to comply with what the president said. For instance, Impala Platinum and Zimplats were building a refinery because that was what Mugabe wanted. Interviewee 4 (2017) concluded that there was a danger of losing mining properties, in other words, expropriation, in Zimbabwe in the same way as the farms of tobacco producers had been seized. Issues of this kind also derived from Zimbabwe's peripheral position since the lack of domestic business reduced the number of cautious policy choices.

As a result of the fractured SBRs during the late years of Mugabe's presidency, the existing mining firms, such as Zimplats and Impala Platinum, carried on but there was no new investment in Zimbabwe (Interviewee 3, 2017):

> It just set a couple of sets to work with 51% that's it. Also, they don't engage. In fact, the mining industry in Zimbabwe is decimated. There is almost no new investment. I think the biggest . . . there is platinum mining which is Zimplat already black empowered. I think they can survive a lot because they have got big operations down here, and they helped their name across the border. Supply materials . . . they can get these; they can make an arrangement to fulfil the staff like that. So, their existing mines are carried on, but a lot of projects aren't going well. There is no big investment there.

President Mnangagwa relaxed the 51 per cent black ownership rule in regard to Zimbabwe's mineral resources except for diamonds and platinum and thus located himself in a business-friendly position (Dzirutwe, 2018a; Turak, 2018). Zimbabwe's Finance Minister Mthuli Ncube announced that the ZANU-PF government was seeking to scrap the 51 per cent indigenised ownership rule from the diamond and platinum sectors and that foreigners would be allowed to own 100 per cent of their investments (Njini *et al.*,

2019). Ncube also said that the government would replace the IEE Act with a 'business-friendly' Economic Empowerment Act, "which will be consistent with the current thrust 'Zimbabwe is open for business'" in August 2019 (ZimTreasury, 2019).

The former president of the Zimbabwe Miners' Federation Henrietta Rushwaya stated that the indigenous miners were selling their stakes to the foreign investors for hard currency because they did not have adequate resources to stay in the business (Vinga, 2019):

> Indigenous miners are surrendering controlling stakes of their mines in order to stay in business and the disadvantages of this are that revenue generated from production is shifted to the majority stakeholders and buyers which is then repatriated out of Zimbabwe.

This shows that the 51 per cent indigenised ownership rule of Mugabe did not work and that after it was dropped indigenised miners had started to make money from their stakes. This created more opportunities for foreign investors, but such sales were not beneficial for the country's economy as they were sold very cheaply.

Following the end of Mugabe's presidency in November 2017, some Western mining companies signalled new investments in the Zimbabwean mining industry (*BBC World Service*, 2018). China also started to invest in Zimbabwe after the relaxation of 51 per cent indigenised ownership rule (Dzirutwe, 2018a; Turak, 2018). RioZim announced a US$1.2 billion investment in a power plant project near the Sengwa coalfield in the northwest of the country along with the Chinese-owned National Energy Investment Group under Mnangagwa's 'Zimbabwe is open for business' policy (Marawanyika, 2018). In addition to this huge project, the Russian diamond company Alrosa, majority-owned by the Russian government and reportedly amongst the world's largest diamond producers, declared that it will reinvest in Zimbabwe's diamond sector in the near future (Njini *et al.*, 2019). Moreover, one of the largest investments in the mining sector during Mnangagwa's presidency came from a Cypriot mining company, Karo Mining Holdings, which signed a US$4.2 billion deal to develop a platinum mine and refinery in Zimbabwe (Dzirutwe, 2018b). The CEO of De Beers also talked positively about the change in Harare and said that the company was excited about what was happening in Zimbabwe (Njini, 2018c).

Anglo American Platinum opened the completed Unki Mine Smelter in Shurugwi, a small town in the Midlands Province (*Mining Review*, 2019). Anglo American Platinum is one of the most significant investors in the Zimbabwean mining industry as it has invested more than half a billion US dollars in mining extraction activities and the social infrastructure since 2008.

Along with the Unki Mine Smelter, the company has implemented several projects in farming, sanitation, the water infrastructure, economic development, employment, the roads infrastructure, and capacity building in cooperation with the Mnangagwa government (*Mining Review*, 2019).

The new government in Harare has openly invited foreign investors to the country, particularly to the mining industry. It is obvious that Zimbabwe's mining sector has always needed foreign investors because indigenised investors are not capable of managing significant investments. Zimbabwean SBRs had never consolidated for long periods under Mugabe's presidency after the Fast-Track Land Invasion Programme and the incidents following it. However, the new president in Harare has been seeking more FDIs to the country and producing policies to attract them. In consequence, even though the consolidation of relations between the mining industry and Harare might be on the right track after the coup in 2017, the new government needs to develop this business-friendly climate more by making real changes such as scrapping the 51 per cent indigenised ownership rule in the industry.

COMPARING SBRS IN SOUTH AFRICA AND ZIMBABWE UNDER THE MAJORITY RULES

I argue that countries' position in the MWS and policy choices regarding the mining industry and the Chinese presence shaped SBRs in the respective mining industries of South Africa and Zimbabwe during their respective periods of economic transformation. The first point of distinction between these countries is their different political transition processes. Whilst black majority rule in Zimbabwe was established because of the guerrilla warfare during the 1970s, South Africa underwent a relatively democratic transition during the late 1980s and early 1990s. For instance, Andreasson (2007, p. 286) argued that "Zimbabwean state-business relations have . . . always been more complicated and volatile than in South Africa . . . This is partly due to a more 'militant' history of the liberation struggle in Zimbabwe." However, incidents like the Marikana massacre suggest that South Africa has also sometimes experienced volatile incidents like Zimbabwe under majority rule. Also, the more sophisticated political institutions and industrial progress in South Africa provided a solid base for a relatively democratic transition because of the country's semiperipheral position in the MWS. On the other hand, as a peripheral country, Zimbabwe had less-developed political institutions and industrial progress than South Africa had under the previous white minority rule. Moreover, the ANC was more liberal than ZANU during the early years of black majority rule and this eased the consolidation of SBRs in South Africa's mining industry.

As part of a semiperipheral country, the domestic and sophisticated mining industry in South Africa is an advantage when it comes to solving problems within the country's boundaries. On the other hand, Zimbabwe's mining industry was highly dependent on foreign mining investments from semiperipheral and core countries of the MWS such as China, South Africa, Canada, and the United Kingdom. Hence, the instability in the mining sector causes unreliable and weak linkages between the government and foreign investors in a peripheral country. For example, following the economic sanctions imposed by the core countries in the early 2000s against Zimbabwe, many mining companies had to pull their investments out of the country's mining industry. As a consequence, SBRs in Zimbabwe fractured during the 2000s due to sanctions. On the other hand, the ANC and Mandela worked jointly and constantly with white business leaders such as Harry Oppenheimer and with IFIs to guarantee the foreign and domestic affirmation of its market credentials during the early years of the postapartheid period (*see* Peet, 2002, p. 73 cited in Andreasson, 2007, p. 279). Although President Mbeki encountered tensions with the mining industry, relations were stable during the 2000s to some extent. The only visible fracturing of SBRs occurred under the Zuma presidency during the mid-2010s when South Africa applied to join the BRIC countries. However, following the election of Ramaphosa, SBRs were consolidated again with the amendment of the third Mining Charter in 2018.

Indeed, the reason behind that fracturing might be that peripheral countries have fewer alternatives than semiperipheral countries in terms of foreign investors. In other words, peripheral countries are more dependent than semiperipheral countries on foreign investors because of the lack of sophisticated domestic industries and of diversified commodity products. The domination of foreign investors in the Zimbabwean mining industry caused fluctuations in terms of SBRs whereas domestic or national actors were only active in the small-scale mining industry (Saunders & Caramento, 2017, p. 14). Nolke and Claar (2013, p. 45) argued that domestic capital dominance is better than international dominance:

> The South African economy is dominated by (various factions of) domestic capital, in close collaboration with (various factions of) the state. This is a major advantage vis-à-vis the dominance of international capital (e.g. subsidiaries of multinational companies, affiliates of global banks)

The presence of domestic mining capital in South Africa not only eased the periods of negotiation but also identified actors over time. On the one hand, the semiperipheral position of South Africa affects its domestic outlook in terms of economic activities and therefore affects the policy options. Therefore the more developed internal political and economic structure in

South Africa might ease consolidation of its SBRs over time. On the other hand, the peripheral position of Zimbabwe and its undeveloped domestic mining sector affect the country's options regarding foreign investors. These restricted options cause a volatile atmosphere in terms of the consolidation of SBRs over time.

The ANC developed policies for promoting black entrepreneurs, particularly in the mining industry, to compete with domestic, white-owned mining corporates. Nolke and Claar (2013, p. 45) pointed out a trajectory within the South African mining industry during the postapartheid era and stated that "close networks between white capital and public authorities have been complemented by close networks between black capital and public authorities." The existence of the powerful traditional domestic capital forced the ANC to empower a rival new domestic capital among the black majority of semiperipheral South Africa. This could be another example of how the majority rule has attempted to get involved in the TCC as not only the politicians but also the stakeholders (Sklair, 2002; 2001; 2000; 1997).

On the other hand, peripheral Zimbabwe has had fewer opportunities for domestic capital investments than semiperipheral South Africa and ZANU-PF politicians largely remained merely within the state fraction of TCC. The mining industry in Zimbabwe has been owned traditionally by foreign investors and there were not enough spaces for the black entrepreneurs in Zimbabwe following the end of white-minority rule. Indeed, domestic governments favour foreign investors, who "demand natural resources and interest in new markets," because of the existence of the weak state agencies in the most of sub-Saharan African countries (Andreasson, 2013). Therefore the ZANU-PF only supported party-linked black entrepreneurs as the government did not want to promote a black bourgeoisie beyond its control (Hammar, 2014). Andreasson (2007, p. 286) claimed that the ZANU-PF government was less successful than the ANC by "fostering a new 'indigenous' business elite" during the first twenty-five years of the postindependence period. In addition, Shumba (2018, p. 90) believed that "the economic indigenisation and empowerment programmes favoured only the politically connected elite and trusted foreign investors of Chinese and South African capital who did not pose a threat to the ruling elite's power aspirations." Andreasson (2007, p. 287) compared promoting black entrepreneurs in both countries:

> To the degree that new economic groups, with some independence from the state, have emerged following independence in Zimbabwe they have not enjoyed the same prolific rise to positions of influence, nor have they been as smoothly integrated with the old establishment and its international compatriots as have new economic groups in South Africa. Essentially Zimbabwe lacks the 'star cast' of new black businessmen, accepted as bona fide businessmen

> in international financial circles, that has developed in South Africa (such as Randall's 'activist capitalists').

The different approaches towards promoting black business as a competitor of domestic white business or foreign investors in semiperipheral South Africa and peripheral Zimbabwe demonstrate the priorities of majority governments during the economic transformation.

Although both Harare and Pretoria pursued liberalisation and indigenisation policies following the end of their respective white-minority rules in 1980 and 1994, the outcomes were different. State-market relations were shaped by two historical trajectories in southern Africa: neoliberalisation and the structural transformation of the region's postcolonial, postapartheid economies (Andreasson, 2007, pp. 275–76). On the one hand, South Africa pursued a homegrown liberalisation policy, namely GEAR, during the mid and late 1990s whereas Zimbabwe pursued a World Bank-supported liberalisation, namely ESAP, like other sub-Saharan African countries during the early 1990s. As I have suggested in this study, GEAR was a more detailed and sophisticated policy than ESAP. Consequently, Zimbabwe experienced an authoritarian regime and violent land redistribution after the failure of its neoliberalisation policies whilst South Africa underwent a less troubled decade during the 2000s in terms of SBRs.

Moreover, South Africa pursued a gradual indigenisation policy through three respective mining charters which required 15 per cent, 26 per cent and 30 per cent black ownership in the mining industry, despite some extreme initiatives under Zuma's presidency during the mid-2010s due to the suspended third Mining Charter draft. On the other hand, between the late 2000s and the late 2010s, Zimbabwe pursued an extreme indigenisation rule regarding its mining industry with a 51 per cent black ownership requirement. In fact, all three accepted mining charters in South Africa were negotiated by the government, business, and labour. In contrast, the Zimbabwean IEE was applied by the ZANU-PF government without any negotiations with other parties. For instance, Interviewee 4 (2017) compared the expropriation laws in South Africa and Zimbabwe and claimed that in South Africa the investors did not have to worry about it; but those investors did not have that same comfort in Zimbabwe through the constitution:

> So, one thing about South Africa is certain, that expropriation is not allowed in the constitution [Although it was on the agenda of South African politics recently]. It is protected by Section 26 . . . even if the ANC or the Economic Freedom Fighters (EFF) wanted to expropriate . . . they cannot. They are going to have to change the constitution. If any government wants to change the constitution, they need a two-thirds majority. Other parties will not be allowed to

> do it. Even a combination of the EFF and the ANC might not even achieve that. Those are probably the parties that will want it the most. In Zimbabwe, you do not have that comfort. I think one thing that keeps us together is the constitution. The constitution is in our judiciary, it is the best and the media of course [support it]. So, there is media freedom. If you are in Zimbabwe you go to trial, then to jail, and you get hanged whatever. That is the difference.

Indeed, the ANC government under Zuma has been accused of state capture because of his personal relations with the Gupta family during the mid-2010s. Both South Africa and Zimbabwe have been in a more optimistic position in terms of their SBRs since the end of the Zuma and Mugabe administrations.

The Chinese presence in the South African and Zimbabwean mining industries was a new phenomenon during the late 2000s. China's relationship with semiperipheral South Africa and peripheral Zimbabwe differed on some major points. For example, following the breakdown between Zimbabwe and Western countries, financial institutions and therefore mining corporates created an important opportunity for non-Western investors such as China and South Africa. In addition, the authoritarian rule in Zimbabwe eased the rapid inclusion of Chinese state-owned and private mining companies through the Look East policy. Hence, Chinese mining firms worked closely with the ZANU-PF government under the Mugabe presidency from the late 2000s to late 2010s. On the other hand, China's inclusion in South Africa's mining industry was relatively slow as the domestic mining industry of South Africa did not give many opportunities for Chinese state-owned and private investors even though they had already invested in some mining companies such as Sibanye-Stillwater and Wesizwe Platinum. China has therefore played a more significant role in Zimbabwe's mining industry than in South Africa's in terms of SBN. Chinese investments in Zimbabwe reconfigured the SBRs regarding the mining industry from the late 2000s to mid-2010s. Meanwhile, internal factors might be more decisive than external factors in South Africa in terms of SBRs during the postapartheid era. It should be noted that South Africa had more options than Zimbabwe to build economic and political ties with alternatives to the core and semiperipheral countries. Ultimately, it can be said that the Chinese presence or core demands might be less determinant than Pretoria's policy choices in South Africa.

CONCLUSION

In this chapter, I have analysed the final outcome of the research, namely the consolidation or fracturing of SBRs in peripheral and semiperipheral countries of the MWS which experienced postwhite minority regimes, namely

South Africa and Zimbabwe respectively. Shumba (2018, p. 3) conceptualised that a twenty-first century developing state's relationship with business contains embedded autonomy (*see* also Evans, 2012; Schneider, 1998; Haggard & Maxfield, 1997; Evans, 1989), which includes the fact that in the collaboration between the state and capital, the state "retains autonomy to formulate and pursue developmental goals." For instance, the early years of the postapartheid period and the latest government under the presidency of Ramaphosa are significant examples of the collaboration between the state and capital in a developing country. On the other hand, if a stable relationship between the government and the business community is under the threat of the domination and capturing of the state by the ruling elite, this might destabilise SBRs. So promoting the ZANU-PF-linked entrepreneurs, politicians, and military officers during the last two decades of the thirty-seven-year Mugabe administration was an example of the domination and capturing of the state by the ruling elite. The Zuma government also became an example of state capture through the ruling power of the ANC during the mid-2010s. The lack of collaboration between the government and business might cause the fracturing of SBRs in developing countries through the capture of the state by the ruling elite.

Thus, in this chapter, I have focused on understanding the respective SBRs of South Africa and Zimbabwe by comparing their mining industries under majority rule. I have illustrated the outcomes of the previous chapters of the research by discussing SBRs of South Africa and Zimbabwe in the subsequent sections.

NOTE

1. GFCF: Gross Fixed Capital Formation.

Conclusion

In this conclusion, I summarise the key discussion of this study and the findings of the research. I also show the limits of the study itself in terms of the selected cases and the selected research method and data collection techniques. I make some suggestions for future studies and practice and consider the wider implications of the consolidation and fracturing of SBRs beyond the SBN.

RESEARCH FINDINGS

The present study was designed to determine the effects of a country's position in the MWS, its policy choices on liberalisation and indigenisation, and China's economic and political presence in order to understand why SBRs tend to consolidate or fracture over time in posttransition communities such as South Africa and Zimbabwe. This study also has examined the nature of the mining industry during the economic transformation in both countries. The findings have shown the differences between the domestic and the foreign-dominated mining sectors of both countries. The complex relationship between the majority governments, white-owned and black empowered businesses, and China's state-owned and private mining firms has been explored in this study.

This study set out to develop the assumptions that in the implementation of economic liberalisation policies in peripheral and semiperipheral countries without China's significant economic and political presence during the neoliberal transformation of sub-Saharan Africa, SBRs are consolidated. On the one hand, South Africa's domestic mining industry was under pressure from isolationist policies during the last two decades of the apartheid regime and welcomed the first phase of the economic transformation, which was the country's turn to neoliberalism (Andreasson, 2003; 2001; Carmody, 2002; Bond 2000; Williams & Taylor, 2000; Fine & Rustomjee, 1996). On the other hand, as a peripheral country, Zimbabwe's domestic mining industry was not powerful or sophisticated even though its agricultural activities and manufacturing sector were controlled by the white-owned domestic business community (Simpson & Hawkins, 2018, p. 3; Bond & Manyanya, 2003, p. 17). The major investors in Zimbabwe's mining industry were Western core mining corporates during the first two decades of the majority rule and they welcomed the implementation of antistatist liberalisation policies (Mamdani, 2008; Raftopoulos & Phimister, 2004; Bond & Manyanya, 2003; Dashwood, 2000; Raftopoulos, 1996). As a result of their economic transformation policies, the relationship between the majority governments and the mining industries in South Africa and Zimbabwe resulted in consolidation but not with the same duration. I have argued that the SBRs in both peripheral and semiperipheral countries would be consolidated when they apply liberalisation policies and the Chinese presence is insignificant. The findings of the current study reveal that the third assumption on semiperipheral countries was more accurate than the first assumption on peripheral countries. In Zimbabwe, SBRs were consolidated but the mismanagement of the Mugabe administration, as well as the increasing domestic pressures from the indigenised Zimbabweans for land invasions during the late 1990s, changed this trajectory and SBRs were fractured during the early 2000s. On the other hand, the consolidated relationship between the ANC government and the South African mining sector might have sometimes deteriorated slightly but did not fracture until the radical approach of Zuma and an increasing Chinese economic and political presence in southern Africa from the early 2010s to the mid-2010s.

The findings suggest that semiperipheral countries are less fragile than peripheral countries in terms of being susceptible to pressures from external powers and to shifts in policy choices during periods of economic transformation (Wallerstein, 2011b). This fragile structure of peripheral countries makes their SBRs vulnerable to swift policy changes during economic transformation (Simpson & Hawkins, 2018). Although some have argued that Zimbabwe developed a supposedly homegrown neoliberal project of ESAP (Dashwood, 2000), it was an IMF and World Bank-sponsored policy as a result of the pressures applied by these IFIs and private finance during the early 1990s (Bond & Manyanya, 2003). In Zimbabwe, the ZANU-PF government did not introduce indigenisation policies until relations with Western investors fractured during the early 2000s (Zvoushe *et al.*, 2017; Andreasson, 2010a). On the other hand, the ANC government developed a homegrown neoliberal project in South Africa without pressure from the IFIs or private finance during the mid-1990s (Seekings & Nattrass, 2011; Bond, 2000). At the same time, initial BEE policies were adopted by the ANC government in 1998 and the second phase of economic transformation started without relations between the government and the domestic mining industry being fractured (Van Wyk, 2009; Handley, 2008; Andreasson, 2007; Carmody, 2002). These two policy choices were the beginning of the economic transformation in both countries.

Another example of the irresistible pressures of external powers was the Western economic sanctions imposed on Zimbabwe during the early 2000s after the implementation of the Fast-Track Land Reform in 2000 (Farley, 2008; Muzondidya, 2007; Moyo & Yeros, 2005; Hammar *et al.*, 2003). As a result of the implementation of the land invasion policy, the Western core investors cancelled their activities in Zimbabwe and SBRs were fractured (Raftapoulos & Phimister, 2004, pp. 368–69). Also, the implementation of the 51 per cent indigenised ownership rule in the early 2010s ended with the fracturing of the relationship between the ZANU-PF government and Chinese state-owned mining companies (Zimnisky, 2014; Bond & Sharife, 2012). Following this fracture, Mugabe lost his last saviour and faced a coup in 2017 after a thirty-seven-year-presidency. This was another example of the vulnerability of peripheral countries to external pressures. In semiperipheral countries, however—for instance, in South Africa—domestic pressures are more decisive than external pressures in terms of SBRs. The SBRs were fractured under the Zuma presidency during the mid-2010s fuelled by the state-capture inquiry and the president stepped down without any external pressure (Renwick, 2018; Basson & Toit, 2017; Myburgh, 2017). The domestic mining industry in South Africa was also decisive in determining the degree of racial transformation with several Mining Charters from 2004 onwards (Chamber of Mines of South Africa, 2018a).

The current study assumed that if a noncore country discards liberalisation policies and adopts indigenisation policies as the second phase of economic transformation (Bowman, 2019; Shumba, 2018; Zvoushe *et al.*, 2017; Leon, 2012; Magure, 2012; Cargill, 2010; Saunders, 2009; Tangri & Southall, 2008; Andreasson, 2011; 2007; 2006; Bond, 2000), the Chinese economic and political presence in that country might increase (Andreasson, 2015; Burgess & Beilstein, 2013; Shelton & Kabemba, 2012; Gonzalez-Vicente, 2011; Carmody & Owusu, 2007; Shaw *et al.*, 2007). It was expected that the implementation of an indigenisation policy without significant Chinese presence in a peripheral country would result in the fracturing of and in a semiperipheral country would result in the consolidation of SBRs. However, as a result of moving away from core countries and towards semiperipheral emerging powers such as China, the fractured SBRs in a peripheral country might be consolidated with the help of a significant Chinese presence (Spiegel, 2014; Maguwu, 2013; Towriss, 2013; Bond & Sharife, 2012). On the other hand, China's significant presence might fracture the consolidated SBRs as Chinese investments establish competition with the domestic semiperipheral mining industry (Shelton & Kabemba, 2012; Carmody & Taylor, 2010; Schoeman, 2007).

The findings suggest that China's significant political and economic presence in a peripheral country has more effect on SBRs than in a semiperipheral country. China's economic and political presence affected the mining industries of both South Africa and Zimbabwe over the last fifteen years (Andreasson, 2015; Burgess & Beilstein, 2013; Shelton & Kabemba, 2012; Gonzalez-Vicente, 2011; Carmody & Owusu, 2007; Shaw *et al.*, 2007). In Zimbabwe, the Chinese presence increased with the Look East policy and the ZANU-PF government replaced core Western technology and money with semiperipheral actors such as South Africa and China (Alao, 2014; Chun, 2014; Bourne, 2011; Youde, 2007). Chinese state-owned and private mining companies gathered a special agreement from the ZANU-PF government and were exempted from the indigenisation rule until the mid-2010s (Zimnisky, 2014; *Bulawayo24 News*, 2013; *Mining Technology*, 2013; Bond & Sharife, 2012). Nevertheless, when Mugabe drove foreign-owned mining firms out of the Marange diamond field in 2013, the relationship between Zimbabwe and China was fractured (*The Guardian*, 2016; Jamasmie, 2012b).

On the other hand, South Africa developed bilateral relations with China after the end of apartheid (Alden & Wu, 2016; Grimm *et al.*, 2014; Shelton & Kabemba, 2012; Le Pere & Shelton, 2007; Payne & Veney, 1998). South Africa's involvement in the BRIC alliance in 2011 developed the Sino-South African relationship in the realms of policy and economy (Bond, 2018; 2013a; Garcia, 2017a; Alden & Schoeman, 2015; 2013; Garcia & Bond, 2015; Taylor, 2014; Carmody, 2013; Vickers, 2012). Chinese state-owned and private mining companies invested in South Africa's mining industry with joint ventures with South African state-owned BEE companies, such as IDC (Harvey, 2014; Carmody, 2013; Jamasmie, 2012b). However, Chinese money and technology did not find the same space that they found in Zimbabwe as the domestic mining sector of South Africa was already sophisticated (Burgess & Beilstein, 2013; Carmody, 2011; Andreasson, 2007; Fine & Rustomjee, 1996). Despite this, increasing Chinese investments in South Africa's mining sector compensated for decreasing investments from other investors (Grimm *et al.*, 2014, pp. 20–21). Even so, the Chinese economic and political presence in South Africa was not as decisive as in Zimbabwe in terms of the fracturing or consolidation of SBRs over time. I argued that the SBRs in peripheral countries would consolidate and in semiperipheral countries would fracture when they apply indigenisation policies and the Chinese presence is significant. The findings show that the second assumption on peripheral countries was more accurate than the fourth assumption on semiperipheral countries.

I have argued that policy shifts in the periphery are more rapid and have more effect on the fluctuations of SBRs over time than in the semiperiphery. Zuma, for instance, said that although the political transition had been completed, a radical economic transformation was inevitable as economic freedom in South Africa remained largely elusive in 2017 (*HuffPost South Africa*, 2017). This was a significant shift from previous ANC governments because the policy of Pretoria had never been as extreme or radical as that (Van Wyk, 2009, pp. 45–47). It was a kind of aggressive reaction from Zuma and southern African politics had experienced this under Mugabe's presidency (Saunders & Caramento, 2017). Mugabe stated, for instance, that "the white man . . . is our real enemy . . . is not indigenous to Africa. Africa is for Africans. Zimbabwe is for Zimbabweans" in 2000 after the implementation of the Fast-Track Land Reform (Gaffey, 2017). Nevertheless, in both countries, probusiness presidents are now in office and it can be expected that the liberalisation policies might come back to some extent.

Although the current study is based on a small sample of participants, the findings suggest that Harare and Pretoria constantly changed their economic transformation policies under majority rule. However, South Africa's transformation has been more gradual than the rapid policy shifts of Zimbabwe (Warikandwa & Osode, 2017; Makwiramiti, 2011; Andreasson, 2011; 2010a). The results of this study indicate that the business sector does not support constant changes in policies, which create uncertainty in the market. The heavy requirements of the indigenisation policies and legislative requirements in regard to mining rights also create uncertainty for business (Doro & Kufakurinani, 2018; Leon, 2012). Insufficient resources for procurement, managerial positions (especially the lack of educated women) and indigenised investors have been another concern for business in both countries (Arya & Bassi, 2011; Cargill, 2010; Fauconnier & Mathur-Helm, 2008; Tangri & Southall, 2008; Ponte *et al.*, 2007; Southall, 2007). These findings contribute in several ways to our understanding of why SBRs either consolidate or fracture by looking at posttransition South Africa and Zimbabwe.

Notwithstanding the relatively limited sample, this study offers valuable insights into the mining sectors of South Africa and Zimbabwe with the help of the fieldwork which was conducted and the analysis of secondary data throughout the research process. The findings provide a deeper insight into SBRs regarding the mining sectors of developing countries from the MWS perspective. The study also contributes to our understanding of the effects of China's economic and political presence in South Africa and Zimbabwe, and to existing knowledge of the political economy of South Africa and Zimbabwe by providing a fuller analysis of SBRs under majority rule.

The findings are subject to at least three limitations. First, the general focus of this study was on developing countries with a history of the settler-colonial rule. This restricts the generalisation of the findings to the wider world. The results therefore might not be applicable to the highly industrialised core countries of the MWS. Although the generalizability of the findings is limited to a few countries, it might be productive to compare the indigenisation experiences of Malaysia and Nigeria with the experiences of South Africa and Zimbabwe using the MWS theory. This also applies more widely to countries experiencing transitions in the context of divided societies. Second, with regard to the research methods, some limitations need to be acknowledged. Additional data, such as surveys, questionnaires, or focus group discussions on the operations of the active mining firms in South Africa and Zimbabwe might have strengthened the findings of the current study (Yin, 2010; Coppedge, 1999). The scope of this study was limited in terms of time, money, and gaining access to the broad range of mining firms. Third, another limitation of this study is that it has only considered the context of the mining sector because the extractive industries have been significant for colonisers, governments, and investors, as well as the key constituents of the political economy of southern Africa (Andreasson, 2010b; Arrighi *et al.*, 2010; Farley, 2008; Amin *et al.*, 1987; Shaw, 1974; Denoon *et al.*, 1972; Bowman, 1968). Another study on other sectors, such as manufacturing or agriculture in South Africa and Zimbabwe, might uncover additional effects of a country's place in the MWS, its policy choices, and the economic and political presence of China on the fracturing or consolidation of SBRs.

RECOMMENDATIONS FOR PRACTICE AND FUTURE RESEARCH

The present study can serve a base for future studies and I suggest that it would be interesting to assess the effects of the wider implications of the fracturing or consolidation of SBRs in South Africa and Zimbabwe beyond the SBN. For instance, the higher inequality rates between black and white South Africans, which was one of the reasons behind the implementation of B-BBEE, in South Africa was an issue which the newly elected ANC government had to address (Arya & Bassi, 2011; Cargill, 2010; Tangri & Southall, 2008; Southall, 2007; Andreasson, 2006). After a fifteen-year period, the consolidation of SBRs did not produce development in South Africa in terms of "strong growth or poverty reduction" because of unimpressive economic growth performance, income poverty, and inequality from the mid-1990s to early 2010s (Seekings & Nattrass, 2011, p. 339). Higher rates of inequality among races in South Africa are therefore one of the most visible manifestations of the unachieved and unsuccessful economic transformation in

South Africa (Bond, 2018; Nolke & Claar, 2013, pp. 46–47; Seekings, 2013, pp. 316–17).

Skilled employment rates and unemployment rates within races are indicators of the inequality among the races. According to a Statistics South Africa (2016) report on employment, unemployment, skills, and economic growth in South Africa, 61 per cent of white South Africans were defined as skilled whereas only 18 per cent of the black workforce were defined as skilled. In other words, only 3 per cent of white South Africans were recorded as low skilled but 34 per cent of black South Africans were low skilled (Statistics South Africa, 2016). Moreover, black and coloured youth unemployment rates in South Africa were recorded at 39.4 per cent and 35.3 per cent respectively in 2014. On the other hand, the unemployment rate for white youth was only 9.6 per cent in 2014 (Statistics South Africa, 2016). The investigation of SBRs in South Africa has shown that economic transformation policies were not completed and did not provide the expected outcomes for redressing the disadvantages of the apartheid period. Despite this, the accomplished targets of the Mining Charter have been a success for economic transformation to some extent (Chamber of Mines of South Africa, 2018a). This might be a positive example for other countries which need to redress inherited colonial imbalances.

On the other hand, the economic transformation in Zimbabwe has had more destructive effects on domestic business and economic growth since the end of white-minority rule (Zvoushe *et al.*, 2017; Raftopoulos, 2013; Magure, 2013; 2012; Brett, 2005; Raftopoulos & Phimister, 2004; Hammar *et al.*, 2003; Bond & Manyanya, 2003). The policy choices under majority rule have been rapid and incautious (Shumba, 2018; Hammar *et al.*, 2003; Bond & Manyanya, 2003). The ZANU-PF government implemented several policies for attracting foreign investors to the country but none of them produced the expected outcomes (Magure 2013; 2012). The first phase of economic transformation started with the implementation of ESAP as an economic liberalisation policy for attracting foreign investors in 1991. The Look East policy was implemented for creating alternatives to Western investors in 2002. Although the ZANU-PF government implemented the IEE, Beijing, for example, was granted 'special mining rights' for Zimbabwe's uranium and diamond sectors (*Bulawayo24 News*, 2013; *Mining Technology*, 2013).

Despite these efforts, the ZANU-PF government failed to attract more investors to Zimbabwe for enhancing economic growth. Also, the government implemented the IEE policy for redressing the imbalances of the white-minority rule, but these policies were restricted to ZANU-PF-linked politicians, military officers, and individuals. The current study has also shown that the economic transformation policies in Zimbabwe did not produce the expected outcomes but fell behind the economic transformation in South Africa. In South Africa, at least some of the targets of the Mining Charter have already been achieved over the last fifteen years (Chamber of Mines of South Africa, 2018a) but in Zimbabwe, the new government removed the 51 per cent indigenised ownership rule and backed down from the IEE Act of 2007 (Dzirutwe, 2018a; Turak, 2018). The investigation of the fracturing or consolidation of SBRs might reveal the success of the new government's 'Zimbabwe is open for business' policy or in other words, the new attempt to liberalise the economy.

A further study could assess the long-term effects of the new governments in Harare and Pretoria on the consolidation or fracturing of SBRs in the mining industry. Further studies regarding the role of business associations, such as the Chamber of Mines of Zimbabwe and the Minerals Council South Africa, during the economic transformation period would be worthwhile (*see* Taylor, 2012; Te Velde, 2006). Further work would be useful to fully understand the implications of implementing indigenisation policies in other industries in addition to the mining sector. The effects of the implementation of the BEE policy on the wine industry, for example, have already been discussed (Herman, 2012; Moseley, 2008; Toit *et al.*, 2008; Janssens *et al.*, 2006; Williams, 2005).

Further research is required to better understand the complex linkages between the labour force, the government, and business in South Africa and Zimbabwe during the economic transformation since this current study did not include an analysis of the relationship in regard to labour (Horwitz & Jain, 2011; Mensah & Benedict, 2010; Iheduru, 2002). The largely black-dominated labour force, including trade unions, has an effect on domestic pressures for adopting empowerment policies on behalf of the historically disadvantaged populations (Bond & Mottiar, 2013; Seekings & Nattrass, 2011; Chinguno, 2010; Nattrass & Seekings, 2010; Van Wyk, 2009; Bond, 2001; Fine & Rustomjee, 1996). The collusive behaviour between the ANC government, the white-owned and the black empowered businesses during the wildcat strikes and Marikana massacre could be analysed from the perspective of the labour force.

The mantra of 'Zimbabwe is open for business' and the removal of the 51 per cent indigenised ownership rule except for the platinum and diamond industries have been signs of a rapid policy shift in Harare (Dzirutwe, 2018a; Marawanyika, 2018; Turak, 2018). This shift is not a new thing for a peripheral country such as Zimbabwe, as the former president Mugabe had attempted either the liberalisation or the indigenisation of the economy many times. On the other hand, in South Africa as a semiperipheral country, the policy shifts are less rapid than in peripheral Zimbabwe and it is expected that the new president Ramaphosa might not liberalise the economy too much like his counterpart Mnangagwa (Mattes, 2018; Monteiro & Gumede, 2018).

Nevertheless, Ramaphosa as a member of the business sector attempted to find solutions for the ongoing crises between the mining industry and the ANC and the new Mining Charter was redrafted in 2018 (Van Vuuren, 2018b).

The issue of extreme and gradual policy choice is an intriguing one which could be usefully explored in further studies. In this research, I have analysed the two phases of economic transformation but not considered their implementation methods. Another possible area of future research would be investigating why peripheral countries are more eager to adopt extreme policies than gradual policies. On the one hand, the modification of the suspended third Mining Charter was a sign of a gradual and cautious approach by Ramaphosa. On the other hand, the rapid liberalisation of the indigenised business in Zimbabwe was an expectation of a swift response from foreign investors by Mnangagwa.

I have explained that constant policy changes, heavy requirements of economic empowerment and indigenisation legislation, and radical transformation attempts by the two governments have created uncertainties in terms of SBRs in South Africa and Zimbabwe. This has sometimes resulted in the fracturing the relationship between the governments and businesses in both countries. Nevertheless, consulting business as part of the economic transformation and creating more dialogue between the governments and the businesses resulted in the consolidation of SBRs in both countries. More balanced and negotiated policies might therefore produce more-stable SBRs in both countries. Reducing the tensions between the governments and the businesses—or in other words, the consolidation of SBRs—might enhance the development in transition economies such as South Africa and Zimbabwe. Although in both countries political transition has been completed, the unfinished economic transformation still hinders the redressing of the legacies of white minority rule. In order to complete their economic transformation, both South Africa and Zimbabwe need to attract more investments, which might be either domestic or foreign, and to stabilise their business environments.

Appendix 1

LIST OF INTERVIEWEES

Pseudonym of interviewee	*Positions at time of interview, and relevant previous positions*	*Date and place*
Interviewee 1	Leadership position at *a gold mining corporation*	2 November 2017, Johannesburg
Interviewee 2	Leadership position at *a private communications consultancy*	3 November 2017, Johannesburg
Interviewee 3	Leadership position at a *private mineral consulting*	6 November 2017, Johannesburg
Interviewee 4	Leadership position at *a nonprecious mineral corporation*	10 November 2017, Johannesburg
Interviewee 5	Professor of political economy in South Africa	20 November 2017, Johannesburg
Interviewee 6	Mining lawyer and leadership position at *a global law firm*	20 July 2018, Online Conversation
Interviewee 7	Leadership position at *an international financial organization*	16 August 2018, Online Conversation

Appendix 2

INTERVIEW QUESTIONS

My interviews are able to explore the following topics:

1. Government policy choices relating to the mining industries
2. The Chinese economic presence in South Africa/Zimbabwe
3. SBRs in South Africa/Zimbabwe

I do not ask questions related to the MWS theory as the potential interviewees might not be able to have required background for the theory and its assumptions on South Africa and Zimbabwe. Interview Questions [to be modified depending on whether they are directed at government or business actors in South Africa and/or Zimbabwe]:

1. What do you think about shifts in the government's approach to the mining industry, from policies emphasising liberalisation (e.g., GEAR/ESAP) to policies emphasising indigenisation (e.g., Black Economic Empowerment/Indigenisation and Economic Empowerment)?
2. How have government policies relating to the mining industry affected relations between these industries and the government?
3. How have the government policy choices on mining industries (B-BBEE/IEE) of South Africa and Zimbabwe affected to find solutions for the posttransition divisions, for instance, inequality of opportunity and unemployment among different races? Do you think these kinds of policies have affected the relationship between government and mining corporates negatively?
4. Do you think that government policy intended to foster black empowerment/indigenisation in the mining industry creates opportunities or barriers for Chinese state-owned or private enterprises and other companies?

5. What is your view on the Chinese government and business involvement in the mining industry?
6. Do you think it is feasible to expect that Chinese capital and mining extractive technologies can substitute Western capital and technologies in South Africa and Zimbabwe?
7. What has been the overall impact of Chinese economic involvement and the policy choices relating to the mining industry on relations between the government and the business sector more generally in South Africa and Zimbabwe?

References

Acemoglu, D., Johnson, S. and Robinson, J.A. (2001) 'The colonial origins of comparative development: An empirical investigation,' *The American Economic Review*, American Economic Association, vol. 91, no. 5, pp. 1369–401.

Acemoglu, D. and Robinson, J.A. (2017) 'The economic impact of colonialism,' in Michalopoulos, S. and Papaioannou, E. (eds.), *The Long Economic and Political Shadow of History*, London, CEPR Press, vol. 1. A Global View, pp. 81–87.

AFP (2018) 'Mining industry eager for S. African leadership change,' *RFI*, 6 February. Available at: https://www.rfi.fr/en/contenu/20180206-mining-industry-eager-safrican-leadership-change (Accessed 24 May 2022).

African Development Bank Group (2018) *Statistics*, African Development Bank Group. Available at https://www.afdb.org/en/documents/document/southern-africa-economic-outlook-2018-100846 (Accessed 28 September 2018).

Agnew, J. (2010) 'Emerging China and critical geopolitics: Between world politics and Chinese particularity,' *Eurasian Geography and Economics*, vol. 51, no. 5, pp. 569–82.

Ahwireng-Obeng, F. and McGowan, P.J. (1998) 'Partner or hegemon? South Africa in Africa: Part One,' *Journal of Contemporary African Studies*, vol. 16, no. 1, pp. 5–38.

Akçalı, E. and Korkut, U. (2015) 'Urban transformation in Istanbul and Budapest: Neoliberal governmentality in the EU's semi-periphery and its limits,' *Political Geography*, vol. 46, pp. 76–88.

Akyüz, Y. (2012) *The Staggering Rise of the South?* Working Paper, Geneva, UNCTAD and South Centre.

Alao, A. (2014) 'China and Zimbabwe: The context and contents of a complex relationship,' *South African Institute of International Affairs (SAIIA)*, SAIIA Occasional Papers, no. 202.

Alden, C. (2013) 'China and Africa,' in *Routledge Handbook of African Politics*, London, Routledge, pp. 414–25.

Alden, C., Large, D. and Soares de Oliveira, R. (eds.) (2008) *China Returns to Africa: A Rising Power and a Continent Embrace*, New York, Columbia University Press.

Alden, C. and Schoeman, M. (2013) 'South Africa in the company of giants: The search for leadership in a transforming global order,' *International Affairs*, vol. 89, no. 1, pp. 111–29.

———. (2015) 'South Africa's symbolic hegemony in Africa,' *International Politics*, vol. 52, no. 2, pp. 239–54.

Alden, C. and Vieira, M.A. (2005) 'The new diplomacy of the South: South Africa, Brazil, India and trilateralism,' *Third World Quarterly*, vol. 26, no. 7, pp. 1077–95.

Alden, C. and Wu, Y.-S. (2016) 'South African foreign policy and China: Converging visions, competing interests, contested identities,' *Commonwealth & Comparative Politics*, vol. 54, no. 2, pp. 203–31.

Alexander, P. (2013) 'Marikana, turning point in South African history,' *Review of African Political Economy*, vol. 40, no. 138, pp. 605–19.

———. (2016) 'Marikana Commission of Inquiry: From narratives towards history,' *Journal of Southern African Studies*, vol. 42, no. 5, pp. 815–39.

Allen, K. (2015) 'Six collapsing commodities,' *Guardian*, 27 July. Available at https://www.theguardian.com/business/2015/jul/27/the-commodities-rout-why-prices-are-falling (Accessed 13 September 2019).

Ambe-Uva, T. (2017) 'Whither the state? Mining codes and mineral resource governance in Africa,' *Canadian Journal of African Studies / Revue canadienne des études africaines*.

Amin, S., Chitala, D. and Mandaza, I. (1987) *SADCC: Prospects for Disengagement and Development in Southern Africa*, United Nations University Press.

Amisi, B., Bond, P., Kamidza, R., Maguwu, F. and Peek, B. (2015) 'BRICS corporate snapshots during African extractivism,' in Garcia, A. and Bond, P. (eds.), *BRICS: An Anticapitalist Critique*, Chicago, Haymarket Books, pp. 97–116.

Ampiah, K. and Naidu, S. (2008) 'Introduction—Africa and China in the post-Cold War era,' in Ampiah, K. and Naidu, S. (eds.), *Crouching Tiger, Hidden Dragon? Africa and China*, Scottsville, South Africa, University of KwaZulu-Natal Press, pp. 3–19.

Amsden, A. H. (1992) *Asia's Next Giant: South Korea and Late Industrialization*, New York, Oxford University Press.

Andreasson, S. (2001) 'Divergent paths of development: The modern world-system and democratization in South Africa and Zambia,' *Journal of World-Systems Research*, vol. 7, no. 2, pp. 175–223.

———. (2003) "Economic reforms and 'virtual democracy' in South Africa and Zimbabwe: The incompatibility of liberalisation, inclusion and development," *Journal of Contemporary African Studies*, vol. 21, no. 3.

———. (2006) "The African national congress and its critics: 'predatory liberalism,' black empowerment and intra-alliance tensions in post-apartheid South Africa," *Democratization*, vol. 13, no. 2, pp. 303–22.

———. (2007) "The resilience of comprador capitalism: 'New' economic groups in southern Africa," in Jilberto, A.E.F. and Barbara, H. (eds.), *Big Business and Economic Development: Conglomerates and Economic Groups in Developing Countries and Transition Economies under Globalization*, London, Routledge, pp. 274–96.

———. (2010a) 'Confronting the settler legacy: Indigenisation and transformation in South Africa and Zimbabwe,' *Political Geography*, vol. 29, no. 8, pp. 424–33.

———. (2010b) *Africa's Development Impasse: Rethinking the Political Economy of Transformation*, London, Zed Books.

———. (2011) 'Africa's prospects and South Africa's leadership potential in the emerging markets century,' *Third World Quarterly*, vol. 32, no. 6, pp. 1165–81.

———. (2013) 'Elusive agency: Africa's persistently peripheral role in international relations,' in Brown, W. and Harman, S. (eds.), *African Agency in International Politics*, London; New York, Routledge, pp. 143–57.

———. (2015) 'Varieties of resource nationalism in sub-Saharan Africa's energy and minerals markets,' *The Extractive Industries and Society*, vol. 2, no. 2, pp. 310–19.

Armitage, J. (2013) 'Nelson Mandela is gone, but South Africa will thrive says Anglo.' Available at http://www.independent.co.uk/news/business/news/nelson-mandela-is-gone-but-south-africa-will-thrive-says-anglo-9001809.html (Accessed 12 September 2019).

Arrighi, G., Aschoff, N. and Scully, B. (2010) 'Accumulation by dispossession and its limits: The Southern Africa paradigm revisited,' *Studies in Comparative International Development*, vol. 45, no. 4, pp. 410–38.

Arrighi, G. and Drangel, J. (1986) 'The stratification of the world-economy: An exploration of the semiperipheral zone,' *Review (Fernand Braudel Center)*, vol. 10, no. 1, pp. 9–74.

Arrighi, G., Hopkins, T.K. and Wallerstein, I.M. (1989) *Antisystemic Movements*, London; New York, Verso Books.

Arya, B. and Bassi, B. (2011) 'Corporate social responsibility and broad-based black economic empowerment legislation in South Africa: Codes of good practice,' *Business & Society*, vol. 50, no. 4, pp. 674–95.

Austin, K.F., McKinney, L.A. and Thompson, G. (2012) 'Agricultural trade dependency and the threat of starvation,' *International Journal of Sociology*, vol. 42, no. 2, pp. 68–89.

Ayee, J. R. A. (2013) 'The developmental state experiment in Africa: The experiences of Ghana and South Africa,' *The Round Table*, Routledge, vol. 102, no. 3, pp. 259–80.

Babones, S. (2005) 'The country-level income structure of the world-economy,' *Journal of World-Systems Research*, vol. 11, no. 1, pp. 29–55.

———. (2015) 'What is world-systems analysis? Distinguishing theory from perspective,' *Thesis Eleven*, pp. 3–20.

Babones, S. and Chase-Dunn, C. (eds.) (2012) *Routledge Handbook of World-Systems Analysis*, Abingdon, Oxon; New York, Routledge.

Balaev, M. (2012) 'Economic-political interaction in the core/periphery hierarchy,' in Babones, S. and Chase-Dunn, C. (eds.), *Routledge Handbook of World-Systems Analysis*, Abingdon, Oxon; New York, Routledge, pp. 224–25.

Baran, P. A. (1968) *The Political Economy of Growth*, New York, monthly review press.

Barber, L. (2006) 'Nasty Nick,' *Observer*, 15 January. Available at https://www.theguardian.com/theobserver/2006/jan/15/features.magazine97 (Accessed 24 January 2023).

Barma, N., Ratner, E. and Weber, S. (2007) 'A world without the West,' *The National Interest*, no. 90, pp. 23–30.

Basson, A. and Toit, P.D. (2017) *Enemy of the People: How Jacob Zuma stole South Africa and How the People Fought Back*, Johannesburg, Jonathan Ball Publishers.

Baxter, R. (2009) *The global economic crisis and its impact on South Africa and the country's mining industry*, Challenges for Monetary Policy-makers in Emerging Markets, Conference Series 2008, Johannesburg, South African Reserve Bank.

BBC News (1998) 'Tiny in name, not in nature,' *BBC News*, 26 July. Available at http://news.bbc.co.uk/2/hi/uk_news/139614.stm (Accessed 24 January 2023).

———. (2002a) 'South African mines charter welcomed,' 10 October. Available at http://news.bbc.co.uk/1/hi/business/2316123.stm (Accessed 12 September 2019).

———. (2002b) "An 'emissary of Beelzebub'," *BBC News*, 22 July. Available at http://news.bbc.co.uk/2/hi/uk_news/england/2143994.stm (Accessed 24 January 2023).

———. (2004) 'SA mining giant rows with Mbeki,' 13 September. Available at http://news.bbc.co.uk/1/hi/world/africa/3651266.stm (Accessed 12 September 2019).

———. (2008) "UK tycoon 'arrested in Zimbabwe'," *BBC News*, 26 January. Available at http://news.bbc.co.uk/2/hi/uk_news/7210688.stm (Accessed 24 January 2023).

BBC World Service (2018) 'Is Zimbabwe open for business?' Business Daily—BBC World Service. Available at https://www.bbc.co.uk/programmes/w3cswgkx (Accessed 27 September 2018).

Beeson, M. and Li, F. (2015) 'What consensus? Geopolitics and policy paradigms in China and the United States,' *International Affairs*, vol. 91, no. 1, pp. 93–109.

Behuria, P., Buur, L. and Gray, H. (2017) 'Studying political settlements in Africa,' *African Affairs*, vol. 116, no. 464, pp. 508–25.

Bell, C. and Pospisil, J. (2017) 'Navigating inclusion in transitions from conflict: The formalised political unsettlement,' *Journal of International Development*, vol. 29, no. 5, pp. 576–93.

Bennett, A. (2004) 'Case study methods: Design, use, and comparative advantages,' in Sprinz, D.F. and Wolinsky-Nahmias, Y. (eds.), *Models, Numbers, and Cases: Methods for Studying International Relations*, Ann Arbor, University of Michigan Press, pp. 19–55.

Berger, G. (1999) 'Towards an analysis of the South African media and transformation, 1994–99,' *TRANSFORMATION*, vol. 38, pp. 82–116.

Berger, I. (2009) *South Africa in World History*, New York, Oxford University Press.

Bergesen, A. (1990) 'Turning world-system theory on its head,' *Theory, Culture & Society*, vol. 7, no. 2, pp. 67–81.

Bernstein, H. (1971) 'Modernization theory and the sociological study of development,' *The Journal of Development Studies*, vol. 7, no. 2, pp. 141–60.

Besada, H. and O'Bright, B. (2016) 'Maturing Sino-Africa relations,' *Third World Quarterly*.

Beveridge, F.C. (1991) 'Taking control of foreign investment: A case study of indigenisation in Nigeria,' *International & Comparative Law Quarterly*, vol. 40, no. 2, pp. 302–33.

Bieler, A. and Morton, A.D. (2004) 'A critical theory route to hegemony, world order and historical change: Neo-Gramscian perspectives in international relations,' *Capital & Class*, vol. 28, no. 1, pp. 85–113.

———. (2014) "Uneven and combined development and unequal exchange: The second wind of neoliberal 'free trade'?" *Globalizations*, vol. 11, no. 1, pp. 35–45.

Black, C.E. (1966) *The Dynamics of Modernization—A Study in Comparative History*, New York, Harper & Row.

Boatca, M. (2006) 'Semiperipheries in the world-system: Reflecting Eastern European and Latin American experiences,' *Journal of World-Systems Research*, vol. 12, no. 2, pp. 321–46.

Bond, P. (1999) 'Uneven development,' in O'Hara, P. (ed.), *The Encyclopaedia of Political Economy*, London; New York, Routledge, pp. 1198–200.

———. (2000) *Elite Transition: From Apartheid to Neoliberalism in South Africa*, London; Sterling, VA: Pietermaritzburg, South Africa, Pluto Press.

———. (2001) 'Radical rhetoric and the working class during Zimbabwean nationalism's dying days,' *Journal of World-Systems Research*, vol. 7, no. 1, pp. 52–89.

———. (2013a) "Sub-imperialism as lubricant of neoliberalism: South African 'deputy sheriff' duty within BRICS," *Third World Quarterly*, vol. 34, no. 2, pp. 251–70.

———. (2013b) 'Financialization, corporate power, and South African subimperialism,' in Cox, R.W. (ed.), *Corporate Power and Globalization in US Foreign Policy*, London; New York, Routledge, pp. 114–32.

———. (2014) 'Marikana's meaning for crisis management: An instance of South Africa's resource curse,' in Schuerkens, U. (ed.), *Global Management, Local Resistances: Theoretical Discussion and Empirical Case Studies*, New York, Routledge, pp. 192–219.

———. (2015) 'BRICS and the sub-imperial location,' in Garcia, A. and Bond, P. (eds.), *BRICS: An Anticapitalist Critique*, Chicago, Haymarket Books, pp. 15–26.

———. (2018) 'South African and global governance: Policy influence generated in conflict from above and below,' in Everatt, D. (ed.), *Governance in South Africa*, unpublished book, Johannesburg, Wits University Press.

Bond, P. and Manyanya, M. (2003) *Zimbabwe's Plunge: Exhausted Nationalism, Neoliberalism and the Search for Social Justice*, 2nd ed., Pietermaritzburg, University of KwaZulu-Natal Press.

Bond, P. and Mottiar, S. (2013) 'Movements, protests and a massacre in South Africa,' *Journal of Contemporary African Studies*, vol. 31, no. 2, pp. 283–302.

Bond, P. and Sharife, K. (2012) 'Zimbabwe's clogged political drain and open diamond pipe,' *Review of African Political Economy*, vol. 39, no. 132, pp. 351–65.

Bourne, R. (2011) *Catastrophe: What Went Wrong in Zimbabwe?* London, Zed Books.

Bowman, A. (2019) 'Black Economic Empowerment policy and state-business relations in South Africa: The case of mining,' *Review of African Political Economy*.

Bowman, L.W. (1968) 'The subordinate state system of Southern Africa,' *International Studies Quarterly*, vol. 12, no. 3, pp. 231–61.

Braudel, F. (1958) 'Histoire et Sciences sociales: La longue durée,' *Annales. Histoire, Sciences Sociales*, vol. 13, no. 4, pp. 725–753.

Brautigam, D. (2009) *The Dragon's Gift: The Real Story of China in Africa*, Oxford; New York, Oxford University Press.

Brautigam, D., Rakner, L. and Taylor, S. (2002) 'Business associations and growth coalitions in sub-Saharan Africa,' *The Journal of Modern African Studies*, vol. 40, no. 4, pp. 519–47.

Bremmer, I. and Johnston, R. (2009) 'The rise and fall of resource nationalism,' *Survival*, vol. 51, no. 2, pp. 149–58.

Breslin, S. (2013) 'China and the global order: Signalling threat or friendship?' *International Affairs*, vol. 89, no. 3, pp. 615–34.

Breslin, S. and Taylor, I. (2008) "Explaining the rise of 'human rights' in analyses of Sino-African relations," *Review of African Political Economy*, vol. 35, no. 115, pp. 59–71.

Brett, E.A. (1985) *The World Economy since the War: The Politics of Uneven Development*, Macmillan International Higher Education.

———. (2005) 'From corporatism to liberalization in Zimbabwe: Economic policy regimes and political crisis, 1980–97,' *International Political Science Review / Revue internationale de science politique*, vol. 26, no. 1, pp. 91–106.

Brownell, J. (2010) *The Collapse of Rhodesia: Population Demographics and the Politics of Race*, London; New York, Tauris Academic Studies.

Bulawayo24 News (2013) 'China set to start mining Zimbabwe's uranium deposits.' Available at https://bulawayo24.com/index-id-news-sc-national-byo-28427.html (Accessed 16 September 2019).

Burgess, S. and Beilstein, J. (2013) 'This means war? China's scramble for minerals and resource nationalism in Southern Africa,' *Contemporary Security Policy*, vol. 34, no. 1, pp. 120–43.

Burke, J. (2018) "How South Africa's 'Ramaphoria' turned into 'Ramageddon'," *Observer*, 9 September. Available at https://www.theguardian.com/world/2018/sep/09/cyril-ramaphosa-allies-long-walk-mandela-south-african-dream (Accessed 26 June 2019).

Burke, P. (2013) *The French Historical Revolution: Annales School 1929–1989*, New York, John Wiley & Sons.

Buzan, B. (2011) 'The inaugural Kenneth N. Waltz annual lecture a world order without superpowers: Decentred globalism,' *International Relations*, vol. 25, no. 1, pp. 3–25.

Calì, M., Mitra, S. and Purohit, P. (2011) 'Measuring state-business relations within developing countries: An application to Indian states,' *Journal of International Development*, vol. 23, no. 3, pp. 394–419.

Calì, M. and Sen, K. (2011) 'Do effective state business relations matter for economic growth? Evidence from Indian states,' *World Development*, vol. 39, no. 9, pp. 1542–57.

Callahan, W. A. (2008) 'Chinese visions of world order: Post-hegemonic or a new hegemony?' *International Studies Review*, vol. 10, no. 4, pp. 749–61.

Campbell, B. (2003) ‘Factoring in governance is not enough: Mining codes in Africa, policy reform and corporate responsibility,’ *Minerals & Energy—Raw Materials Report*, vol. 18, no. 3, pp. 2–13.

Campbell, H. (2008) ‘China in Africa: Challenging US global hegemony,’ *Third World Quarterly*, vol. 29, no. 1, pp. 89–105.

Cardoso, F.H. (1977) ‘The consumption of dependency theory in the United States,’ *Latin American Research Review*, vol. 12, no. 3, pp. 7–24.

———. (1979) *Dependency and Development in Latin America*, Berkeley, University of California Press.

Cargill, J. (2010) *Trick or Treat: Rethinking Black Economic Empowerment*, Auckland Park, South Africa, Jacana Media.

Carmody, P. (1998) ‘Constructing alternatives to structural adjustment in Africa,’ *Review of African Political Economy*, vol. 25, no. 75, pp. 25–46.

———. (2002) ‘Between globalisation and (post) apartheid: The political economy of restructuring in South Africa,’ *Journal of Southern African Studies*, vol. 28, no. 2, pp. 255–75.

———. (2011) *The New Scramble for Africa*, Cambridge, Polity Press.

———. (2012) ‘Another BRIC in the wall? South Africa’s developmental impact and contradictory rise in Africa and beyond,’ *The European Journal of Development Research*, vol. 24, no. 2, pp. 223–41.

———. (2013) *The Rise of the BRICS in Africa: The Geopolitics of South-South Relations*, London, Zed Books.

———. (2017) ‘The geopolitics and economics of BRICS’ resource and market access in Southern Africa: Aiding Development or Creating Dependency?’ *Journal of Southern African Studies*.

Carmody, P.R. and Owusu, F.Y. (2007) ‘Competing hegemons? Chinese versus American geo-economic strategies in Africa,’ *Political Geography*, vol. 26, no. 5, pp. 504–24.

Carmody, P. and Taylor, I. (2010) ‘Flexigemony and force in China’s resource diplomacy in Africa: Sudan and Zambia compared,’ *Geopolitics*, vol. 15, no. 3, pp. 496–515.

Carmody, P. and Taylor, S. (2003) ‘Industry and the urban sector in Zimbabwe’s political economy,’ *African Studies Quarterly*, vol. 7, no. 2, pp. 53–80.

Cawood, R.C. and Minnitt, F.T. (1998) ‘A historical perspective on the economics of the ownership of mineral rights ownership,’ *Journal of the Southern African Institute of Mining and Metallurgy*, vol. 98, no. 7, pp. 369–76.

Chabane, N., Roberts, S. and Goldstein, A. (2006) ‘The changing face and strategies of big business in South Africa: more than a decade of political democracy,’ *Industrial and Corporate Change*, vol. 15, no. 3, pp. 549–77.

Chamber of Mines of South Africa (2017) ‘Chamber of Mines notes outcome of 54th ANC national conference leadership election,’ media statement. Available at https://www.mineralscouncil.org.za/industry-news/media-releases/2017/send/29-2017/526-chamber-of-mines-notes-outcome-of-54th-anc-national-conference-leadership-election.

———. (2018a) *MINE SA 2017: Fact and Figures Pocketbook*, Johannesburg.

———. (2018b) 'Chamber welcomes election of President Cyril Ramaphosa,' media statement. Available at https://www.mineralscouncil.org.za/industry-news/media-releases/2018/send/35-2018/542-chamber-welcomes-election-of-president-cyril-ramaphosa.

———. (2018c) 'Chamber of Mines applauds President Ramaphosa's commitment to ethical leadership, and to putting South Africa first,' media statement. Available at https://www.mineralscouncil.org.za/industry-news/media-releases/2018/send/35-2018/543-chamber-of-mines-applauds-president-ramaphosa-s-commitment-to-ethical-leadership-and-to-putting-south-africa-first.

Chase-Dunn, C. and Grimes, P. (1995) 'World-systems analysis,' *Annual Review of Sociology*, vol. 21, no. 1, pp. 387–417.

Chase-Dunn, C. and Hall, T.D. (1997) *Rise and Demise: Comparing World Systems*, Boulder, CO, Westview Press.

Chase-Dunn, C., Kawano, Y. and Brewer, B.D. (2000) 'Trade globalization since 1795: Waves of integration in the world-system,' *American Sociological Review*, vol. 65, no. 1, pp. 77–95.

Chase-Dunn, C. and Rubinson, R. (1977) 'Toward a structural perspective on the world-system,' *Politics & Society*, vol. 7, no. 4, pp. 453–76.

Cheru, F. and Obi, C. (eds.) (2010) *The Rise of China and India in Africa: Challenges, Opportunities and Critical Interventions*, London; New York; Uppsala, Zed Books.

Chesseman, N. (2013) 'Nationalism, one-party states, and military rule,' in *Routledge Handbook of African Politics*, London, Routledge, pp. 11–23.

Chidaushe, M. (2007) 'China's grand re-entrance into Africa—Mirage or oasis?' in *African Perspectives on China in Africa*, Pambazuka Press, pp. 107–18.

Chin, G. and Helleiner, E. (2008) 'China as a creditor: A rising financial power?' *Journal of International Affairs*, vol. 62, no. 1, pp. 87–102.

Chinguno, C. (2010) 'Trade unions and workers in the periphery: Forging new forms of solidarity?' *J. Workplace Rights*, vol. 15, no. 3–4, pp. 367–86.

Christensen, B.V. (2010) *China in Africa: A Macroeconomic Perspective*, SSRN Scholarly Paper, Rochester, NY, Social Science Research Network.

Chun, Z. (2014) 'China-Zimbabwe Relations: A Model of China-Africa Relations?' *South African Institute of International Affairs (SAIIA)*, SAIIA Occasional Papers, no. 205.

Chutel, L. and Kopf, D. (2018) 'South Africa's troubled rand has turned the corner against the US dollar.' *QUARTZ*, 24 January. Available at https://qz.com/africa/1188420/south-african-rand-zar-is-up-versus-the-us-dollar-first-time-since-2015/ (Accessed 13 September 2019).

Clark, N.L. and Worger, W.H. (2011) *South Africa: The Rise and Fall of Apartheid*, 2nd ed., Harlow, UK; New York, Routledge.

Clelland, D.A. (2012) 'Surplus drain and dark value in the modern world-system,' in Babones, S. and Chase-Dunn, C. (eds.), *Routledge Handbook of World-Systems Analysis*, Abingdon, Oxon; New York, Routledge, pp. 197–205.

Cohen, M. and Mkokeli, S. (2017) 'Zuma's plan to retain sway in South Africa,' *Bloomberg.com*, 23 April. *Bloomberg.com*. Available at https://www.bloomberg

.com/news/articles/2017-04-23/zuma-s-plan-to-retain-sway-in-south-africa-keep-power-in-family (Accessed 7 September 2018).

Collier, D. (1993) 'The comparative method,' in Finifter, A.W. (ed.), *Political Science: The State of the Discipline II*, Washington D.C., APSA, pp. 105–19.

Coppedge, M. (1999) 'Thickening thin concepts and theories: Combining large N and small in comparative politics,' *Comparative Politics*, vol. 31, no. 4, pp. 465–76.

Dansereau, S. (2005) 'Win-win or new imperialism? Public-private partnerships in Africa mining,' *Review of African Political Economy*, vol. 32, no. 103, pp. 47–62.

Dansereau, S. and Zamponi, M. (2005) 'Zimbabwe—The Political Economy of Decline: Discussion Paper 27,' Uppsala, Nordic Africa Institute, p. 43.

Dashwood, H.S. (2000) *Zimbabwe: The Political Economy of Transformation*, Toronto; Buffalo; London, University of Toronto Press.

Davenport, T.R.H. and Saunders, C. (2000) *South Africa*, London, Palgrave Macmillan UK.

Davies, R. (2012) 'Afrikaner capital elites, neo-liberalism and economic transformation in post-apartheid South Africa,' *African Studies*, vol. 71, no. 3, pp. 391–407.

Demissie, F. (1998) 'In the shadow of the gold Mines: Migrancy and mine housing in South Africa,' *Housing Studies*, Routledge, vol. 13, no. 4, pp. 445–69.

Deng, Y. and Wang, F.-L. (2004) *China Rising: Power and Motivation in Chinese Foreign Policy*, Lanham, MD, Rowman & Littlefield Publishers.

Denoon, D., Nyeko, B. and Webster, J.B. (1972) *Southern Africa since 1800*, London, Longman.

Di John, J. and Putzel, J. (2009) *Political Settlements*, Issues Paper, Birmingham, GSDRC. Available at https://gsdrc.org/wp-content/uploads/2015/06/EIRS7.pdf.

Diao, X., Hazell, P. and Thurlow, J. (2010) 'The role of agriculture in African development,' *World Development*, The Future of Small Farms, vol. 38, no. 10, pp. 1375–83.

Doro, E. and Kufakurinani, U. (2018) 'Resource curse or governance deficit? The role of parliament in Uganda's oil and Zimbabwe's diamonds,' *Journal of Southern African Studies*, vol. 44, no. 1, pp. 43–57.

Dos Santos, T. (1970) 'The structure of dependence,' *The American Economic Review*, vol. 60, no. 2, pp. 231–36.

Dosse, F. (1994) *New History in France: The Triumph of the Annales*, Urbana, University of Illinois Press.

Downes, G. (2009) 'China and India—The new powerhouses of the semi-periphery?' in Worth, O. and Moore, P. (eds.), *Globalization and the 'New' Semi-Peripheries*, International Political Economy Series, London, Palgrave Macmillan UK, pp. 102–19.

DTI, (2003) *South Africa's Economic Transformation: A Strategy for Broad-Based Black Economic Empowerment*, Pretoria, Department of Trade & Industry (DTI).

Dzirutwe, M. (2018a) 'Zimbabwe changes law limiting majority ownership by the state to . . . ,' *Reuters*, 19 March. Available at https://www.reuters.com/article/us-zimbabwe-economy/zimbabwe-changes-empowerment-law-limiting-majority-ownership-to-diamond-and-platinum-idUSKBN1GV1ES (Accessed 10 September 2018).

———. (2018b) 'Zimbabwe hopes to transform mining sector with $4.2 bln platinum deal,' *Reuters*, 22 March. Available at https://www.reuters.com/article/zimbabwe-mining-idINL8N1R4258 (Accessed 25 May 2022).

Edwards, S. (1984) *The order of liberalization of the external sector in developing countries*, International Finance Section, Dept. of Economics, Princeton University.

Emmanuel, A. (1972) *Unequal exchange: A study of the imperialism of trade*, New York, Monthly Review Press.

England, A. (2011) 'CIC buys 25% stake in Shanduka,' *Financial Times*, 22 December. Available at https://www.ft.com/content/a8ded20a-2cc3-11e1-aaf5-00144feabdc0 (Accessed 21 November 2018).

Evans, M. (2007) *Karl Marx*, London, Routledge.

Evans, P. (1992) 'The state as problem and solution: Predation, embedded autonomy, and structural change,' in Haggard, S. and Kaufman, R.R. (eds.), *The Politics of Economic Adjustment: International Constraints, Distributive Conflicts, and the State*, Princeton, NJ, Princeton University Press, pp. 139–81.

———. (1997) 'State structures, government–business relations, and economic transformation,' in Maxfield, S. and Schneider, B.R. (eds.), *Business and the State in Developing Countries*, Cornell Studies in Political Economy, Ithaca, NY; London, Cornell University Press, pp. 63–87.

Evans, P.B. (2012) *Embedded Autonomy: States and Industrial Transformation*, Princeton, NJ, Princeton University Press.

Farley, J. (2008) *Southern Africa*, London, Routledge.

Fauconnier, A. and Mathur-Helm, B. (2008) 'Black Economic Empowerment in the South African mining industry: A case study of Exxaro Limited,' *South African Journal of Business Management*, vol. 39, no. 4, pp. 1–14.

Fine, B., Ashman, S. and Newman, S. (2011) 'The crisis in South Africa: Neoliberalism, financialization and uneven and combined development,' *Socialist Register*, vol. 47, pp. 174–95.

Fine, B. and Rustomjee, Z. (1996) *The Political Economy of South Africa: From Minerals-Energy Complex to Industrialisation*, Boulder, CO, Perseus.

Forster, R. (1978) 'Achievements of the Annales School,' *The Journal of Economic History*, vol. 38, no. 1, pp. 58–76.

Foster, J.B. and Holleman, H. (2014) 'The theory of unequal ecological exchange: A Marx-Odum dialectic,' *The Journal of Peasant Studies*, vol. 41, no. 2, pp. 199–233.

Fragile State Index (2016) *Fragile State Index, 2016*, The Fund for Peace.

France24 (2018) "China's Xi pledges $60 billion to Africa, says 'no strings attached'." Available at https://www.france24.com/en/20180903-china-xi-jinping-pledges-60-billion-africa-investment-summit-beijing (Accessed 25 May 2022).

Frank, A.G. (2009) *Capitalism and Underdevelopment in Latin America: Historical Studies of Chile and Brazil*, Revised ed., New York; London, Monthly Review Press.

Freedom House (2016) *Freedom in the World: Anxious Dictators, Wavering Democracies: Global Freedom under Pressure*, New York.

Freund, B. (2007) 'South Africa as developmental state?' *Africanus*, vol. 37, no. 2, pp. 191–97.

Frey, R.S., Gellert, P.K. and Dahms, H.F. (2018) *Ecologically Unequal Exchange: Environmental Injustice in Comparative and Historical Perspective*, Springer.

Friedberg, A.L. (2005) 'The future of U.S.-China relations: Is conflict inevitable?' *International Security*, vol. 30, no. 2, pp. 7–45.

Friedberg, A.L. (2018) 'Competing with China,' *Survival*, vol. 60, no. 3, pp. 7–64.

Gaffey, C. (2017) "'I have beaten Christ' and other memorable quotes from Zimbabwe's Robert Mugabe." Available at https://www.newsweek.com/best-quotes-robert-mugabe-zimbabwe-coup-713072 (Accessed 11 September 2018).

Gao, C. (2017) "China and Zimbabwe Are Still 'Good Brothers'." Available at https://thediplomat.com/2017/11/china-and-zimbabwe-are-still-good-brothers/ (Accessed 9 September 2019).

Gapper, J. (2016) 'A requiem for Anglo American, the octopus of South Africa.' Available at https://www.ft.com/content/5ba52f88-d55d-11e5-829b-8564e7528e54 (Accessed 12 September 2019).

Garcia, A. (2017a) 'BRICS investment agreements in Africa: more of the same?' *Studies in Political Economy*, vol. 98, no. 1, pp. 24–47.

———. (2017b) 'Nonwestern periphery and its paradoxes: Reflections for struggles in the 21st century,' *Journal of World-Systems Research*, vol. 23, no. 2, pp. 499–504.

Garcia, A. and Bond, P. (eds.) (2015) *BRICS: An Anticapitalist Critique*, Chicago, Haymarket Books.

Guardian (1990) 'Tiny Rowland: Portrait of the bastard as a rebel—Nick Davies.' Available at https://www.nickdavies.net/1990/08/01/tiny-rowland-portrait-of-the-bastard-as-a-rebel/ (Accessed 24 January 2023).

Gellert, P.K. (2012) 'Extraction and the world-system,' in Babones, S. and Chase-Dunn, C. (eds.), *Routledge Handbook of World-Systems Analysis*, Abingdon, Oxon; New York, Routledge, pp. 404–05.

Gerring, J. (2004) 'What is a case study and what is it good for?' *The American Political Science Review*, vol. 98, no. 2, pp. 341–54.

Gilpin, R. (1981) *War and Change in World Politics*, Cambridge; New York, Cambridge University Press.

———. (1987) *The Political Economy of International Relations*, Princeton, NJ, Princeton University Press.

Global Witness (2017) *An Inside Job Zimbabwe: The State, the Security Forces, and a Decade of Disappearing Diamonds*, London, Global Witness.

Goko, C. (2019) 'How Ramaphoria is taking hold of the markets.' Available at https://www.fin24.com/Markets/how-ramaphoria-is-taking-hold-of-the-markets-20190510 (Accessed 26 June 2019).

Goldfrank, W.L. (2000) 'Paradigm regained? The rules of Wallerstein's world-system method,' *Journal of World-Systems Research*, vol. 6, no. 2, pp. 150–95.

———. (2012) 'Wallerstein's world-system: Roots and contributions,' in Babones, S. and Chase-Dunn, C. (eds.), *Routledge Handbook of World-Systems Analysis*, Abingdon, Oxon; New York, Routledge, pp. 97–103.

Golley, J. and Song, L. (2011) *Rising China: Global Challenges and Opportunities*, Canberra; Beijing, Anu E Press.

Golooba-Mutebi, F. and Hickey, S. (2013) *Investigating the Links between Political Settlements and Inclusive Development in Uganda: Towards a Research Agenda*, Working Paper, Manchester, ESID. Available at https://www.effective-states.org/working-paper-20/?cn-reloaded=1 (Accessed 24 January 2023).

Golub, P.S. (2013) "From the New International Economic Order to the G20: How the 'Global South' is restructuring world capitalism from within," *Third World Quarterly*, vol. 34, no. 6, pp. 1000–15.

Gonzalez-Vicente, R. (2011) 'China's engagement in South America and Africa's extractive sectors: New perspectives for resource curse theories,' *The Pacific Review*, vol. 24, no. 1, pp. 65–87.

Good, K. (1976) 'Settler colonialism: Economic development and class formation,' *The Journal of Modern African Studies*, vol. 14, no. 4, pp. 597–620.

Goodfellow, T. (2014) 'Rwanda's political settlement and the urban transition: Expropriation, construction and taxation in Kigali,' *Journal of Eastern African Studies*, Routledge, vol. 8, no. 2, pp. 311–29.

Goodman, D. and Segal, G. (2013) *China Rising: Nationalism and Interdependence*, New York, Routledge.

Gore, C. (2000) 'The rise and fall of the Washington consensus as a paradigm for developing countries,' *World Development*, vol. 28, no. 5, pp. 789–804.

Gowan, P. (2004) 'Contemporary intra-core relations and world systems theory,' *Journal of World-Systems Research*, vol. 10, no. 2, pp. 471–500.

Gray, H. and Whitfield, L. (2014) *Reframing African Political Economy: Clientelism, Rents and Accumulation as Drivers of Capitalist Transformation*, Working Paper, Working Paper Series. Available at https://www.econstor.eu/handle/10419/224793 (Accessed 24 January 2023).

Grimm, S., Kim, Y. and Anthony, R. (2014) *South African Relations with China and Taiwan: Economic Realism and the 'One-China' Doctrine*, Stellenbosch, Centre for Chinese Studies, Stellenbosch University.

Groenewald, Y. (2018) "Chamber of Mines welcomes new Minister Mantashe as 'man of integrity'." Available at https://www.fin24.com/Companies/Mining/chamber-of-mines-welcomes-new-minister-mantashe-as-man-of-integrity-20180227 (Accessed 26 June 2019).

Gumede, W. (2011) *Delivering a Democratic Developmental State in South Africa*, Policy Brief, Midrand, Development Bank of South Africa. Available at https://www.dbsa.org/sites/default/files/media/documents/2021-02/Policy%20Brief%20No.%201%20Delivering%20a%20democratic%20developmental%20state%20in%20South%20Africa_0.pdf (Accessed 23 January 2023).

———. (2012) 'South Africa: Marikana is a turning point | William Gumede,' *Guardian*, 29 August. Available at https://www.theguardian.com/commentisfree/2012/aug/29/marikana-turning-point-south-africa (Accessed 13 September 2019).

Haggard, S. and Kaufman, R.R. (eds.) (1992) *The Politics of Economic Adjustment: International Constraints, Distributive Conflicts, and the State*, Princeton, NJ, Princeton University Press.

———. (1997) 'The political economy of democratic transitions,' *Comparative Politics*, vol. 29, no. 3, pp. 263–83.

Haggard, S., Maxfield, S. and Schneider, B.R. (1997) 'Theories of business and business-state relations,' in Maxfield, S. and Schneider, B.R. (eds.), *Business and the State in Developing Countries*, Cornell Studies in Political Economy, Ithaca, NY; London, Cornell University Press, pp. 36–60.

Halper, S. (2010) *The Beijing Consensus: How China's Authoritarian Model Will Dominate the Twenty-First Century*, ReadHowYouWant.com.

Hammar, A. (2014) 'The paradoxes of class: Crisis, displacement and repositioning in post-2000 Zimbabwe,' in Hammar, A. (ed.), *Displacement Economies in Africa: Paradoxes of Crisis and Creativity*, London; New York, Zed Books, pp. 79–106.

Hammar, A. and Raftopoulos, B. (2003) 'Zimbabwe's Unfinished Business: Rethinking Land, State and Nation,' in Hammar, A., Raftopoulos, B., and Jensen, S. (eds.), *Zimbabwe's Unfinished Business*, Harare, Weaver Press, pp. 1–47.

Hammar, A., Raftopoulos, B. and Jensen, S. (eds.) (2003) *Zimbabwe's Unfinished Business: Rethinking Land, State and Nation in the Context of Crisis*, Harare, Weaver Press.

Handley, A. (2008) *Business and the State in Africa: Economic Policy-Making in the Neo-Liberal Era*, Cambridge; New York, Cambridge University Press.

Hansell, S. (1996) 'Clive S. Menell, 65, mining executive in South Africa,' *New York Times*, 25 July. Available at https://www.nytimes.com/1996/07/25/world/clive-s-menell-65-mining-executive-in-south-africa.html (Accessed 13 September 2019).

Harvey, R. (2014) *Nationalism with Chinese Characteristics: How Does It Affect the Competitiveness of South Africa's Mining Industry?* Governance of Africa's Resources Programme, Policy Briefing, Johannesburg, The South African Institute of International Affairs.

Hawkins, T. (2004) 'Crisis in Zimbabwe,' *Whitehall Papers*, vol. 62, no. 1, pp. 31–43.

Hawthorn, G. (1993) 'Sub-Saharan Africa,' in Held, D. (ed.), *Prospects for Democracy: North, South, East, West*, Cambridge, Polity Press, pp. 330–54.

Hendrix, C.S. and Noland, M. (2014) *Confronting the Curse: The Economics and Geopolitics of Natural Resource Governance*, Peterson Institute for International Economics.

Hentz, J.J. (2005) *South Africa and the Logic of Regional Cooperation*, Bloomington, Indiana University Press.

Herbst, J. (1990) 'The structural adjustment of politics in Africa,' *World Development*, vol. 18, no. 7, pp. 949–58.

———. (2014) *States and Power in Africa: Comparative Lessons in Authority and Control*, 2nd ed., Princeton, NJ, Princeton University Press.

Herman, A. (2012) 'Tactical ethics: How the discourses of Fairtrade and Black Economic Empowerment change and interact in wine networks from South Africa to the UK,' *Geoforum*, Themed issue: Spatialities of Ageing, vol. 43, no. 6, pp. 1121–30.

Hilson, A., Hilson, G. and Dauda, S. (2019) 'Corporate social responsibility at African mines: Linking the past to the present,' *Journal of Environmental Management*, vol. 241, pp. 340–52.

Hlongwane, S. (2012) 'Cyril Ramaphosa's Marikana email batters ANC heavy-weight's reputation,' *Guardian*, 24 October. Available at https://www.theguardian

.com/world/2012/oct/24/cyril-ramaphosa-lonmin-email-reputation (Accessed 13 September 2019).

Hopkins, T.K. (1982) 'The study of the capitalist world-economy: Some introductory considerations,' in Hopkins, T.K. and Wallerstein, I. (eds.), *World-Systems Analysis: Theory and Methodology*, Beverly Hills, CA, Sage Publications, pp. 9–38.

Hopkins, T.K. and Wallerstein, I. (eds.) (1980) *Processes of the World-System*, Political economy of the world-system annuals, Beverly Hills, CA, Sage Publications.

———. (1982) *World-Systems Analysis: Theory and Methodology*, Beverly Hills, CA, SAGE Publications.

Hopkins, T.K., Wallerstein, I. and Associates (1982) 'Patterns of development of the modern world-system,' in Hopkins, T.K. and Wallerstein, I. (eds.), *World-Systems Analysis: Theory and Methodology*, Beverly Hills, CA, Sage Publications, pp. 41–82.

Hornborg, A. (2009) 'Zero-sum world: Challenges in conceptualizing environmental load displacement and ecologically unequal exchange in the world-system,' *International Journal of Comparative Sociology*, vol. 50, no. 3–4, pp. 237–62.

———. (2012) *Global Ecology and Unequal Exchange: Fetishism in a Zero-Sum World*, New York, Routledge.

Hornborg, A., McNeill, J.R. and Alier, J.M. (2007) *Rethinking Environmental History: World-system History and Global Environmental Change*, Lanham, MD, Rowman Altamira.

Horwitz, F.M. and Jain, H. (2011) 'An assessment of employment equity and broad based Black Economic Empowerment developments in South Africa,' *Equality, Diversity and Inclusion: An International Journal*, vol. 30, no. 4.

Howard, M.C. and King, J.E. (1989) *A History of Marxian Economics, Vol. I: 1883–1929*, Princeton, NJ, Princeton University Press.

HuffPost South Africa (2017) *Full Text: President Jacob Zuma's Freedom Day Speech*. Available at https://www.huffingtonpost.co.uk/2017/04/27/full-text-president-jacob-zumas-freedom-day-speech_a_22058132/ (Accessed 25 May 2022).

Hume, N. (2018) 'Rio Tinto warns of threat from rising costs and resource nationalism.' Available at https://www.ft.com/content/8991ce20-5845-11e8-bdb7-f6677d2e1ce8 (Accessed 13 September 2019).

Hung, H.-F. (2017) 'Hegemonic crisis, comparative world-systems, and the future of Pax Americana,' *Journal of World-Systems Research*, vol. 23, no. 2, pp. 637–48.

Huppert, G. (1982) 'Lucien Febvre and Marc Bloch: The creation of the annales,' *The French Review*, vol. 55, no. 4, pp. 510–13.

Iheduru, O.C. (2002) 'Social concertation, labour unions and the creation of a black bourgeoisie in South Africa,' *Commonwealth & Comparative Politics*, vol. 40, no. 2, pp. 47–85.

Ikenberry, G.J. (2011) 'The future of the liberal world order: Internationalism after America,' *Foreign Affairs*, vol. 90, no. 3, pp. 56–68.

IMF (1980) *International Monetary Fund Annual Report 1980*, Washington D.C., IMF.

Industrial Development Corporation (2019) *2019 Integrated Report*, Pretoria, Industrial Development Corporation. Available at https://www.idc.co.za/financial-results/2019-annual-report/.

Intellidex (2015) *The Value of BEE Deals*, Sandton.

International Trade Centre (2016) *Annual Report 2015*.

IOL News (1999) 'Mbeki hails mining law as a pacemaker,' *IOL News*. Available at https://www.iol.co.za/business-report/economy/mbeki-hails-mining-law-as-a-pacemaker-780104 (Accessed 12 September 2019).

———. (2016) 'Zimbabwe shuts 7 diamond companies,' *IOL News*. Available at https://www.iol.co.za/news/africa/zimbabwe-shuts-7-diamond-companies-1988239 (Accessed 20 September 2019).

IRIN News (2005) "Zimbabwe: 'Look East' policy staves off collapse with grants and deals—Zimbabwe." Available at https://reliefweb.int/report/zimbabwe/zimbabwe-look-east-policy-staves-collapse-grants-and-deals (Accessed 16 September 2019).

Islamogu-Inan, H. (2004) *The Ottoman Empire and the World-Economy*, Cambridge, Cambridge University Press.

Jackson, N., Want, M.V.D. and Malesa, G. (2013) 'Resource nationalism: Africa,' *Without Prejudice*, vol. 13, no. 4, pp. 20–22.

Jackson, R.H. and Rosberg, C.G. (1982) 'Why Africa's weak states persist: The empirical and the juridical in statehood,' *World Politics*, vol. 35, no. 1, pp. 1–24.

Jamasmie, C. (2012a) 'Rio Tinto and Anglo sell Palabora to Chinese group,' *MINING.COM*. Available at https://www.mining.com/rio-tinto-and-anglo-sell-palabora-to-chinese-group-91994/ (Accessed 10 September 2019).

———. (2012b) "Zimbabwe 'owns' majority of all foreign mining companies," *MINING.COM*. Available at https://www.mining.com/zimbabwe-owns-majority-of-all-foreign-mining-companies/ (Accessed 13 September 2019).

———. (2016) 'Zimbabwe orders diamond miners to halt operations,' *MINING.COM*. Available at https://www.mining.com/zimbabwe-orders-diamond-miners-to-halt-operations/ (Accessed 13 September 2019).

Jansen, J.D. (1990) 'Curriculum policy as compensatory legitimation? A view from the periphery,' *Oxford Review of Education*, vol. 16, no. 1, pp. 29–38.

Janssens, W., Sefoko, N., Rooyen, J. van and Bostyn, F. (2006) 'Measuring perceived BEE in the South African wine industry,' *Agrekon*, vol. 45, no. 4, pp. 381–405.

Jaquette, J.S. (1982) 'Women and modernization theory: A decade of feminist criticism,' *World Politics*, vol. 34, no. 2, pp. 267–84.

JCI Limited (2019) *Corporate Profile*. Available at https://jcimining.co.za/about-us/.

Jenkins, C. (1997) 'The politics of economic policy-making in Zimbabwe,' *The Journal of Modern African Studies*, vol. 35, no. 4, pp. 575–602.

Jilberto, A.E.F. and Hogenboom, B. (eds.) (2007) *Big Business and Economic Development: Conglomerates and Economic Groups in Developing Countries and Transition Economies Under Globalisation*, London; New York, Routledge.

Jordaan, E. (2012) 'South Africa, multilateralism and the global politics of development,' *The European Journal of Development Research*, vol. 24, no. 2, pp. 283–99.

Jorgenson, A.K. (2010) 'World-economic integration, supply depots, and environmental degradation: A study of ecologically unequal exchange, foreign investment dependence, and deforestation in less developed countries,' *Critical Sociology*, vol. 36, no. 3, pp. 453–77.

Kadzere, M. (2018) 'Zim, China seal $1bn power deal: Investment to create 25 000 jobs: New ferrochrome smelters to be set up.' Available at https://www.herald.co.zw/zim-china-seal-1bn-power-deal%E2%80%A2-investment-to-create-25-000-jobs-%E2%80%A2-new-ferrochrome-smelters-to-be-set-up/ (Accessed 9 September 2019).

Kanyenze, G., Jauch, H., Kanengoni, A.D., Madzwamuse, M. and Muchena, D. (eds.) (2016) *Towards Democratic Development States in Southern Africa*, Harare, Weaver Press.

Karombo, T. (2018) 'Zimbabwe's new diamond policy allows more than 49% foreign ownership,' *IOL Business Report*. Available at https://www.iol.co.za/business-report/international/zimbabwes-new-diamond-policy-allows-more-than-49-foreign-ownership-18382315 (Accessed 20 September 2019).

Kasaba, R. (1988) *The Ottoman Empire and the World Economy: The Nineteenth Century*, Albany, NY, SUNY Press.

Kay, G. (1975) *Development and Underdevelopment: A Marxist Analysis*, 2nd ed., London, Macmillan.

Kay, W. (1995) 'He just could not go quietly,' *Independent*, 3 March. Available at https://www.independent.co.uk/voices/he-just-could-not-go-quietly-1609793.html (Accessed 24 January 2023).

Kelsall, T. (2018) *Thinking and Working with Political Settlements: The Case of Tanzania*, Working Paper, London, ODI. Available at https://odi.org/en/publications/thinking-and-working-with-political-settlements-the-case-of-tanzania / (Accessed 24 January 2023).

Kelsall, T. and vom Hau, M. (2020) *Beyond Institutions: Political Settlements Analysis and Development*, Working Paper, Barcelona, IBEI. Available at https://www.ibei.org/en/beyond-institutions-political-settlements-analysis-and-development_208952 (Accessed 24 January 2023).

Keohane, R. O. (2005) *After Hegemony: Cooperation and Discord in the World Political Economy*, Princeton, NJ, Princeton University Press.

Kerr, S. and England, A. (2013) 'Mugabe in the money with gems lifeline.' Available at https://www.ft.com/content/c9a33556-9213-11e2-851f-00144feabdc0 (Accessed 20 September 2019).

Khan, M.H. (2010) *Political Settlements and the Governance of Growth-Enhancing Institutions*, London, SOAS. Available at https://eprints.soas.ac.uk/id/eprint/9968 (Accessed 24 January 2023).

———. (2017) 'Political settlements and the analysis of institutions,' *African Affairs*, vol. 117, no. 469, pp. 636–55.

Kollmeyer, C. (2009) 'Consequences of North-South trade for affluent countries: A new application of unequal exchange theory,' *Review of International Political Economy*, vol. 16, no. 5, pp. 803–26.

Kragelund, P. (2012) "Bringing 'indigenous' ownership back: Chinese presence and the Citizen Economic Empowerment Commission in Zambia," *The Journal of Modern African Studies*, vol. 50, no. 3, pp. 447–66.

Kuzawa, K. (2015) 'Indigenisation changes fuel rent-seeking,' *Zimbabwe Independent*. Available at https://www.theindependent.co.zw/2015/03/29/indigenisation-changes-fuel-rent-seeking/ (Accessed 10 September 2018).

Le Pere, G. and Shelton, G. (2007) *China, Africa and South Africa: South-South Co-operation in a Global Era*, Institute for Global Dialogue.

Lee, M.C. (2006) 'The 21st century scramble for Africa,' *Journal of Contemporary African Studies*, vol. 24, no. 3, pp. 303–30.

Lee, R.E. (ed.) (2013) *The Longue Duree and World-Systems Analysis*, Albany, NY, SUNY Press.

Lenin, V.I. (1963) 'Imperialism, the highest stage of capitalism,' in *Lenin's Selected Works*, Moscow, Progress Publishers, pp. 667–766.

Leon, P. (2012) 'Whither the South African mining industry?' *Journal of Energy & Natural Resources Law*, vol. 30, no. 1, pp. 5–27.

Li, M. (2005) 'The rise of China and the demise of the capitalist world-economy: Exploring historical possibilities in the 21st century,' *Science & Society*, vol. 69, no. 3, pp. 420–48.

———. (2008) *The Rise of China and the Demise of the Capitalist World Economy*, New York, NYU Press.

Lipton, M. (1986) *Capitalism and Apartheid: South Africa, 1910–1986*, Cape Town, David Philip Publishers.

Lodge, T. (2009) 'The South African developmental state?' *Journal of Southern African Studies*, Routledge, vol. 35, no. 1, pp. 253–61.

Louw, P.E. (2004) *The Rise, Fall, and Legacy of Apartheid*, Westport, CT, Greenwood Publishing Group.

Love, J. (2005) *Southern Africa in World Politics: Local Aspirations and Global Entanglements*, Boulder, CO, Westview Press.

Lucas, J. (1997) 'The politics of business associations in the developing world,' *The Journal of Developing Areas*, vol. 32, no. 1, pp. 71–96.

Luce, M. (2015) 'Sub-imperialism, the highest stage of dependent capitalism,' in Garcia, A. and Bond, P. (eds.), *BRICS: An Anticapitalist Critique*, Chicago, Haymarket Books, pp. 27–44.

Macharia, J. and Cropley, E. (2018) 'Zuma quits, ending scandal-plagued term as South African president,' *Reuters*, 15 February. Available at https://www.reuters.com/article/us-safrica-politics-idUSKCN1FY0HM (Accessed 25 May 2022).

MacLean, S.J. (1997) 'The Effects of Structural Adjustment on Civil Society in Zimbabwe: Implications for Canadian Aid Policy,' *Canadian Journal of Development Studies / Revue canadienne d'études du développement*, vol. 18, no. 3, pp. 463–84.

———. (2002) 'Mugabe at war: The political economy of conflict in Zimbabwe,' *Third World Quarterly*, vol. 23, no. 3, pp. 513–28.

Maclean, S.J., Quadir, F. and Shaw, T.M. (1997) 'Structural adjustment and the response of civil society in Bangladesh and Zimbabwe: A comparative analysis,' *New Political Economy*, vol. 2, no. 1, pp. 149–64.

Macupe, B. (2017) 'Zwane: ANC delegates want 50% black owners in mining industry.' Available at https://mg.co.za/article/2017-07-04-zwane-anc-delegates-displeased-with-mining-charters-black-ownership-targets/ (Accessed 13 September 2019).

Magure, B. (2012) 'Foreign investment, black economic empowerment and militarised patronage politics in Zimbabwe,' *Journal of Contemporary African Studies*, vol. 30, no. 1, pp. 67–82.

———. (2013) 'Foreign investment, black economic empowerment and militarised patronage politics in Zimbabwe,' in Moore, D., Kriger, N., and Raftopoulos, B. (eds.), *'Progress' in Zimbabwe? The Past and Present of a Concept and a Country*, New York, Routledge, pp. 67–82.

Maguwu, F. (2013) 'Marange diamonds and Zimbabwe's political transition,' *Journal of Peacebuilding & Development*, vol. 8, no. 1, pp. 74–78.

Makambe, E.P. (1994) 'The exploitation and abuse of African labour in the colonial economy of Zimbabwe, 1903–1930: A lopsided struggle between labour and capital,' *Transafrican Journal of History*, Gideon Were Publications, vol. 23, pp. 81–104.

Makochekanwa, A., Hurungo, J.T. and Kambarami, P. (2012) *Zimbabwe's Experience with Trade Liberalization*, research paper, Nairobi, African Economic Research Consortium.

Makwiramiti, A.M. (2011) 'In the name of economic empowerment: A case for South Africa and Zimbabwe,' *Polity.org.za*.

Mamdani, M. (2008) 'Lessons of Zimbabwe,' *London Review of Books*, 4 December.

Mandel, E. (1969) *Marx Economic Theory*, New York, NYU Press.

Mangongera, C. (2014) 'A new twilight in Zimbabwe: The military vs. democracy,' *Journal of Democracy*, vol. 25, no. 2, pp. 67–76.

Maponga, O. and Maxwell, P. (2001) 'The fall and rise of African mining,' *Minerals & Energy—Raw Materials Report*, vol. 16, no. 3, pp. 9–27.

Marais, H. (2001) *South Africa: Limits to Change: The Political Economy of Transition*, 2nd ed., London; Cape Town, Zed Books.

Marawanyika, G. (2013) 'Zimbabwe proposes state control of metal marketing,' *Bloomberg.com*, 6 May. Available at https://www.bloomberg.com/news/articles/2013-05-05/zimbabwe-proposes-mineral-deposit-auctions-policy-shows (Accessed 16 September 2019).

———. (2018) 'RioZim evaluating bids for investors in Zimbabwe power plant,' *Bloomberg.com*, 17 May. Available at https://www.bloomberg.com/news/articles/2018-05-17/riozim-evaluating-bids-for-investors-in-zimbabwe-power-plant (Accessed 13 September 2019).

Marks, S. (2007) 'Introduction,' in *African Perspectives on China in Africa*, Oxford, Pambazuka Press, pp. 1–14.

Marks, S. and Manji, F. (2007) *African Perspectives on China in Africa*, Oxford, Pambazuka Press.

Martin, W.G. (2008) 'South Africa's subimperial futures: Washington consensus, Bandung consensus, or peoples' consensus?' *African Sociological Review / Revue Africaine de Sociologie*, vol. 12, no. 1, pp. 124–34.

———. (2013a) "South Africa and the 'new scramble for Africa': Imperialist, sub-imperialist, or victim?" *Agrarian South: Journal of Political Economy*, vol. 2, no. 2, pp. 161–88.

———. (2013b) *South Africa and the World Economy: Remaking Race, State, and Region*, Rochester, NY, University of Rochester Press.

Marx, K. (1990) *Capital: Critique of Political Economy v. 1* (trans. B. Fowkes), London; New York, Penguin Classics.

Masinga, L. (2018) '#ZumaRecall: Business leadership SA welcomes ANC NEC decision,' *IOL News*. Available at https://www.iol.co.za/news/politics/zumarecall-business-leadership-sa-welcomes-anc-nec-decision-13266152 (Accessed 26 June 2019).

Mason, R. (2016) 'China's impact on the landscape of African International Relations: Implications for dependency theory,' *Third World Quarterly*, pp. 1–13.

Matomela, D. (2011) 'Wesizwe eyes consolidation with neighbours' *IOL Business Report*, 15 July. Available at https://www.iol.co.za/business-report/economy/wesizwe-eyes-consolidation-with-neighbours-1099548 (Accessed 21 November 2018).

Mattes, R. (2018) 'Ramaphoria in South Africa: Just a honeymoon, or the start of true love?.' Available at http://theconversation.com/ramaphoria-in-south-africa-just-a-honeymoon-or-the-start-of-true-love-97789 (Accessed 26 June 2019).

Maunganidze, L. (2016) 'Zimbabwe: Institutionalized corruption and state fragility,' in Olowu, D. and Chanie, P. (eds.), *State Fragility and State Building in Africa: Cases from Eastern and Southern Africa*, United Nations University Series on Regionalism, Cham, Springer International Publishing, pp. 39–60.

Mavhunga, C. (2018) 'US ambassador to Zimbabwe: Sanctions removal linked to genuine reforms.' Available at https://www.voanews.com/a/us-ambassador-to-zimbabwe-sanctions-removal-genuine-reforms/4529865.html (Accessed 25 May 2022).

Mawowa, S. (2013) 'The political economy of artisanal and small-scale gold mining in central Zimbabwe,' *Journal of Southern African Studies*, vol. 39, no. 4, pp. 921–36.

Maxfield, S. and Schneider, B.R. (eds.) (1997) *Business and the State in Developing Countries*, Cornell Studies in Political Economy, Ithaca, NY; London, Cornell University Press.

Mazarire, G.C. (2013) 'ZANU-PF and the Government of National Unity 2009–12,' in Raftopoulos, B. (ed.), *The Hard Road to Reform. The Politics of Zimbabwe's Global Political Agreement*, Harare; Port Shepstone, Weaver Press, pp. 71–116.

McGowan, P.J. (1993) "The 'new' South Africa: Ascent or descent in the world system?" *South African Journal of International Affairs*, vol. 1, no. 1, pp. 35–61.

McGowan, P.J. and Ahwireng-Obeng, F. (1998) 'Partner or hegemon? South Africa in Africa: Part Two,' *Journal of Contemporary African Studies*, vol. 16, no. 2, pp. 165–95.

Mearsheimer, J.J. (2006) 'China's unpeaceful rise,' *Current History*, vol. 105, pp. 160–62.

Meng, Y. (2017) 'South Africa still waiting for its largest ever Chinese-invested steel mill,' *Africa-China Reporting Project*. Available at https://africachinareporting.com/south-africa-still-waiting-for-its-largest-ever-chinese-invested-steel-mill/ (Accessed 25 May 2022).

Menon, S. (2018) 'SA's economic growth for 2018 gets off to a dire start.' *BusinessLIVE,* 10 May. Available at https://www.businesslive.co.za/bd/economy/2018-05-10-sas-economic-growth-for-2018-gets-off-to-a-dire-start/ (Accessed 11 September 2018).

Mensah, S.N.-A. and Benedict, E. (2010) 'Entrepreneurship training and poverty alleviation,' *African Journal of Economic and Management Studies*, vol. 1, no. 2

Meredith, M. (2003) *Our Votes, Our Guns: Robert Mugabe and the Tragedy of Zimbabwe*, New York, Public Affairs.

Mgojo, M. (2018) 'New mining council aims to reboot sector amid growing hope,' *BusinessLIVE*, 24 May. Available at https://www.businesslive.co.za/bd/opinion/2018-05-24-new-mining-council-aims-to-reboot-sector-amid-growing-hope/ (Accessed 6 June 2018).

Minerals Council South Africa (2018) 'Minerals Council South Africa's response to the publication of the Mining Charter,' media statement. Available at https://www.mineralscouncil.org.za/industry-news/media-releases/2018/send/35-2018/640-minerals-council-south-africa-s-response-to-the-publication-of-the-mining-charter.

———. (2019) 'Minerals Council South Africa welcomes new cabinet, congratulates Minister Mantashe on appointment to enhanced role,' media statement. Available at https://www.mineralscouncil.org.za/industry-news/media-releases/2019/send/50-2019/736-minerals-council-south-africa-welcomes-new-cabinet-congratulates-minister-mantashe-on-appointment-to-enhanced-role.

———. (2013) 'Mining in Zimbabwe—Has the tide turned for investment?' *Mining Technology | Mining News and Views Updated Daily*. Available at https://www.mining-technology.com/features/feature-mining-in-zimbabwe-has-the-tide-turned-investment/ (Accessed 16 September 2019).

Ministry of Finance and Economic Development (@ZimTreasury) (2019) "The Indigenisation and Economic Empowerment Act will be repealed and replaced by the Economic Empowerment Act, which will be consistent with the current thrust 'Zimbabwe is Open for Business' #MidTermBudget2019," Twitter. Available at https://twitter.com/zimtreasury/status/1156924396235350016 (Accessed 13 September 2019).

Mkandawire, P.T. and Soludo, C.C. (eds.) (2003) *African Voices on Structural Adjustment: A Companion to Our Continent, Our Future*, Ottawa: Trenton, NJ: Dakar, Senegal, IDRC; Africa World Press; Council for the Development of Social Science Research in Africa.

MOFCOM (2018) 'A BRICS success story.'

Mondliwa, P. and Roberts, S. (2021) 'The political economy of structural transformation: Political settlements and industrial policy in South Africa,' in Andreoni, A., Mondliwa, P., Roberts, S., and Tregenna, F. (eds.), *Structural Transformation in South Africa: The Challenges of Inclusive Industrial Development in a Middle-Income Country*, Oxford University Press, pp. 312–36.

Monteiro, A. and Gumede, A. (2018) 'Business confidence at three-year high on Ramaphosa.' Available at https://www.moneyweb.co.za/news/economy/business-confidence-at-three-year-high-on-ramaphosa/ (Accessed 26 June 2019).

Moore, D., Kriger, N. and Raftopoulos, B. (eds.) (2013) *'Progress' in Zimbabwe?: The Past and Present of a Concept and a Country*, New York, Routledge.

Moseley, W.G. (2008) 'Fair trade wine: South Africa's post-apartheid vineyards and the global economy,' *Globalizations*, vol. 5, no. 2, pp. 291–304.

Mothabi, T. (2016) 'A need for developmental intervention in South Africa,' in Kanyenze, G., Jauch, H., Kanengoni, A. D., Madzwamuse, M., and Muchena, D. (eds.), *Towards Democratic Development States in Southern Africa*, Harare, Weaver Press, pp. 52–105.

Moyo, G. (2016) 'The curse of military commercialism in state enterprises and parastatals in Zimbabwe,' *Journal of Southern African Studies*, vol. 42, no. 2, pp. 351–64.

Moyo, S. and Yeros, P. (2005) 'Land occupations and land reform in Zimbabwe: Towards the national democratic revolution,' in Moyo, S. and Yeros, P. (eds.), *Reclaiming the Land: The Resurgence of Rural Movements in Africa, Asia and Latin America*, London, Zed Books, pp. 165–208.

———. (2015) 'Scramble, resistance and a new non-alignment strategy,' in Garcia, A. and Bond, P. (eds.), *BRICS: An Anticapitalist Critique*, Chicago, Haymarket Books, pp. 246–50.

Mukwereza, L. (2013) 'Reviving Zimbabwe's agriculture: The role of China and Brazil,' *IDS Bulletin*, vol. 44, no. 4, pp. 116–26.

Murombo, T. (2010) 'Law and the indigenisation of mineral resources in Zimbabwe: Any equity for local communities?,' *Southern African Public Law (SA Public Law)*, vol. 25, no. 2, pp. 568–89.

———. (2013) 'Regulating mining in South Africa and Zimbabwe: Communities, the environment and perpetual exploitation,' *Law, Environment and Developmental Journal*, vol. 9, no. 1, pp. 31–49.

Musekiwa, N. (2016) 'The impact of fragility on social services: The case of Zimbabwean State, 2000–2008,' in Olowu, D. and Chanie, P. (eds.), *State Fragility and State Building in Africa: Cases from Eastern and Southern Africa*, United Nations University Series on Regionalism, Cham, Springer International Publishing, pp. 91–112.

Muzondidya, J. (2007) 'Jambanja: Ideological ambiguities in the politics of land and resource ownership in Zimbabwe,' *Journal of Southern African Studies*, vol. 33, no. 2, pp. 325–41.

Myburgh, P.-L. (2017) *The Republic of Gupta—A Story of State Capture*, Cape Town, South Africa, Penguin.

National Bureau of Statistics of China (2017) *National Bureau of Statistics of China Annual Data*. Available at http://www.stats.gov.cn/english/Statisticaldata/AnnualData/ (Accessed 5 September 2017).

Nattrass, N. and Seekings, J. (2010) 'State, Business and Growth in Post-Apartheid South Africa,' in *IPPG Discussion Paper 34*, Manchester, Research Programme Consortium for Improving Institutions for Pro-Poor Growth.

Nelson, F. (2013) 'Zimbabwe is booming—But its future lies in Chinese hands,' *Telegraph*, 1 August. Available at https://www.telegraph.co.uk/news/worldnews/africaandindianocean/zimbabwe/10216403/Zimbabwe-is-booming-but-its-future-lies-in-Chinese-hands.html (Accessed 16 September 2019).

Njini, F. (2018a) 'Implats says Zimbabwe agrees to waive 51% ownership law,' *Bloomberg.com*, 13 September. Available at https://www.bloomberg.com/news/articles/2018-09-13/impala-platinum-says-zimbabwe-agrees-to-waive-51-ownership-law (Accessed 26 September 2018).

———. (2018b) 'SA's gold industry nears end of decades-long death spiral.' Available at https://www.businesslive.co.za/bd/companies/mining/2018-12-09-sas-gold-industry-nears-end-of-decades-long-death-spiral/ (Accessed 12 September 2019).

———. (2018c) 'De Beers eyes Zimbabwe, DRC after gaining S. Africa permits,' *Bloomberg.com*, 6 February. Available at https://www.bloomberg.com/news/articles/2018-02-06/de-beers-eyes-zimbabwe-congo-after-gaining-south-africa-permits (Accessed 13 September 2019).

Njini, F. and Burkhardt, P. (2018) 'South Africa's new mining charter to credit past black deals,' *Bloomberg.com*, 15 June. Available at https://www.bloomberg.com/news/articles/2018-06-15/s-africa-draft-mine-charter-recognises-past-empowerment-deals (Accessed 13 September 2019).

Njini, F., Marawanyika, G. and Sguazzin, A. (2019) 'Zimbabwe to scrap platinum and diamond mine ownership rules,' *Bloomberg.com*, 6 March. Available at https://www.bloomberg.com/news/articles/2019-03-06/zimbabwe-to-scrap-local-mine-ownership-rule-to-boost-investment (Accessed 13 September 2019).

Njini, F., Mkokeli, S. and Burkhardt, P. (2018) "AngloGold chairman warns South Africa on 'reckless' mining rules," *Bloomberg.com*, 20 July. Available at https://www.bloomberg.com/news/articles/2018-07-20/anglogold-chairman-warns-south-africa-on-reckless-mining-rules (Accessed 13 September 2019).

Nölke, A. and Claar, S. (2013) 'Varieties of capitalism in emerging economies,' *Transformation: Critical Perspectives on Southern Africa*, vol. 81, no. 1, pp. 33–54.

Nyabereka, M.C. (2017) 'An exploration of the effects of structural adjustment and BRICS engagement on development in Zimbabwe over the Periods 1991–1995 and 2009–2013,' *Politikon*, vol. 44, no. 1.

Nyakudya, M. (2013) 'Sanctioning the government of national unity: A review of Zimbabwe's relations with the West in the framework of the Global Political Agreement,' in Raftopoulos, B. (ed.), *The Hard Road to Reform: The Politics of Zimbabwe's Global Political Agreement*, Harare; Port Shepstone, Weaver Press, pp. 171–210.

OECD (2017) *African Economic Outlook 2017: Entrepreneurship and Industrialisation*, Paris, Organisation for Economic Co-operation and Development. Available at: https://www.oecd-ilibrary.org/development/african-economic-outlook-2017_aeo-2017-en (Accessed: 24 May 2022).

Ojakorotu, V. and Kamidza, R. (2018) 'Look East policy: The case of Zimbabwe-China political and economic relations since 2000,' *India Quarterly*, vol. 74, no. 1, pp. 17–41.

Olowu, D. and Chanie, P. (2016) 'Introduction: Renewed interest in state weakness and fragility,' in Olowu, D. and Chanie, P. (eds.), *State Fragility and State Building in Africa: Cases from Eastern and Southern Africa*, United Nations University Series on Regionalism, Cham, Springer International Publishing, pp. 1–17.

Onis, Z. and Aysan, A. F. (2000) 'Neoliberal globalisation, the nation-state and financial crises in the semi-periphery: A comparative analysis,' *Third World Quarterly*, vol. 21, no. 1, pp. 119–39.

Overholt, W.H. (2010) 'China in the global financial crisis: rising influence, rising challenges,' *The Washington Quarterly*, vol. 33, no. 1, pp. 21–34.

Pamuk, S. (1987) *The Ottoman Empire and European Capitalism, 1820–1913: Trade, Investment and Production*, Cambridge University Press.

Paus, E., Prime, P. and Western, J. (2009) *Global Giant: Is China Changing the Rules of the Game?* New York, Palgrave Macmillan.

Payne, R.J. and Veney, C.R. (1998) 'China's post-Cold War African policy,' *Asian Survey*, vol. 38, no. 9, pp. 867–79.

Pedersen, P.O. and McCormick, D. (1999) 'African business systems in a globalising world,' *The Journal of Modern African Studies*, vol. 37, no. 1, pp. 109–35.

Peet, R. (2002) 'Ideology, discourse, and the geography of hegemony: From socialist to neoliberal development in postapartheid South Africa,' *Antipode*, vol. 34, no. 1, pp. 54–84.

Petras, J. (1981) 'Dependency and world system theory: A critique and new directions,' *Latin American Perspectives*, vol. 8, no. ¾, pp. 148–55.

Phimister, I. (2011) 'The collapse of Rhodesia: Population demographics and the politics of race,' *The Journal of Imperial and Commonwealth History*, vol. 39, no. 3, pp. 518–19.

Ponte, S., Roberts, S. and Van Sittert, L. (2007) "'Black Economic Empowerment': Business and the state in South Africa," *Development and Change*, vol. 38, no. 5, pp. 933–55.

Pratley, N. (2015) 'Global mining industry faces up to a deep malaise,' *Guardian*, 24 July. Available at https://www.theguardian.com/business/2015/jul/24/global-mining-industry-faces-up-to-a-deep-malaise (Accessed 13 September 2019).

Prebisch, R. (1959) 'Commercial policy in the underdeveloped countries,' *The American Economic Review*, vol. 49, no. 2, pp. 251–73.

Pretorius, F. (2014) *A History of South Africa: From the Distant Past to the Present Day*, Pretoria, Protea Book House.

Prinsloo, L. and Njini, F. (2018) 'Top Sibanye holders are said to show support for Lonmin deal,' 31 August. Available at https://www.bloomberg.com/news/articles/2018-08-31/top-sibanye-holders-are-said-to-indicate-support-for-lonmin-deal (Accessed 21 November 2018).

PWC (2016) *Mine 2016: Slower, Lower, Weaker . . . But Not Defeated*, Annual review of global trends in the mining industry, PWC.

Qobo, M. (2010) "Refocusing South Africa's economic diplomacy: The 'African Agenda' and emerging powers," *South African Journal of International Affairs*, vol. 17, no. 1, pp. 13–28.

Qobo, M. and Dube, M. (2015) 'South Africa's foreign economic strategies in a changing global system,' *South African Journal of International Affairs*, vol. 22, no. 2, pp. 145–64.

Qobo, M. and Soko, M. (2015) 'The rise of emerging powers in the global development finance architecture: The case of the BRICS and the New Development Bank,' *South African Journal of International Affairs*, vol. 22, no. 3, pp. 277–88.

Qureshi, M.S. and Te Velde, D.W. (2013) 'State-business relations, investment climate reform and firm productivity in sub-Saharan Africa,' *Journal of International Development*, vol. 25, no. 7, pp. 912–35.

Radice, H. (2009) 'Halfway to paradise? Making sense of the semi-periphery,' in Worth, O. and Moore, P. (eds.), *Globalization and the 'New' Semi-Peripheries*, International Political Economy Series, London, Palgrave Macmillan UK, pp. 25–39.

Raftopoulos, B. (1996) *Race and Nationalism in a Post-colonial State*, SAPES Books.

———. (2003) 'The state in crisis authoritarian nationalism, selective citizenship and distortions of democracy in Zimbabwe,' in Hammar, A., Raftopoulos, B., and Jensen, S. (eds.), *Zimbabwe's Unfinished Business: Rethinking Land, State and Nation in the Context of Crisis*, Harare, Weaver Press, pp. 217–41.

———. (ed.) (2013) *The Hard Road to Reform. The Politics of Zimbabwe's Global Political Agreement*, Harare; Port Shepstone, Weaver Press.

Raftopoulos, B. and Compagnon, D. (2003) 'Indigenization, the state bourgeoisie and neo-authoritarian politics,' in Darnolf, S. and Laakso, L. (eds.), *Twenty Years of Independence in Zimbabwe: From Liberation to Authoritarianism*, International Political Economy Series, London, Palgrave Macmillan UK, pp. 15–33.

Raftopoulos, B. and Mlambo, A. (eds.) (2009) *Becoming Zimbabwe: A History from the Pre-colonial Period to 2008*, Harare, Weaver Press.

Raftopoulos, B. and Phimister, I. (2004) 'Zimbabwe now: The political economy of crisis and coercion,' *Historical Materialism*, vol. 12, no. 4, pp. 355–82.

Ramo, J.C. (2004) *The Beijing Consensus*, London, Foreign Policy Centre.

Reddy, N. (2015) 'BRICS after the Durban and Fortaleza summits,' in Garcia, A. and Bond, P. (eds.), *BRICS: An Anticapitalist Critique*, Chicago, Haymarket Books, pp. 274–78.

Renwick, R. (2018) *How to Steal a Country—State Capture and Hopes for the Future in South Africa*, London, Biteback Publishing.

Republic of South Africa (2002) 'Mineral and Petroleum Resources Development Act, No 28 of 2002,' Government Gazette, 448(23922).

———. (2004a) 'Broad-Based Black Economic Empowerment Act, No 53 of 2003,' Government Gazette, 463(25899).

———. (2004b) 'Broad-Based Socio-Economic Empowerment Charter for the South African Mining Industry, Notice No: 1639 of 2004,' Government Gazette, 2661:617.

———. (2010) 'Amendment of the Broad-Based Socio-Economic Empowerment Charter for the South African Mining and Minerals Industry,' Government Gazette, 543(33573).

———. (2017) 'Broad-Based Socio-Economic Empowerment Charter for the South African Mining and Minerals Industry, 2017 (Draft).'

Republic of Zimbabwe (2008) 'Indigenisation and Economic Empowerment Act, Chapter 14:33,' Government Gazette, Acts 14/2007, 5/2011.

———. (2018) 'The Finance Act, 2018 (No. 1 of 2018),' Government Gazette, 14 March 2018.

Reserve Bank of Zimbabwe (2019) *Macro-Economic Indicators*. Available at https://www.rbz.co.zw/index.php/research/markets/macro-economic-indicators (Accessed 13 September 2019).

Reuters (2018) "China-Africa relations enters 'Golden Age'–Ramaphosa," *Africanews*. Available at http://www.africanews.com/2018/09/06/china-africa-relations-enters-golden-age-ramaphosa// (Accessed 22 November 2018).

Rice, J. (2007) 'Ecological unequal exchange: International trade and uneven utilization of environmental space in the world system,' *Social Forces*, vol. 85, no. 3, pp. 1369–92.

Riseborough, J. and Latham, B. (2015) 'Rio Tinto exits Zimbabwe after selling diamond mine,' *Bloomberg.com*, 26 June. Available at https://www.bloomberg.com/news/articles/2015-06-26/rio-tinto-exits-zimbabwe-after-selling-diamond-mine (Accessed 28 September 2018).

Robinson, W.I. (2011) 'Giovanni Arrighi: Systemic cycles of accumulation, hegemonic transitions, and the rise of China,' *New Political Economy*, vol. 16, no. 2, pp. 267–80.

Rodney, W. (1972) *How Europe Underdeveloped Africa*, London, Bogle-L'Ouverture Publications.

Rogers, P.D. (2007) 'Dragon with a heart of darkness? Countering Chinese influence in Africa,' *Joint Force Quarterly*, no. 47, pp. 22–27.

Ross, R. (1999) *Status and Respectability in the Cape Colony, 1750–1870: A Tragedy of Manners*, Cambridge, Cambridge University Press.

Sartori, G. (1970) 'Concept misformation in comparative politics,' *The American Political Science Review*, vol. 64, no. 4, pp. 1033–53.

———. (1991) 'Comparing and miscomparing,' *Journal of Theoretical Politics*, vol. 3, no. 3, pp. 243–57.

Saunders, R. (2009) 'Crisis, capital, compromise: Mining and empowerment in Zimbabwe,' *African Sociological Review / Revue Africaine de Sociologie*, vol. 12, no. 1.

———. (2011) 'Zimbabwe: Liberation nationalism—Old and born-again,' *Review of African Political Economy*, vol. 38, no. 127, pp. 123–34.

Saunders, R. and Caramento, A. (2017) 'An extractive developmental state in Southern Africa? The cases of Zambia and Zimbabwe,' *Third World Quarterly*, vol. 39, no. 6, pp. 1166–90.

Saunders, R. and Nyamunda, T. (eds.) (2016) *Facets of Power: Politics, Profits and People in the Making of Zimbabwe's Blood Diamonds*, Avondale, Harare: Johannesburg, Weaver Press.

Scarnecchia, T. (2008) *The Urban Roots of Democracy and Political Violence in Zimbabwe: Harare and Highfield, 1940–1964*, Rochester, NY, University of Rochester Press.

Schmidt, H.I. (2013) *Colonialism and Violence in Zimbabwe: A History of Suffering*, Oxford, James Currey.

Schneider, B.R. and Maxfield, S. (1997) 'Business, the state, and economic performance in developing countries,' in Maxfield, S. and Schneider, B.R. (eds.), *Business and the State in Developing Countries*, Cornell Studies in Political Economy, Ithaca, NY; London, Cornell University Press, pp. 3–35.

Schoeman, M. (2007) 'China in Africa: The rise of hegemony?' *Strategic Review for Southern Africa*, vol. 29, no. 2, p. 74.

Schubert, J., Engel, U. and Macamo, E. (eds.) (2018a) *Extractive Industries and Changing State Dynamics in Africa: Beyond the Resource Curse*, New York, Routledge.

———. (2018b) 'Introduction,' in Schubert, J., Engel, U., and Macamo, E. (eds.), *Extractive Industries and Changing State Dynamics in Africa: Beyond the Resource Curse*, New York, Routledge, pp. 1–21.

Schubert, T. and Sooryamoorthy, R. (2009) 'Can the centre–periphery model explain patterns of international scientific collaboration among threshold and industrialised countries? The case of South Africa and Germany,' *Scientometrics*, vol. 83, no. 1, pp. 181–203.

Schwartz, N.D. and Creswell, J. (2015) 'A global chill in commodity demand hits America's heartland,' *New York Times*, 23 October. Available at https://www.nytimes.com/2015/10/25/business/energy-environment/americas-heartland-feels-a-chill-from-collapsing-commodity-prices.html (Accessed 10 September 2018).

Seawright, J. and Gerring, J. (2008) 'Case selection techniques in case study research: A menu of qualitative and quantitative options,' *Political Research Quarterly*, vol. 61, no. 2, pp. 294–308.

Seccombe, A. (2018a) 'Cyril Ramaphosa brings hope for mining, says Mbazima,' 9 February. Available at https://www.businesslive.co.za/bd/companies/mining/2018-02-09-cyril-ramaphosa-brings-hope-for-mining-says-mbazima/ (Accessed 6 June 2018).

———. (2018b) 'Creating black capitalists will not come at the expense of mining sector, says Gwede Mantashe,' *Business Day*. Available at https://www.businesslive.co.za/bd/companies/mining/2018-05-23-creating-black-capitalists-will-not-come-at-the-expense-of-mining-sector-says-gwede-mantashe/ (Accessed 6 June 2018).

Seekings, J. (2013) 'Social policy,' in *Routledge Handbook of African Politics*, London, Routledge, pp. 309–21.

Seekings, J. and Nattrass, N. (2011) 'State-business relations and pro-poor growth in South Africa,' *Journal of International Development*, vol. 23, no. 3, pp. 338–57.

Sen, K. (ed.) (2013a) *State-Business Relations and Economic Development in Africa and India*, Routledge-ERIA Studies in Development Economics, 1st edition., New York, Routledge.

———. (2013b) 'State-business relations and economic development in Africa and India: The analytical issues,' in Sen, K. (ed.), *State-Business Relations and Economic Development in Africa and India*, Routledge-ERIA Studies in Development Economics, 1st edition., New York, Routledge, pp. 1–14.

Sen, K. and Te Velde, D.W. (2009) 'State-business relations and economic growth in sub-Saharan Africa,' *Journal of Development Studies*, vol. 45, no. 8, pp. 1267–83.

———. (2013) 'State-business relationships and economic growth in sub-Saharan Africa,' in Sen, K. (ed), *State-Business Relations and Economic Development in Africa and India*, Routledge-ERIA Studies in Development Economics, 1st edition., New York, Routledge, pp. 57–68.

Shaw, T.M. (1974) 'Southern Africa: Co-operation and conflict in an international sub-system,' *The Journal of Modern African Studies*, vol. 12, no. 4, pp. 633–55.

———. (1978) 'Inequalities and interdependence in Africa and Latin America: Sub-imperialism and semi-industrialism in the semi-periphery,' *Cultures et développement*, vol. 10, no. 2, pp. 231–63.

Shaw, T.M., Cooper, A.F. and Antkiewicz, A. (2007) 'Global and/or regional development at the start of the 21st century? China, India and (South) Africa,' *Third World Quarterly*, vol. 28, no. 7, pp. 1255–70.

Shelton, G. and Kabemba, C. (eds.) (2012) *Win-Win Partnership: China, Southern Africa and the Extractive Industries*, Johannesburg, Southern Africa Resource Watch.

Shumba, J.M. (2018) *Zimbabwe's Predatory State*, Pietermaritzburg, South Africa, University of KwaZulu-Natal Press.

Sklair, L. (1997) 'Social movements for global capitalism: The transnational capitalist class in action,' *Review of International Political Economy*, vol. 4, no. 3, pp. 514–38.

———. (2000) 'The transnational capitalist class and the discourse of globalisation,' *Cambridge Review of International Affairs*, vol. 14, no. 1, pp. 67–85.

———. (2001) *The Transnational Capitalist Class*, New York, Wiley.

———. (2002) 'The transnational capitalist class and global politics: Deconstructing the corporate-state connection,' *International Political Science Review*, vol. 23, no. 2, pp. 159–74.

Smith, D. (2013) 'South African mining deep in crisis as ANC considers peacekeeping force,' *Guardian*, 4 June. Available at https://www.theguardian.com/business/2013/jun/04/south-african-mining-crisis-peacekeeping-force (Accessed 13 September 2019).

Smith, N. and Harvey, D. (2008) *Uneven Development: Nature, Capital, and the Production of Space*, 3rd ed., Athens, University of Georgia Press.

Smith, S. (1982) 'Class analysis versus world systems: Critique of Samir Amin's typology of under-development,' *Journal of Contemporary Asia*, vol. 12, no. 1, pp. 7–18.

Snyder, D. and Kick, E.L. (1979) 'Structural position in the world system and economic growth, 1955–1970: A multiple-network analysis of transnational interactions,' *American Journal of Sociology*, vol. 84, no. 5, pp. 1096–126.

Sorensen, P. (2011) 'Mining in South Africa: A mature industry?' *International Journal of Environmental Studies*, vol. 68, no. 5, pp. 625–49.

Southall, R. (2004) 'The ANC and black capitalism in South Africa,' *Review of African Political Economy*, vol. 31, no. 100, pp. 313–28.

———. (2007) 'Ten propositions about Black Economic Empowerment in South Africa,' *Review of African Political Economy*, vol. 34, no. 3, pp. 67–84.

———. (2012) 'South Africa's fractured power elite,' Johannesburg, University of the Witwatersrand. Available at https://wiser.wits.ac.za/content/south-africas-fractured-power-elite-10262 (Accessed 3 July 2016).

———. (2014) 'Threats to constitutionalism by liberation movements in Southern Africa,' *Africa Spectrum*, vol. 49, no. 1, pp. 79–99.

———. (2018) 'Presidential transitions and generational change in Southern African liberation movements,' *Review of African Political Economy*, vol. 46, no. 159, pp. 143–56.

Spiegel, S.J. (2015) 'Contested diamond certification: Reconfiguring global and national interests in Zimbabwe's Marange fields,' in Grynberg, R. and Mbayi, L. (eds.), *The Global Diamond Industry: Economics and Development Volume II*, London, Palgrave Macmillan UK, pp. 153–80.

Statistics South Africa (2015) *Mining Industry, 2015*, Pretoria, Statistics South Africa.

———. (2018a) *Mining: Production and Sales*, Statistical Release, Pretoria, Statistics South Africa.

———. (2018b) 'The economy shrinks by 0.7% in Q2: 2018,' Statistics South Africa. Available at http://www.statssa.gov.za/?p=11507 (Accessed 11 September 2018).

Stephen, M.D. (2012) 'Rising regional powers and international institutions: The foreign policy orientations of India, Brazil and South Africa,' *Global Society*, vol. 26, no. 3, pp. 289–309.

———. (2014) 'Rising powers, global capitalism and liberal global governance: A historical materialist account of the BRICs challenge,' *European Journal of International Relations*, vol. 20, no. 4, pp. 912–38.

Stiglitz, J.E. (1998) *More Instruments and Broader Goals: Moving toward the Post-Washington Consensus*, Helsinki.

Stoddard, E. and Lewis, B. (2018) 'Political shifts lift investor mood in southern African mining,' *Reuters*, 8 February. Available at https://www.reuters.com/article/us-africa-mining-investment/political-shifts-lift-investor-mood-in-southern-african-mining-idUSKBN1FS1XR (Accessed 5 June 2018).

Stone, S. (2018) 'China commits to pumping investment into SA,' *Fin24*, 3 September. Available at https://www.fin24.com/Economy/china-commits-to-pumping-investment-into-sa-20180903 (Accessed 21 November 2018).

Tang, W. and Pigato, M.A. (2015) *China and Africa: Expanding Economic Ties in an Evolving Global Context*, The World Bank.

Tangri, R. and Southall, R. (2008) 'The politics of Black Economic Empowerment in South Africa,' *Journal of Southern African Studies*, vol. 34, no. 3, pp. 699–716.

Taylor, I. (2006) *China and Africa: Engagement and Compromise*, Milton Park, Abingdon, Oxon; New York, Routledge.

———. (2008) 'Sino-African relations and the problem of human rights,' *African Affairs*, vol. 107, no. 426, pp. 63–87.

———. (2009) "'The South will rise again'? New alliances and global governance: The India-Brazil-South Africa dialogue forum," *Politikon*, vol. 36, no. 1, pp. 45–58.

———. (2011) "South African 'imperialism' in a region lacking regionalism: A critique," *Third World Quarterly*, vol. 32, no. 7, pp. 1233–53.

———. (2014) *Africa Rising: BRICS—Diversifying Dependency*, Woodbridge; New York, James Currey.

———. (2016a) 'Dependency redux: Why Africa is not rising,' *Review of African Political Economy*, vol. 43, no. 147, pp. 8–25.

———. (2016b) 'Meet the new boss—Same as the old boss: South Africa's transition as embourgeoisement,' *Revista Brasileira de Estudos Africanos*, vol. 1, no. 1, pp. 11–39.

Taylor, S.D. (2007) *Business and the State in Southern Africa: The Politics of Economic Reform*, Boulder, CO, Lynne Rienner Publishers.

———. (2012) 'Influence without organizations: State-business relations and their impact on business environments in contemporary Africa,' *Business and Politics*, vol. 14, no. 1, pp. 1–35.

Te Velde, D.W. (2013) 'Measuring state-business relations in sub-Saharan Africa,' in Sen, K. (ed.), *State-Business Relations and Economic Development in Africa and India*, Routledge-ERIA Studies in Development Economics, 1st ed., New York, Routledge, pp. 17–34.

Te Velde, D.W. and Leftwich, A. (2010) *State-Business Relations and Economic Growth in Sub-Saharan Africa: A Review of Case Studies in Ghana, Mauritius, South Africa and Zambia*. Research Programme Consortium for Improving Institutions for Pro-Poor Growth, Manchester, UK.

Tella, O. (2017) 'South Africa in BRICS: The regional power's soft power and soft balancing,' *Politikon*, vol. 44, no. 3, pp. 387–403.

Tevera, D.S. (1996) 'Indigenisation of the Zimbabwean economy and the emerging economic and socio-spatial impacts,' *Eastern Africa Social Science Research Review*, vol. 12, no. 2, pp. 1–12.

Thompson, L.M. (2001) *A History of South Africa*, New Haven, CT, Yale University Press.

Times (2006) 'Jane Kelly meets Nicholas van Hoogstraten,' *Times*, 8 January. Available at https://www.thetimes.co.uk/article/jane-kelly-meets-nicholas-van-hoogstraten-t0q05hfnfvz (Accessed 24 January 2023).

Tipps, D.C. (1973) 'Modernization theory and the comparative study of national societies: A critical perspective,' *Comparative Studies in Society and History*, vol. 15, no. 2, pp. 199–226.

Toit, A.D., Kruger, S. and Ponte, S. (2008) "Deracializing exploitation? 'Black Economic Empowerment' in the South African wine industry," *Journal of Agrarian Change*, vol. 8, no. 1, pp. 6–32.

Towriss, D. (2013) 'Buying loyalty: Zimbabwe's Marange diamonds,' *Journal of Southern African Studies*, vol. 39, no. 1, pp. 99–117.

Transparency International (2019) *Corruption Perception Index 2018*, Transparency International. Available at https://www.transparency.org/cpi2018 (Accessed 9 September 2019).

Tshishonga, N. and De Vries, M.S. (2011) 'The potential of South Africa as a developmental state: A political economy critique.' Available at https://repository.up.ac.za/handle/2263/57700 (Accessed 23 January 2023).

Turak, N. (2018) "Zimbabwe is 'open for business,' new president Emmerson Mnangagwa tells Davos." Available at https://www.cnbc.com/2018/01/24/zimbabwe-is-open-for-business-new-president-emmerson-mnangagwa-tells-davos.html (Accessed 11 September 2018).

Turok, I. (2010) 'Towards a developmental state? Provincial economic policy in South Africa,' *Development Southern Africa*, Routledge, vol. 27, no. 4, pp. 497–515.

UNCTAD (2018) *Country Fact Sheet*, UNCTAD and South Centre.

United Nations Development Programme (2015) *Human Development Report 2015*, New York.

———. (2016) *Human Development Report 2016*, New York.

Van Evera, S. (1997) *Guide to Methods for Students of Political Science*, Ithaca, NY, Cornell University Press.

Van Vuuren, R.J. (2018a) 'SA Chamber of Mines renamed: Minerals Council South Africa.' Available at https://www.miningreview.com/sa-chamber-mines-renamed-minerals-council-south-africa/ (Accessed 15 August 2018).

———. (2018b) 'All eyes on Gwede Mantashe to resolve impasse in the mining sector.' Available at https://www.miningreview.com/eyes-gwede-mantashe-resolve-impasse-mining-sector/ (Accessed 6 June 2018).

Van Wyk, J.-A. (2009) *Cadres, Capitalists, Elites and Coalitions: The ANC, Business and Development in South Africa*, Working Paper.

Verhoef, G. (2004) 'Economic empowerment and performance: Strategies towards indigenisation/BEE and the performance of such enterprises in Nigeria and South Africa, since the early 1970s to 2002,' *Journal for Contemporary History*, vol. 29, no. 2, pp. 92–118.

Vickers, B. (2012) 'Towards a new aid paradigm: South Africa as African development partner,' *Cambridge Review of International Affairs*, vol. 25, no. 4, pp. 535–56.

Vieira, M.A. and Alden, C. (2011) 'India, Brazil, and South Africa (IBSA): South-South cooperation and the paradox of regional leadership,' *Global Governance: A Review of Multilateralism and International Organizations*, vol. 17, no. 4, pp. 507–28.

Vinga, A. (2019) 'High costs force indigenous miners to lease chrome mines to Chinese,' *NewZimbabwe.com*. Available at https://www.newzimbabwe.com/high-costs-force-indigenous-miners-to-lease-chrome-mines-to-chinese/ (Accessed 13 September 2019).

Wagner, P. (1993) *A Sociology of Modernity*, London; New York, Routledge.

Wallerstein, I. (1974a) *The Modern World-System 1: Capitalist Agriculture and the Origins of the European World-Economy in the Sixteenth Century*, London, Academic Press.

———. (1974b) 'The rise and future demise of the world capitalist system: Concepts for comparative analysis,' *Comparative Studies in Society and History*, vol. 16, no. 4, pp. 387–415.

———. (ed.) (1975) *World Inequality: Origins and Perspectives on the World System*, Nottingham, Spokesman.

———. (1976) 'Semi-peripheral countries and the contemporary world crisis,' *Theory and Society*, vol. 3, no. 4, pp. 461–83.

———. (1979a) *The Capitalist World-Economy: Essays*, Cambridge, Cambridge University Press.

———. (1979b) 'The Ottoman Empire and the capitalist world-economy: Some questions for research,' *Review (Fernand Braudel Center)*, vol. 2, no. 3, pp. 389–98.

———. (1980) *The Modern World-System 2: Mercantilism and the Consolidation of the European World-Economy, 1600–1750*, London, Academic Press.

———. (1982) 'World-systems analysis: Theoretical and interpretative issues,' in Hopkins, T. K. and Wallerstein, I. (eds.), *World-Systems Analysis: Theory and Methodology*, Beverly Hills, CA, SAGE Publications, pp. 91–103.

———. (1989) *The Modern World-System 3: Second Era of Great Expansion of the Capitalist World-Economy, 1730–1840s*, London, Academic Press.

———. (2004) *Modern World-System in the Longue Duree*, Boulder, CO, Paradigm.

———. (2006) *World-Systems Analysis: An Introduction*, 4th ed., Durham; London, Duke University Press.

———. (2011a) *The Modern World-System: Centrist Liberalism Triumphant, 1789–1914 v. 4*, Berkeley, University of California Press.

———. (2011b) *The Modern World-System I, Capitalist Agriculture and the Origins of the European World-Economy in the Sixteenth Century*, 20th ed., Berkeley, University of California Press.

———. (2012) 'Conclusion: World-systems analysis as a knowledge movement,' in Babones, S. and Chase-Dunn, C. (eds.), *Routledge Handbook of World-Systems Analysis*, Abingdon, Oxon; New York, Routledge.

Wanmali, S. and Islam, Y. (1997) 'Rural infrastructure and agricultural development in Southern Africa: A centre-periphery perspective,' *The Geographical Journal*, vol. 163, no. 3, pp. 259–69.

Warikandwa, T.V. and Osode, P.C. (2017) "Regulating against business 'fronting' to advance Black Economic Empowerment in Zimbabwe: Lessons from South Africa," *Potchefstroom Electronic Law Journal*, vol. 20, no. 1.

Wearden, G. (2008) 'Mining giant defends Zimbabwe investment,' *Guardian*, 25 June. Available at https://www.theguardian.com/business/2008/jun/25/angloamericanbusiness.zimbabwe (Accessed 16 September 2019).

Webb, M.C. and Krasner, S.D. (1989) 'Hegemonic stability theory: An empirical assessment,' *Review of International Studies*, vol. 15, no. 2, pp. 183–98.

Weiner, D. (1991) 'Socialist transition in the capitalist periphery: A case study of agriculture in Zimbabwe,' *Political Geography Quarterly*, vol. 10, no. 1, pp. 54–75.

West, M.O. (2014) 'China, Africa and the Bandung idea, then and now,' *Agrarian South: Journal of Political Economy*, vol. 3, no. 1, pp. 111–23.

Wild, F. and Cohen, M. (2013) 'Waiting for the rainbow: Villagers lament Motsepe's empty promises.' Available at https://mg.co.za/article/2013-07-24-african-rainbow-minerals-and-patrice-motsepes-un-met-promises (Accessed 9 September 2019).

Willem te Velde, D. (2006) 'Measuring state-business relations in sub-Saharan Africa,' in *IPPG Discussion Paper 4*, Manchester, Research Programme Consortium for Improving Institutions for Pro-Poor Growth.

Willems, W. (2011) "'Powerful centre' versus 'powerless periphery'? Postcolonial encounters, global media and nationalism in the 'Zimbabwe crisis'," in Ndlovu-Gatsheni, S. and Muzondidya, J. (eds.), *Redemptive or Grotesque Nationalism? Rethinking Contemporary Politics in Zimbabwe*, Oxford, Peter Lang, pp. 315–48.

Williams, G. (2005) 'Black Economic Empowerment in the South African wine industry,' *Journal of Agrarian Change*, vol. 5, no. 4, pp. 476–504.

Williams, P. and Taylor, I. (2000) "Neoliberalism and the political economy of the 'new' South Africa," *New Political Economy*, vol. 5, no. 1, pp. 21–40.

Williamson, J. (1990) 'What Washington means by policy reform,' in Williamson, J. (ed.), *Latin American Adjustment: How Much Has Happened?* Washington D.C., Institute for International Economics, pp. 5–20.

———. (1993) "Democracy and the 'Washington consensus'," *World Development*, SPECIAL ISSUE, vol. 21, no. 8, pp. 1329–36.

World Bank (1981) *Accelerated Development in Sub-Saharan Africa: An Agenda for Action*, The World Bank.

———. (2016) *World Development Indicators 2016*, Washington D.C.

———. (2019) *Doing Business 2019: Training for Reform*, Washington D.C.. Available at https://www.doingbusiness.org/content/dam/doingBusiness/media/Annual-Reports/English/DB2019-report_web-version.pdf.

World Economic Forum (2017) *The Global Competitiveness Report 2017–2018*, Insight Report, Geneva, The World Economic Forum.

Worth, O. and Moore, P. (2009) *Globalization and the 'New' Semi-Peripheries*, New York, Springer.

Wren, C.S. (1991) 'Mandela group may shift on nationalization,' *New York Times*, 24 February. Available at https://www.nytimes.com/1991/02/24/world/mandela-group-may-shift-on-nationalization.html (Accessed 12 September 2019).

Xing, L. and Christensen, S.F. (2012) *The Rise of China: The Impact on Semi-periphery and Periphery Countries*, Aalborg University Press.

Xiong, M. (2014) 'Rosa Luxemburg and the theory of underdevelopment,' *International Critical Thought*, vol. 4, no. 4, pp. 491–98.

Yin, R.K. (2010) *Qualitative Research from Start to Finish*, New York, Guilford Press.

Youde, J. (2007) 'Why look east? Zimbabwean foreign policy and China,' *Africa Today*, vol. 53, no. 3, pp. 3–19.

Youé, C. (2018) 'Settler colonialism or colonies with settlers?' *Canadian Journal of African Studies / Revue canadienne des études africaines*.

Young, C. (2004) 'The end of the post-colonial state in Africa? Reflections on changing African political dynamics,' *African Affairs*, vol. 103, no. 410, pp. 23–49.

Zhao, S. (2015) 'Rethinking the Chinese world order: The imperial cycle and the rise of China,' *Journal of Contemporary China*, vol. 24, no. 96, pp. 961–82.

Zimbabwe Independent, T. (2006) 'Mining policy worries SA,' *Zimbabwe Independent*. Available at https://www.theindependent.co.zw/2006/03/10/mining-policy-worries-sa/ (Accessed 12 September 2019).

Zimbabwe National Statistics Agency (2018) *Facts and Figures 2017*, Harare, Zimbabwe National Statistics Agency.

Zimnisky, P. (2014) 'Marange may not be the world's largest diamond producer for much longer,' *MINING.COM*. Available at https://www.mining.com/web/marange-may-not-be-the-worlds-largest-diamond-producer-for-much-longer/ (Accessed 20 September 2019).

Zvobgo, C.J.M. (2009) *A History of Zimbabwe, 1890–2000 and Postscript, Zimbabwe, 2001–2008*, Newcastle upon Tyne, Cambridge Scholars.

Zvoushe, H., Uwizeyimana, D. E. and Auriacombe, C.J. (2017) 'Indigenisation, politics of exclusion, and problematics of autochthony in Zimbabwe's redistribution agenda,' *Administratio Publica*, vol. 25, no. 4, pp. 122–45.

Index

About the Author

Sinan Baran is a lecturer in the Department of International Relations at Kırşehir Ahi Evran University. He holds a PhD in politics from Queen's University Belfast (United Kingdom) and a master's degree in African studies from Ankara University (Turkey). His research fields cover comparative politics, Modern World-System theory, the political economy of Africa, and emerging powers in Africa. He is the author of *Congo Wars* (*Kongo Savaşları* in Turkish) (Phoenix, 2016).

www.ingramcontent.com/pod-product-compliance
Ingram Content Group UK Ltd.
Pitfield, Milton Keynes, MK11 3LW, UK
UKHW041452071026
15587UKWH00010B/824

9 781666 920024